The Economics and Politics
of World Sugar Policies

STUDIES IN INTERNATIONAL TRADE POLICY

Studies in International Trade Policy includes works dealing with the theory, empirical analysis, political, economic, legal relations, and evaluations of international trade policies and institutions.

General Editor: Robert M. Stern

John H. Jackson and Edwin A. Vermulst, Editors. *Antidumping Law and Practice: A Comparative Study*

John Whalley, Editor. *Developing Countries and the Global Trading System.* Volumes 1 and 2

John Whalley, Coordinator. *The Uruguay Round and Beyond: The Final Report from the Ford Foundation Project on Developing Countries and the Global Trading System*

John S. Odell and Thomas D. Willett, Editors. *International Trade Policies: Gains from Exchange between Economics and Political Science*

Alan V. Deardorff and Robert M. Stern. *Computational Analysis of Global Trading Arrangements*

Jagdish Bhagwati and Hugh T. Patrick, Editors. *Aggressive Unilateralism: America's 301 Trade Policy and the World Trading System*

Ulrich Kohli. *Technology, Duality, and Foreign Trade: The GNP Function Approach to Modeling Imports and Exports*

Robert M. Stern, Editor. *The Multi-Lateral Trading System: Analysis and Options for Change*

J. Michael Finger, Editor. *Antidumping: How It Works and Who Gets Hurt*

Stephen V. Marks and Keith E. Maskus, Editors. *The Economics and Politics of World Sugar Policies*

The Economics and Politics of World Sugar Policies

Edited by Stephen V. Marks and
Keith E. Maskus

Ann Arbor

THE UNIVERSITY OF MICHIGAN PRESS

ISBN 0-472-10428-4
Published in the United States of America by
The University of Michigan Press
Manufactured in the United States of America

1996   1995   1994   1993   4   3   2   1

A CIP catalogue record for this book is available from the British Library.

Preface

On May 23, 1990, the U.S. Department of State held a conference on "Sugar Markets in the 1990s." Given the importance of sugar in the context of broader aspects of international trade policies and international disputes over farm policies, and given the initiation of congressional debate on the 1990 U.S. farm bill, it was deemed useful to draw together a variety of perspectives on sugar. The presentations included analytical treatments of sugar markets and policies by leading scholars in agricultural economics, critical commentaries on these analyses, and a panel in which sugar policy experts from government, business, and academia engaged in a frank discussion of current and prospective problems in the sugar arena.

The editors of this volume were both participants in the conference and have been visiting scholars in the Bureau of Economic and Business Affairs of the U.S. Department of State. We believed the papers and commentaries presented would be of great interest to those working in both agricultural economics and international economics. However, because the Department of State's interest lay primarily in sponsoring the conference and encouraging the exchange of views therein, it made no plans for wider dissemination.

Accordingly, we took it upon ourselves to make the insights of the conference available to a wider audience. The contributions to this volume are outgrowths of research prepared for the conference and in its aftermath. The conference was held in the public domain, and our decision to publish the revised, extended, and updated versions of these research papers and commentaries was taken without the endorsement or control of the Department of State or the United States government. The opinions expressed in this volume are not necessarily their own.

On the other hand, the conference could not have been held without the commitment of financial and logistical support from several institutions. In particular, credit is due to Gordon C. Rausser and the generous support of the U.S. Agency for International Development. Thanks are due as well to Walter Armbruster and the Farm Foundation, Assistant Secretary Douglas P. Mulholland and the Bureau of Intelligence and Research in the Department of State, and all those individuals in the Bureau of Economic and Business Affairs who contributed their time and energy. For keeping the conference itself running smoothly, thanks are due to Paul Wonnacott of the Department of State, Jerome R. LaPittus of the Agency for International Development, Robert D. Barry of the U.S. Department of Agriculture, and Geza Feketekuty of the Office of the U.S. Trade Representative. We would also like to thank five discussants for their insightful commentaries on the papers during and after the conference: Robert M. Stern of the University of Michigan, James L. Seale, Jr., of the University of Florida, Ron Lord of the U.S. Department of Agriculture, Jasper Womach of the Congressional Research Service, and Arnold C. Harberger of the University of California at Los Angeles. Finally, we wish to express our debt of gratitude to William G. Dewald of the Department of State. Without his dedication to economic analysis and his passion for sugar, this project would not have been undertaken.

Contents

CHAPTER 1

Introduction

Stephen V. Marks and Keith E. Maskus

The sugar policies of the United States and other industrial nations are among the most controversial of all farm programs worldwide. The past two years have offered opportunities for significant reforms of these policies, both unilaterally by the United States and multilaterally under the General Agreement on Tariffs and Trade (GATT), as part of broader packages of farm policy revisions.

In the United States, 1990 marked a need for new farm legislation, which is reconsidered every five years by Congress. Since 1985, federal supports for sugar, dairy products, and peanuts had remained lavishly generous, even while grains and other commodities met with reduced support. For this reason, the sugar program generated controversy even among farmers, and certainly among powerful industrial users of sweeteners. Its opponents were determined to achieve reform. In the summer of 1990, however, both houses of Congress voted to maintain the status quo, and rejected proposals that would have mandated very modest reforms of the program.[1]

One of the arguments made against such unilateral reform was that it would have amounted to "unilateral disarmament" in the ongoing battle over farm policy between the United States and the European Community (EC), for close on the heels of the U.S. debates on farm legislation came the most critical phase of a major multilateral negotiation on agricultural policy under the Uruguay Round of the GATT. Many observers viewed the U.S. and EC sugar programs as potential targets for at least token reform in the GATT talks. Progress in the negotiations has proved elusive to date, however, with original deadlines long past and no agreement in sight. The primary obstacle to the completion of a broad international agreement—one that would apply to agriculture and numerous other trade-related sectors and issues—has been the adamant opposition of the European Community to the reform of its farm policies.

1. Why Sugar Stands Out

Examination of the economics and politics of sugar markets and policies, we will argue, can provide important insights into the reasons why farm policy reforms in general are so important, and have been so difficult to achieve. But sugar is also an unusual commodity in several ways, one that rewards study on its own terms.

Sugar has historically been one of the few agricultural commodities that could be produced in both temperate and tropical climates, with low-income and high-income countries potentially in direct competition with each other. In the past two decades, moreover, high fructose corn syrup (HFCS) has emerged as a popular substitute for liquid sugar in countries that grow or import corn. The substantial differences in the costs of production across these countries and products have resulted in sugar being one of the most heavily protected farm commodities in the major developed countries of the northern hemisphere. In 1987, for example, governmental subsidies and price supports provided 41 percent of sugar producer revenues in the EC, 67 percent in Japan, 60 percent in the United States, and 54 percent in Canada (Webb, Lopez, and Penn 1990).

The distortive effects of these policies are not necessarily proportional to these numbers. It can be argued, for example, that the global impact of the EC sugar regime is roughly on a par with that of the U.S. program. In any case, because sugar is a homogeneous product, unlike most other agricultural commodities, the tools of economic analysis can be used in a relatively simple manner to measure the distortions that result from these policies. Prior studies of sugar, a number by the contributors to this volume, have shown that industrial-country sugar policies together have made sugar markets among the most egregiously distorted of all agricultural commodity markets and have caused significant global welfare losses. In terms of international equity, these losses have been poorly distributed, with many lower-income developing countries bearing a disproportionate share of the harmful effects. However, the industrial nations themselves are made worse off by their own programs, and thus have their own economic interests in liberalization.

Though it has no real strategic importance, sugar has historically been one of the most highly politicized of commodities traded internationally. Cane sugar was for centuries associated with the development of the European colonies and slavery in the Caribbean and America. In the early nineteenth century, the emergence of beet sugar production in continental Europe brought the European nations into competition and conflict with each other and their colonies. Numerous attempts to reconcile international disputes over sugar since that time have resulted in a succession of failed international sugar agreements.[2]

Even in recent years, sugar policy disputes have been a persistent source of friction in international economic relations. The sugar export subsidies of the European Community were the subject of separate complaints to the GATT by Brazil and Australia in 1978. After GATT panels ruled that the EC regime had depressed the world price, a composite complaint was refiled by a group of ten sugar exporters in 1982 (Harris, Swinbank, and Wilkinson 1983). The EC regime remains subject to sharp criticism in international forums, but the U.S. sugar import quotas have come in for particular criticism in the 1980s.[3] The United States has received complaints about its extension of import quotas to sugar-containing products, its dumping of excess sugar into the Chinese market, and its arbitrary designation of quota shares and the length of the quota year, among other aspects of its sugar policy. Criticism of the U.S. program culminated in a complaint to the GATT by Australia in 1988 that the U.S. import quotas constituted excessive protection that violated GATT rules. A GATT panel agreed with this interpretation in 1989, and the United States accepted its report, but only made essentially cosmetic changes in the program to bring it into compliance.[4]

It is perhaps ironic that the United States made one of the most comprehensive proposals for farm policy reform in the Uruguay Round negotiations, with its call for conversion of existing agricultural trade barriers to their tariff-equivalents, followed by subsequent reductions in tariff rates and internal farm support levels. The controversial U.S. record on sugar clearly did not strengthen the U.S. position in the negotiations.

2. Sugar as a Microcosm of Agriculture

As long as significant sugar policy reforms remain unachieved, it is important that we understand clearly the economic distortions generated by existing policies, and the political obstacles to a more efficient worldwide allocation of resources. Both are objectives of this volume. Sugar brings some important *general* issues in the political economy of agriculture into especially sharp relief, however. We consider these themes in this section. We then summarize the works included in this volume.

2.1 Cost Variations by Nation and Region

As we have pointed out, there are substantial cost differences among the nations involved in sweetener production. In general, sugar is produced at lowest cost from cane grown in certain developing countries, though sugar from beets and sweetener from corn in a few developed countries may be competitive as well.[5] Global liberalization would result in a marked improvement in world resource allocation by moving sugar production to lower-cost areas and limiting the inefficient production of corn-based sweeteners.

There are also significant cost differences within countries or blocs of countries. In the United States, for example, variable costs per unit of cane produced in Hawaii averaged more than double those of cane in Louisiana over 1982–87, while variable unit costs of beets produced in Texas and New Mexico averaged more than double those of beets in the Red River Valley of North Dakota and Minnesota.[6] In the European Community, unit costs of beet sugar in Italy are roughly double those in France.[7] Because industrial-country sugar policies are typical of other agricultural policies in targeting their protection to marginal producers, the cost disparities have meant that there have been substantial rents for lower-cost producers. The existence of these rents in turn has given producers powerful incentives to use the political process to retain their privileged positions.

2.2 World Market Price Volatility

That sugar production is heavily supported around the world is partly a response to the periodic boom-and-bust cycles that sugar markets have experienced historically. Such price cycles are typical of many agricultural commodities for which demand and supply are price-inelastic. Sugar prices have been highly volatile, even in comparison with other farm commodities, however. Typically, the cycle begins with an upward spike in the world price caused by production shortfalls associated with bad weather in some important producing region. After stocks are depleted, producers worldwide react by planting significantly more acreage in sugarcane and sugarbeets. Expanding cane acreage tends to generate structural output surpluses over time because cane, once planted, continues to produce sugar for several years. This feature is exacerbated by the tendency of sugar farmers in most countries to lobby for additional protection to support their additional output. The result is a period of depressed world prices for sugar, generating additional impetus for protection.[8] As a consequence of economic and political dynamics of this sort, monthly world sugar prices ranged from a low of 2.7 U.S. cents per pound to a high of 41.1 U.S. cents per pound during the 1980s.

2.3 High Adjustment Costs

Such volatility might not be a particularly disabling feature of the sugar market if resource adjustments in sugar were easy to make. However, another feature of sugar markets worth noting is that the economic and political costs of adjustment to reduced sweetener production tend to be high. High costs of adjustment are common to most agricultural activities, meaning that farmers have strong incentives to defend their interests in the political process.

In fact, the sugar market may be more susceptible to this problem than others. First of all, much of the land on which sugarcane is grown around the world has few alternative uses, while employment of displaced labor and capital can be particularly difficult in developing countries. Moreover, production of sweeteners from all crops includes at least one processing stage characterized by substantial economies of scale and sunk costs. Thus, even if the land used to grow sugarcane, sugarbeets, or corn could be used in other ways, the owners and operators of cane mills, beet factories, cane refineries, and corn refineries have strong incentives to protect the value of their fixed assets. Further, scale economies generate high levels of industrial concentration in sweetener processing. For example, the top six producers of high fructose corn syrup in the United States control some 88 percent of industry capacity (Barry et al. 1990). Similarly, U.S. beet processing factories are typically organized as cooperatives to which the more than ten thousand farmers who grow beets in the United States surrender their crop. These additional layers of economic concentration facilitate political organization to protect asset values.

2.4 The Dynamics of Technological Change

A final important factor at work in sugar and sweetener markets is that significant technological changes have fundamentally altered the dynamics of protection. We have mentioned the most important such change, the emergence of HFCS as a popular alternative sweetener. The political significance is that this development has forged an alliance between corn and sugar producers and processors in the United States and other industrial countries that has broadened the geographic range of support for sugar intervention.[9] Prospects have now emerged for further technological changes that could revolutionize the sweetener industry in the years ahead. For example, the U.S. patent held by NutraSweet on the artificial sweetener aspartame expires in 1992. This could reduce the price of aspartame and further cut into the markets for caloric sweeteners, with potentially quite negative implications for the level of sugar imports. An array of other artificial sweeteners are contemplated, as are crystalline forms of high fructose corn sweetener. It remains to be seen how the various political forces will accommodate such changes.

3. The Contributions to this Volume

The papers in this volume provide far richer discussion of these and related issues. Written by recognized experts in agricultural economics and the analysis of sugar markets, the papers emphasize the economic analysis of the sugar policies, though important political factors behind the emergence of these policies are examined as well. As the United States and the European Community are the two most important policy-making entities in the world sugar market, the volume gives extensive coverage to their policies—from a variety of perspectives and based on a variety of analytical techniques. Some of the assessments are relatively sympathetic, while others are more critical. The complexity of the policy debates implicit in this volume suggests that the last word is far from in.

3.1 Borrell and Duncan on World Sugar Policies

The first paper is an overview of world sugar markets and policies by Brent Borrell of the Centre for International Economics in Canberra and Ronald Duncan of the World Bank. Previously with the Australian Bureau of Agricultural and Resource Economics (ABARE), Borrell was instrumental in developing the influential SUGABARE model for analyzing global agricultural distortions in the sugar market. He and Duncan examine both the causes and effects of sugar protection in major markets—including the United States, the European Community, Japan, and the Cairns Group—making liberal use of results from the ABARE model.

Borrell and Duncan first document the high levels of governmental support for sugar production in the industrial countries. These supports impose a high cost on the world economy, but a variety of political-economy factors have weighed against significant reform. These factors, which are typical of agriculture in general, include an interest-group incentive structure that favors producer interests, noneconomic rationales for the support of farming, and political institutions that in many cases favor agriculture over other sectors. Moreover, price volatility is both a cause and effect of excessive protection, which results in a global tendency toward excess capacity with consequent harmful impacts on small sugar exporters.

Borrell and Duncan then review the main features of sugar support in industrial countries. The U.S. program has resulted in rapidly rising beet output, significant substitution into HFCS, falling sugar consumption, and rapidly declining imports under quota. Evidence suggests that these trends have markedly diminished the equilibrium world price of sugar, perhaps by as much as 20 to 40 percent in the 1980s. It is clear that the United States is not interested in any associated terms-of-trade gains since it pays the quota-inclusive price to foreign exporters. The economic rents implicit in this arrangement have diminished rapidly, however, and foreign exporters to the U.S. market are largely worse off now. Major exporters into the free market have suffered severe losses, while major importers have gained. Borrell and Duncan estimate that the United States itself has been a big loser in welfare terms from its own sugar protection, suffering net losses of some $1 billion annually over 1982–88.

The authors turn next to a detailed explanation of the complex support program of the EC. The program has provided explicit incentives to farmers to supply the internal market fully (though limited imports from certain developing countries are allowed) and implicit incentives to overproduce and export the excess sugar. This policy has contributed to the destabilization of world markets and has depressed the long-term world sugar price by perhaps 17 percent in the 1980s, imposing large costs on foreign exporters. They note also that Japanese protection has kept sugar prices in Japan far above world prices, leading to markedly lower import demand and further reductions in the international price. They estimate that Japanese consumers lose $2.27, and foreign exporters $2.50 to $3.40, for every $1.00 of benefits to Japanese producers.

In summary, Borrell and Duncan note that, despite considerable uncertainty as to the appropriate modelling techniques, the bulk of the evidence indicates that global intervention in sugar markets has resulted in costly resource misallocations and large transfers from consumers to producers and from net exporters to net importers. Global reductions in protection would help sugar exporters by raising the equilibrium price and, perhaps more importantly, by sharply reducing its volatility. Most countries stand to gain from multilateral liberalization.

The authors conclude with an analysis of the prospects for reform, both multilaterally and within major producing and consuming nations. Despite the apparent welfare gains potentially available, it seems unlikely to them that the critical political will for reform will emerge, given the structural and political dimensions of the problem around the world.

3.2 Schmitz and Christian on U.S. Sugar Policy

In the second paper, Andrew Schmitz and Douglas Christian of the University of California at Berkeley provide a relatively sympathetic assessment of the U.S. sugar program. The current program, based on the use of import quotas to maintain a domestic support price, is the most recent development in more than two centuries of U.S. government intervention in sugar trade.

Schmitz and Christian point out that estimates of the program's costs and benefits to the U.S. economy are highly sensitive to a variety of assumptions about domestic and foreign conditions, including the elasticities of supply and demand in the U.S. sugar market, the extent of user substitution into lower-cost corn sweeteners, the difference between the supported U.S. price and the world price at a point in time, and the extent to which the liberalization of U.S. sugar policy would cause the world price to increase. Calculations from a model developed by Schmitz and others suggest that the net cost of the sugar program to the U.S. economy in 1983 could have been as low as $200 million or as high as $3 billion. In addition, the U.S. sugar import restrictions provide quota rents to countries with access to the U.S. market. However, the authors acknowledge that the current U.S. quotas are so tight that these countries—in the Caribbean, Latin America, Africa, Asia, and Oceania—would be better off if the quotas were relaxed.

Schmitz and Christian emphasize that a number of broader qualifications must be made in any assessment of the U.S. sugar program. For example, though it cannot be known with certainty how dependent the development of the U.S. HFCS industry was on the protection provided by the program, the authors argue that its emergence has been beneficial to the United States. Moreover, the sugar program must be understood within the context of a world sugar market that is affected by the policies of other nations. Given that the policies of many nations tend to depress the world market price, the U.S. import quotas counteract the effects of these policies on U.S. sweetener production and consumption. It is even conceivable that conditions in U.S. sweetener markets would not be much different under globally free trade than under the current program. This suggests the importance of further analysis of the effects of multilateral sugar policy reforms, and that the multilateral route offers the best prospects for significant reform.

Finally, even if the United States overall would benefit from unilateral reform of its sugar program, the political durability of the program may well rule out that option. Foremost among the reasons for this durability is that the program is run at practically no budgetary cost to the U.S. government, unlike most other U.S. farm programs. Moreover, sugar crops remain highly lucrative to many regions of the nation, particularly as federal support for other crops has come under further budgetary pressure. Indeed, the authors examine U.S. House and Senate votes on the level of support provided under the sugar program, and find evidence of a strong relationship between the voting and the presence of sweetener crops or processing facilities in a district or state. Given the broad geographic base of support for sugar protection from cane, beet, and corn producers and processors, the authors suggest that the program will likely be continued for the foreseeable future.

3.3 Marks on the U.S. Sugar Program

Stephen Marks of Pomona College adopts a more critical view of U.S. sugar protection. His main aim is to develop a new partial-equilibrium modelling approach that reflects a high level of institutional detail in sweetener markets and that provides both more accurate and more timely results.

Marks notes that it is impractical to attempt estimation of separate demands for sugar and HFCS from data generated in an integrated sweetener market that underwent substantive dynamic transition in the 1970s and 1980s. Rather, he presumes HFCS substitution now to be completed and irreversible. This allows him to estimate total sweetener demand and to split it into demand for sugar and HFCS based on current market shares.

Based on 1961–88 data, Marks develops behavioral equations for U.S. sweetener demand, the prices of refined sugar and HFCS, and U.S. supplies of cane and beet sugar. He also estimates sugar demand and supply behavior in the rest of the world. His equations perform quite well and result in believable estimates of key elasticities. The model is straightforward and parsimonious, which is an advantage in that it can be easily employed for policy simulation.

After calibration of the model, Marks conducts two policy experiments. The first is to compute the effects of the U.S. sugar program over the period 1984–89 on prices and quantities traded, on the welfare of consumers and producers in the United States and the rest of the world (broken down by major producing country), and on U.S. government revenue. His results suggest that the program has lowered the world equilibrium price of sugar by some 8 to 16 percent in this period. The United States on net is worse off by perhaps $667 million per year, implying that the gains to producers and the government are outweighed by consumer losses and rent transfers. Further, he points out that the producer benefits, despite being quite large per farm, are highly unevenly distributed. Costs per consumer amount to roughly $11 per person per year.

The distinctive result in the paper is that the rest of the world actually gains welfare on net as a result of the U.S. sugar program, by $331 million on average in recent years—even though the rest of the world is a net exporter of sugar, and the U.S. program depresses the world price. The explanation is that the transfer of quota rents from the United States to nations that hold quotas for the U.S. market, plus the gains to sugar-importing nations, exceed the losses to exporting nations. However, Marks does note that certain major exporting countries, such as Thailand and Australia, have suffered heavy losses from the U.S. program.

Despite this result, U.S. liberalization would actually increase world welfare by providing gains to the United States and exporters in excess of the losses to importers and rent recipients. For example, a ten percent cut in the U.S. loan rate (effectively the support price) would generate $117 million in annual global welfare gains, as shown in his second policy experiment.

It is also noteworthy that Marks' estimates of welfare changes associated with the program are much smaller than previous estimates, some of which were based on assumptions of demand and supply elasticities that were questionable. Nonetheless, the basic message remains that U.S. import quotas are harmful to domestic and global welfare and that liberalization would benefit most countries.

3.4 Harris and Tangermann on the EC Sugar Regime

In the fourth paper, Simon Harris of British Sugar Corporation and Stefan Tangermann of the University of Gottingen review the operation of the sugar regime of the European Community since its inception in 1968. They first trace the origins of the European beet sugar industry and the tradition of protection in Western Europe to the early nineteenth century, then survey the much more recent history of the EC sugar regime. The regime includes two quota categories for domestic sugar, each subject to its own support price level. Variable import levies are used to protect the domestic market from imported sugar, though preferential import quotas have been established by the EC for its associated African, Caribbean, and Pacific (ACP) countries. Surplus EC sugar production is sold on world markets. Though producers presumably receive world market prices for this marginal output, it is arguably subject to indirect subsidy of two forms.

The authors next examine a number of recent empirical studies of the effects of multilateral and unilateral agricultural market liberalization by industrial market economies on the world market, the domestic EC market, and the ACP countries. Based on one of these studies, they calculate the implied effects of such liberalization for domestic economic welfare in the Community (a gain of $902 million per year) and quota rents to the ACP countries (a loss of at least $196 million per year).

Harris and Tangermann also examine the evolution of the performance of the Community beet sugar industry in recent years. They argue that under the EC regime the price mechanism has worked well enough to allow rapid productivity increases in beet production and processing, and suggest that international cost comparisons in recent years indicate that EC sugar producers have held their own in international competition. It is notable that some Community members remain among the lowest-cost sugar producers in the world.

Finally, the authors offer a detailed comparison of the EC sugar regime with the U.S. sugar program. There are some clear similarities between the two. For one, economic analysis clearly implies that each lowers global and domestic welfare overall—with domestic consumers and most sugar exporters the losers, and domestic sweetener producers the winners. However, the authors argue that the EC regime is less distorting in certain respects than the U.S. program. In particular, among the differences between the two regimes, two stand out. First, with its tight quota on domestic corn sweetener production, the EC regime has prevented the emergence of additional powerful beneficiaries of the program. Second, under the EC regime, domestic producer prices are more sensitive to movements in world prices than are U.S. producer prices, and sugar stocks are used in a countercyclical manner. The implication is that the EC regime contributes less at the margin to world sugar price volatility than does the U.S. policy.

3.5 Jabara and Valdés on the Developing Countries

The final paper, by Cathy Jabara of the U.S. International Trade Commission and Albert Valdés of the World Bank, is concerned with the implications of global sugar protection for welfare in developing countries. Production supports in the industrial countries—as well as anti-export, import-substitution industrialization policies in many developing countries—have combined to diminish markedly the latter group's share of world sugar exports, despite its traditionally lower production costs.

The authors analyze in detail the effects of protection in the developed countries on welfare in the developing countries. Exporting nations have suffered losses due to lower world prices, falling export volumes, and greater price instability. On the other hand, some developing-country importers have gained. Recent estimation results suggest that protection in the industrial nations has lowered the world price by between 5 and 29 percent and has reduced foreign exchange earnings of poor exporters by between $2.2 billion and $5.1 billion (in 1980 prices) per year. Jabara and Valdés note that these estimates are likely to be understatements of the full costs because they ignore the dynamic benefits of improved resource allocation, faster growth, and diminished "export pessimism" that would ensue from liberalization. Further, the benefits of preferential access to the EC and U.S. markets for quota holders have likely been dissipated by rent-seeking and wasteful inefficiencies.

Jabara and Valdés also describe the widespread intervention in sugar markets by governments in developing countries. It is noteworthy that in sugar-producing countries there are significant direct incentives to produce, yet the indirect penalties from distorted exchange rates, protection for industrial inputs, and high costs for agricultural services significantly offset the direct incentives. Effective support levels for sugar are low or even negative. At the same time, sugar consumption is subsidized or only marginally taxed (except in Thailand). These policies have contributed to the erosion of export positions in sugar. In total, however, the sugar-market distortions in developing countries are low compared to those in the developed countries.

Jabara and Valdés go on to simulate the effects of five potential policy liberalization scenarios in comparison with a baseline simulation of no policy changes over the next 20 years, using a multicommodity model developed by Valdés and Joachim Zietz. The comparisons are to a base period of 1981–83, in which world prices were similar to those today. These simulations are remarkably rich in content and coverage. Under the model's assumptions, the simulations suggest that U.S. liberalization alone would raise the equilibrium world price by 1.8 percent and would substantially raise U.S. sugar imports. In contrast, liberalization in all OECD countries jointly would raise the world price by 14 percent and would limit the growth of U.S. imports. Since U.S. domestic production falls by less under OECD liberalization than under unilateral U.S. liberalization, this scenario lends weight to the view that multilateral reform would help blunt the negative impacts on domestic producers.

Finally, the authors find that full global liberalization (including reform in the developing countries) would actually reduce the world sugar price slightly by greatly expanding production in the lowest-cost developing countries. In this case, higher-cost U.S. producers would suffer a loss in output of up to 10.1 percent. Both importing and exporting developing countries would gain welfare from the consequent improvement in resource allocation, however.

3.6 Five Commentaries on Sugar Policies

The volume concludes with commentaries from five experts on sugar markets and policies, with focus on the assessment of sugar policies and the prospects for sugar markets after the Uruguay Round negotiations under the GATT. The panel of commentators provides a cross section of the interested parties in recent deliberations on U.S. sugar policy in particular, but in the agricultural policy talks under the GATT as well. The first contributor is Bruce Gardner, the U.S. Assistant Secretary of Agriculture for Economics, and a professor of agricultural economics who is a past president of the American Agricultural Economics Association. Second is Thomas Hammer, the President of the Sweetener Users Association, which represents major industrial users of sugar and corn sweeteners in Washington. Third is Eiler Ravnholt, the Vice President for Legislative Affairs of the Hawaiian Sugar Planters Association, and a prominent force on behalf of sugar interests in Washington. Fourth is Daniel Pearson, a public policy analyst for Cargill, Inc., a producer of corn sweeteners and a major worldwide commodity trader. With the last word is D. Gale Johnson, professor of agricultural economics at the University of Chicago and past president of the American Agricultural Economics Association.

NOTES

1. See David S. Cloud, "House and Senate Resist Calls to Alter Course on Farm Bill," *Congressional Quarterly Weekly Report*, July 28, 1990, 2393–5.
2. Mintz (1985) examines the social and economic importance of sugar in modern history. On the international political and economic history of sugar, see the paper by Harris and Tangermann in this volume, and the references cited therein.
3. Maskus (1989) reviews controversies related to the U.S. sugar program through 1987.
4. For details on this episode, see the paper by Schmitz and Christian in this volume.
5. Lord, Barry, and Fry (1989) summarize the findings of an extensive study of production and processing costs of sugar and high fructose corn syrup in the major producing countries.

6. These findings are based on calculations by the authors from data given by McElroy, Ali, Dismukes, and Clauson (1989).
7. See the paper by Harris and Tangermann in this volume, which provides a more complete international cost comparison.
8. Wong, Sturgiss, and Borrell (1990) have cogently identified this phenomenon, and have tested for ratchet effects in the protection of sugar production in their earlier studies cited therein.
9. For further analysis, see the paper by Schmitz and Christian in this volume.

REFERENCES

Barry, Robert D., Luigi Angelo, Peter J. Buzzanell, and Fred Gray. 1990. *Sugar: Background for 1990 Farm Legislation*. U.S. Department of Agriculture, Economic Research Service, Commodity Economics Division. Staff Report No. AGES 9006.

Harris, Simon, Alan Swinbank, and Guy Wilkinson. 1983. *The Food and Farm Policies of the European Community*. Chichester, England: John Wiley.

Lord, Ronald C., Robert D. Barry, and James Fry. 1989. "World Sugar and HFCS Production Costs, 1979/80–1986/87." *Sugar and Sweetener Situation and Outlook Report*. U.S. Department of Agriculture, Economic Research Service, Commodity Economics Division. June.

Maskus, Keith E. 1989. "Large Costs and Small Benefits of the American Sugar Programme." *The World Economy* 12: 85–104.

McElroy, Robert, Mir Ali, Robert Dismukes, and Annette Clauson. 1989. *Costs of Production for Major U.S. Crops, 1975–87*. U.S. Department of Agriculture, Economic Research Services, Agriculture and Rural Economy Division. Staff Report No. AGES 89–22.

Mintz, Sidney W. 1985. *Sweetness and Power: The Place of Sugar in Modern History*. New York: Viking Press.

Webb, Alan J., Michael Lopez, and Renata Penn. 1990. *Estimates of Producer and Consumer Subsidy Equivalents: Government Intervention in Agriculture, 1982–87*. U.S. Department of Agriculture, Economic Research Service, Agriculture and Trade Analysis Division. USDA Statistical Bulletin No. 803.

Wong, Gordon, Robert Sturgiss, and Brent Borrell. 1989. *The Economic Consequences of International Sugar Trade Reform*. Australian Bureau of Agricultural and Resource Economics. Discussion Paper 89.7. Canberra: Australian Government Publishing Service.

CHAPTER 2

A Survey of World Sugar Policies

Brent Borrell and Ronald C. Duncan

1. Introduction

Volatility in world agricultural commodity markets has long given rise to forces that compel farmers to form coalitions that demand policy actions to address their problems caused by price instability and risk. The incentives for consumer groups (and taxpayers) to respond politically to volatile prices are different from those of farmers. The uneven political pressures from the different groups tend to give rise to policy interventions that favor agricultural producers over other groups.

Volatile prices and widespread governmental intervention have long been features of the world sugar market. Prices appear to follow a pattern of short, sharp peaks and extended troughs. Indeed, the sugar market is one of the most volatile of all primary commodity markets. To gain some independence from the volatile world market, producers in most countries have lobbied their governments to operate schemes aimed at controlling domestic prices, supply, and demand. Numerous price, production, trade, and stockholding policies have been devised.

Ultimately, this insulation from the market has greatly distorted production, consumption, trade, and the world price. Under a more liberal trading order, production would tend to shift from subsidized, higher-cost countries like the United States, the European Community (EC), and Japan, to lower-cost countries like Thailand, Australia, Brazil, and other efficient exporting nations. Some of the resources used to produce the world's sugar could therefore be saved for use in other industries, which would generate higher real incomes.

The Uruguay Round of the GATT multilateral trade negotiations has opened an avenue for agricultural trade liberalization. Many special interest groups, however, stand in the way of trade reforms. To achieve durable and effective reforms, measures must be adopted that alter the incentives that bear upon the policy formation process. To provide a framework for assessing the prospects for trade reform in the sugar market, this paper first examines the main features of the farm policy formation process that are relevant to sugar. Some of the key features of existing policies are discussed, and the findings

15

of a number of empirical studies are highlighted to draw attention to the economic costs and welfare effects of such policies. The discussion draws heavily on a recent model of the world market developed by Wong, Sturgiss, and Borrell (1989), and indeed some parts of this paper summarize that work directly. The paper concludes with an assessment of the prospects for reform.

2. The Political Economy of World Sugar Policies

The volatility of world sugar prices is shown in figure 1, which draws on unpublished data from the Australian Bureau of Agricultural and Resource Economics (ABARE). In June 1985 the nominal world market price slumped to an historical low of U.S. 2.8 cents per pound. A decade earlier, in the boom year of 1974, sugar had sold for a brief period at about 120 cents (in 1985 values) and averaged 59 cents for the year. The average real price over the past 35 years (in 1985 values) has been about U.S. 16 cents per pound, and the average cost of production worldwide is estimated at about 20 cents. Because of the volatility of the world market, virtually all countries—even those exporting countries with low production costs—have attempted to insulate their producers from low prices. This protection has both compensated for, and sustained, the long-term excess of costs over export returns.

Among the producing countries, those most exposed to world price volatility are those that export a large share of their production, such as Thailand and Australia. Cuba, although a large exporter, in the past had its exposure reduced through a bilateral trade deal with the Soviet Union, though this arrangement is changing. The producers that are least exposed are those with large domestic markets. In these countries, policies compel consumers and taxpayers to subsidize production and insulate producers from world price fluctuations. The most notable examples in this category have been the United States, the EC, Japan, the former Soviet Union, India, and China.

The sugar policies of major industrial countries have attracted much attention by virtue of the large magnitude of support they offer to producers and their seeming disregard for the high costs incurred. The stated aims of sugar policy in industrial countries are usually stability and maintenance of farm incomes, in the face of volatile prices, and industry expansion. In some cases self-sufficiency has been a consideration, as in Europe and Japan. Intervention is also widespread in developing countries, where a primary aim of policy is to earn or conserve foreign exchange. In high-price years, sugar is a valuable foreign exchange earner for exporting countries but a severe drain on reserves for importers.

The high levels of producer support in Japan, the United States, and the EC have been reflected in their high producer prices in recent decades. In

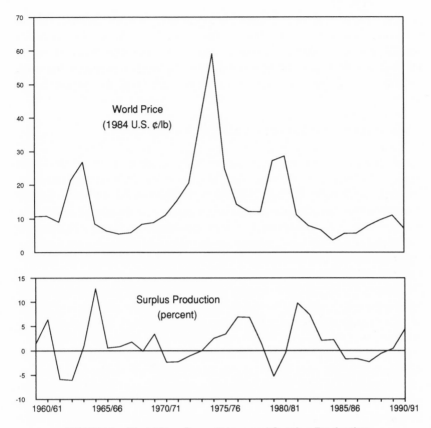

FIGURE 1.   **World Raw Sugar Prices and Surplus Production**

Japan, for example, the producer price in 1986 was 11 times the world price. As well as providing price support, sugar policies have provided a degree of price stability; in all cases producers are protected in times of falling world prices. The European Community's intervention price, received on the bulk of its sugar output, is compared to the world price in figure 1 of the chapter by Harris and Tangermann in this volume. It has been well above the world price at all times except during major world price spikes. The United States is notable for its insulation of producers from world price troughs but not peaks, as shown by figure 2 in the chapter by Schmitz and Christian. It appears that support of producers' incomes is a higher U.S. priority than any benefits from price stability.

While governments and other official institutions have designed policies in part to protect producers from instability in world prices, their policies have also tended to exacerbate world price fluctuations, because increases in supply have not been well synchronized with the rather stable growth in demand. Governments change production controls only after long intervals, and then in large steps. The government-controlled increases in production have come only after world price peaks. The resulting surges in production worldwide have far exceeded increases in consumption, leading to global surplus production as shown in figure 1.

Though high world prices have led to large increases in production, low world prices have not led to large contractions. When world prices fall due to a surge in production, protective policies are activated to support the expanded industries and new fixed investments around the world. This protection of expanded production causes world prices to remain depressed for some years. After a time, consumption again exceeds production, and stocks fall to a level where a large weather-induced drop in production can again lead to a sharp increase in the world price. Price booms and slumps have therefore been a major feature of the market.

Because of the insulation of many domestic markets by their governments, the burden of adjustment is borne by the relatively small unprotected sectors of the world market. To induce the necessary adjustments of supply and demand, the world price must vary more than would otherwise be required.

2.1 Economic Effects of Policy Intervention

Under a trading system in which policy interventions were reduced, so that producers had incentives to respond directly to the world price, producers would be likely to base their production plans on anticipated growth in consumption and on changing market conditions. Severe shortages of sugar and high prices would then be less likely to occur, as would overexpansion and periods of drastically low prices. The price would become less variable.

Whether the average world price level over time would be higher or lower than otherwise is difficult to predict. It is possible that the average world price would increase because of the reduced tendency for higher-cost producers to expand under the stimulus of high support prices. On the other hand, with the removal of supply controls in the lower-cost countries it might be profitable for efficient producers to supply the world market at a price lower than would otherwise prevail.

What is more certain is that there would be a shift in production away from subsidized, higher-cost countries to lower-cost countries. The welfare of producers in efficient exporting countries would be lifted through greater trade opportunities. Sugar prices paid by consumers in importing countries would be lowered, and subsidies paid by taxpayers would be reduced or eliminated.

2.2 The Policy Formation Process

Intervention in the world sugar market began over 300 years ago, when European countries strictly regulated the trade in sugar to facilitate taxation of their sugar-producing colonies (Ballinger 1971). The colonies were forced to export exclusively to the respective mother countries (or their colonies), in which large import duties were exacted. These duties, by increasing the landed price of sugar, indirectly provided an incentive for the establishment of sugar production (especially from beet) in Europe and North America. The sugar industries in these areas therefore grew up heavily dependent on the import taxes, and had a strong interest in this intervention being maintained.

Although sugar policy instruments are considerably more complex nowadays, the political processes in the major developed nations do tend to provide for interventions favorable to growers and processors of sugar and other farm products, for a variety of reasons.

Vested Interests

With few exceptions, groups whose welfare is directly affected by governmental intervention seek to influence policies in their favor. In the higher-cost countries, producer groups influence sugar policies in a fashion that consistently favors producers at the expense of consumers, taxpayers, and producers in other countries. In Japan, the United States, and the European Community, for example, implicit or explicit subsidies have in recent years made up more than half the income of a sugar farmer or sweetener producer. These costs, unless they are budget items, are not usually transparent to consumers, taxpayers, or voters.

The amount that firms or individuals stand to gain from policy interventions will determine their incentive to form "distributional coalitions" (Olsen 1982) to lobby to maintain or increase the protection. Those who incur the costs of the support policies—consumers and taxpayers who bear the direct burden of such subsidies, and other groups such as producers of other goods who incur less obvious economic costs—have *as groups* strong incentives to press for reforms. However, individuals have limited incentives to press for reform because the cost of the policies to individuals (even if clearly perceived) tends to be relatively small. In addition, the costs of forming a strong lobbying organization from a diverse and populous group, such as sugar consumers, are usually quite large in comparison to the benefits to be obtained from policy reform.

Producers, however, may have very large incentives to form coalitions. Relatively small producer groups, who have a great deal of fixed capital in the sweetener industry, have strong incentives to lobby to maintain support. For instance, in the United States, the six large companies that own all the mills and farms in Florida received total support estimated at U.S. $329 million in 1984/85 (in 1984 dollar values) (Borrell, Sturgiss, and Wong 1987). In the same year the estimated cost of the U.S. sugar policy to a U.S. family of four was about $55. Thus, the political will to reform is not strong, even where the benefits of an existing policy are enjoyed by relatively few and the costs exceed the benefits and are borne by many.

Moreover, agricultural support policies have typically been designed to keep the marginal, or least efficient, farmers in business by setting support prices that cover their average costs. The practical effect of this policy is that, while the bulk of small and inefficient farms may earn relatively little net income, the larger and more efficient farms earn significant inframarginal rents from the price supports. This outcome both maldistributes the benefits and provides an incentive for the owners of larger farms and processing facilities to organize themselves on behalf of continued protection. Such organization comes both within specific crops and across crops, implying that often the entire farming sector speaks with a unified voice.[1]

Volatility of Prices

The variability of world market prices may help producer groups achieve regulatory changes that ultimately increase the total level of support they receive. When the world price rises, producers seek political support for increases in either production quotas, producer prices, or subsidized investment, since production controls and fixed domestic prices may clearly disadvantage even some high-cost producers when the world price is high. At the same time, if security of supply and maintenance of foreign exchange reserves are governmental objectives, high prices in the world market may provide an additional stimulus for governments to encourage expansion of domestic production—even if it is not profitable for the economy as a whole.

When prices fall due to a surge in production, producers have a strong incentive to seek protection for the value of their fixed investments. Particularly for a government that has encouraged the previous expansion, it can be politically difficult to reduce protection despite its rising financial and economic costs. High levels of protection are thus given to enlarged industries, lengthening the period of excessive production and depressed prices. Indeed, the expectation of protection against low prices may have encouraged producers to overexpand when given the opportunity to increase production.

It is usually only after a long period of depressed prices, if at all, that some action is taken to decrease levels of support. When world prices fall, the costs of export rebates and stockholding increase, as has happened in recent years in the European Community. Further, the opportunity cost to consumers increases. In Japan, for example, during recent periods in which a high value for the yen has lowered the prices of imported goods, the lower prices for agricultural products have not been passed on to consumers. Though some pressure is being mounted for this to be done (see ABARE 1988), changes are likely to be small and to occur only slowly.

Thus, the high degree of price volatility in the world market tends to help producers in many countries to lobby for changes in policy that ultimately lead to increases in the supported output of their industries, even when prices are low. Paradoxically, such behavior exacerbates world market instability. Intervention is thus both a cause and an effect of instability in world prices. It is also a cause of sustained resource misallocation in the production of sugar and other sweeteners worldwide. Through a shift to freer trade, world prices would tend to become more stabilized, thereby reducing the incentives for producers to lobby for increased intervention. The allocation of resources would improve as well.

Political Institutions

A variety of institutional structures and relationships in the developed countries have historically strengthened the political clout of the farm sector. In the United States, all states have equal representation in the Senate, which lends disproportionate weight to agricultural producers in thinly populated parts of the country. Moreover, the agriculture committees of the U.S. House of Representatives and Senate have traditionally provided sympathetic and convenient forums in which broad coalitions of rural and even urban interests can be formed to assure passage of generous farm legislation. In Japan, the structure of the Diet has traditionally favored the representation of rural over urban interests, while the national system of agricultural cooperatives (*nokyo*) provides a formidable organizational structure and entrenched bureaucratic interest (ABARE 1988).

In Japan and Germany, national farm organizations have especially close ties to prominent political parties.[2] The members of the EC in general feel obliged to pursue the interests of their own farming sectors, regardless of the costs imposed on the Community as a whole. Moreover, as Moyer and Josling (1990) point out, the pace of reform approved in the EC Council of Ministers is set by the inclinations of the most reluctant country, given the informal tradition of unanimity in voting. With the momentum today toward further European economic and political unification, few in Europe want to tackle the potentially divisive reform of agricultural policy.

Noneconomic Rationales

Finally, the farm supports of the developed countries have sometimes been justified on noneconomic grounds. Some countries perceive the need for a large, even if inefficient, domestic farming sector for purposes of sustaining food security. Others consider the support of rural economies, especially through the maintenance of small family farms, to be important for aesthetic and environmental reasons. Many farm supports are rationalized as necessary for sustaining rough income parity between urban and rural workers. Conversely, the practice of penalizing farmers in developing countries has been part of a development strategy to force industrialization and urbanization. This strategy has involved the adoption of exchange-rate and tax policies that have favored industry over agriculture and low agricultural prices that have subsidized food consumption but penalized its production. The combination of these global policies has resulted in a gross misallocation of agricultural resources, both within countries and internationally. Paradoxically, the policies often have not achieved their stated aims, forcing yet additional governmental intervention and economic distortion into the system.

3. Empirical Evidence on the Effects of Intervention

Protectionist agricultural policies have so distorted world markets that it is difficult to determine accurately what form these markets might assume under more liberal trading practices. Nonetheless, some studies analyzing the separate effects of specific country policies have been undertaken, and others have been conducted that look at the joint effects of policies of several countries. Such studies provide important insights about the impacts of intervention and the effectiveness of policy reform.

In reviewing these studies, we pay particular attention to the ABARE sugar model that is laid out by Wong, Sturgiss, and Borrell (1989) and has been used by Sturgiss, Field, and Young (1990) and in World Bank studies. The model presents a detailed partial-equilibrium treatment of major world sugar exporters (Australia, Brazil, and the European Community), importers (the United States, Japan, and China), and the special relationship between the former Soviet Union and Cuba. A residual sector is included for the rest of the world. The model captures numerous complexities in sugar markets, such as asymmetric reactions of policy makers in various countries to changes in world prices, and differential stockholding behavior in various areas. Model parameters are estimated for each major region. Regions are then linked through market-clearing equations. The model is dynamic and may be used for simulating the potential future global effects of policy changes.[3]

3.1 Separate Effects: OECD Countries

Since 1975, the sugar policies of the EC, the United States, and Japan have encouraged greater domestic sweetener production, which has contributed to structural surpluses of sugar and periods of severely low prices in the world market. During this time, the European Community has risen from the status of a net importer to the world's second-largest sugar exporter. During the 1980s, the United States declined from its position as the world's largest importer, accounting for 20 percent of world imports or 5.5 million tons, to a far smaller share of world imports, 3.5 percent or about 1 million tons. (Metric weights are used throughout.) Meanwhile, Japan, the second-largest importer, experienced a 25 percent reduction in imports.

The United States and the European Community have favored certain foreign exporters with restricted access to their high-priced domestic markets as a form of compensation for the depressive effects their policies have on the world price. In the EC, the quotas have been virtually fixed since 1975. In the United States, rents received by quota holders have been declining in line with declining imports.

As we have suggested, apart from lowering the world price, the U.S., EC, and Japanese policies also increase instability in the world price. To equilibrate demand and supply, larger price adjustments are required in the world market than otherwise would be necessary. The lower and less stable prices directly cause resource misallocation and reduce welfare in third countries. Also, by indirectly inducing changes in policies in other countries—for example, to protect producers' incomes—resource allocation and welfare can be indirectly affected. Import quota rents, such as those given by the United States to the Caribbean Basin countries, are another cause of resource misallocation and changes in welfare in and among third countries. Selective allocation of quotas can protect producers in high-cost countries like the Dominican Republic and Jamaica from competition by producers in low-cost countries like Zimbabwe, Swaziland, and Thailand. Moreover, quota rents can be capitalized into factor prices, raising the costs of production and decreasing the long-term international competitiveness of countries heavily protected by quotas.

United States

U.S. sugar consumption and imports have declined due to the technical developments in, and price competitiveness of, alternative sweeteners. These alternatives include high fructose corn syrup (HFCS) and low-calorie sweeteners such as aspartame. The high and stable U.S. price resulting from protection has been a major factor contributing to the declining trend in sugar consumption and imports. Sugar's share of the total U.S. sweetener market fell from 79 percent in 1970 to 41 percent by 1988.

The major feature of U.S. sweetener policy has been the level of protection it has offered not only to sugar producers but also to producers of HFCS. The chief instruments of the policy are a domestic target price and the import quotas that support it. The quotas are determined on the basis of the target price level and anticipated U.S. supply and demand conditions. When the world price rises above the target price, import quotas are not set and domestic prices follow the world price up.

Domestic sugar production is based on both beets and cane, and has increased rapidly in recent years (to 6.7 million tons in 1987/88, from just under 5.5 million tons in 1985/86). This increase has been caused largely by beet growers switching production from wheat to beets in response to declining relative returns from wheat. The size of the increase indicates an increase in the responsiveness of some beet growers to changes in relative prices of wheat and beet since the 1980 farm bill. This increased sensitivity can be explained as a response to the change in sugar price policy. In the 1980s, domestic sugar prices have been more stable than they were previously, and have been announced up to four years in advance. Uncertainty regarding sugar returns has therefore been removed, which has changed the relative attractiveness of beet and wheat production.

HFCS has many of the attributes of sugar and is readily substitutable for it in many uses (for example, soft drinks). In the United States, its costs of production have been low relative to the protected sugar price, enabling its producers to undercut the sugar price and rapidly expand their market share. Corn syrup production is not subject to control in the United States (unlike in the EC). By 1985, HFCS had virtually completed its substitution for sugar in applications in which substitution was relatively easy. Henceforth, HFCS is expected to maintain its share of the caloric sweetener market.

Reduced U.S. import demand for sugar is estimated to have greatly depressed world sugar prices in the 1980s. Sudaryanto (1987) estimated that in 1982/83 U.S. sugar policies depressed the world price by 49 percent. Borrell, Sturgiss, and Wong (1987) estimated a price-depressing effect of 34–50 percent for the period 1982 to 1986. More recently, Sturgiss, Field, and Young (1990) have estimated that sugar policy depressed the price on average by between 21 percent and 33 percent over the period 1982 to 1988, although for some years reductions of up to 48 percent were estimated. Moreover, Sturgiss, Field, and Young estimated that U.S. grain-pricing arrangements depressed the world sugar price a further 9 percent over the period 1986 to 1988.

The work of Borrell, Sturgiss, and Wong (1987) and Sturgiss, Field, and Young (1990) suggests that the impact of U.S. policy has been particularly severe during the depressed phase of the world price cycle, because it is then that the gap between U.S. and world prices is greatest. Borrell, Sturgiss, and Wong (1987) estimate that U.S. policy has increased world price instability by between 8 percent and 12.5 percent. The policy increases the chance of both very low and very high prices. Nonetheless, averaged over the long term (a 20–year period) the depressive effect of U.S. policy is sizable, though not as severe as was the case during the 1980s. Borrell, Sturgiss, and Wong (1987) estimate a reduction in price of 9 percent on average.

There are at least two reasons why the impact of U.S. policy has been so large. First, the increases in domestic production of both HFCS and sugar in the United States had displaced an estimated 68 to 82 percent of previously imported sugar by 1988 (Sturgiss, Field, and Young 1990). Second, consumers and producers elsewhere in the world are mostly unresponsive to changes in the world price. Because declines in the world price cause, at best, small changes in the quantities of sugar supplied and demanded, relatively large falls in the world price are required to induce absorption of the imports displaced from the United States. With so little adjustment in production and consumption, falling prices mostly induce increased stockholding.

Although U.S. policy provides some compensation to quota-holding exporters to help offset the lower world price, for most exporting countries the policy now imposes net costs. The main beneficiaries of the policy have been Japan, the former Soviet Union, and China. Table 1 gives a summary of the estimated costs and benefits of the policy to exporters for selected years.

For Australia, Brazil, the EC, Fiji, and Thailand, U.S. policy imposed hefty costs, at least between 1982 and 1988. Access to the high-priced U.S. market for quota holders was insufficient to provide compensation for the loss of export revenue from the world market. Meanwhile, no compensation of any kind is given to the European Community. It should be noted, however, that the losses to the Community exist because EC policy itself has been so distortionary as to convert the region into a major net sugar exporter. Absent such policy, the region likely would still be a significant net importer, and would gain from the U.S. sugar program.

For the Caribbean Basin countries, access to the high-priced U.S. market is considered to be a form of aid under the U.S. Caribbean Basin Initiative. However, although the benefit was sizable in the early 1980s, in line with the diminishing import quota it has since declined. Indeed, in 1988 at least, the region is estimated to have experienced a net cost. Moreover, considering that these estimates exclude the economic effects associated with resource misallocations arising from distortions to trade, the costs are likely to be greater than reported. Areas that once produced sugar for the U.S. market have been forced out of sugar production, having been unable to compete on the depressed world market. Sturgiss, Field, and Young (1990) report that exports from the region decreased by 0.6 million tons between 1983 and 1988, corresponding to a loss of revenue of $340 million. Given this consideration, the costs of U.S. policies on the region may have outweighed the benefits by as early as 1986.

TABLE 1. Estimated Net Income Transfers to U.S. Trading Partners from U.S. Sugar Policies (in 1988 values, U.S. $ millions)

Crop Year[a]	1982		1984		1986		1988	
Country/Region	Upper Bound	Lower Bound	Upper Bound	Lower Bound	Upper Bound	Lower Bound	Upper Bound	Lower Bound
Argentina			42	21	15	8	7	2
Australia	-7	-34	-76	-194	-78	-244	-227	-526
Brazil	20	-3	-16	-134	-12	-151	-206	-511
Caribbean Basin			198	111	200	132	-5	-110
Dominican Republic			120	84	87	60	5	-40
European Community	-34	-62	-167	-320	-153	-383	-409	-961
Fiji			2	-4	-4	-8	-20	-48
Philippines			83	48	69	56	39	39
Thailand			-54	-110	-79	-193	-177	-390

Source: Sturgiss, Field and Young (1990), tables 12, 13, 14.
[a] September to August.

The Philippines and Argentina may similarly be suffering net costs from the policy when the wider economic effects are taken into account. Like the Caribbean Basin countries, the Philippines has reduced both total exports and exports to the unprotected world market over the 1980s. It was highly dependent on access to the high-priced U.S. market early in the decade. With the subsequent reduction in access to the U.S. market, the Philippines has found itself uncompetitive on the world market. By contrast, Thailand, Fiji, Swaziland, Zimbabwe, and Malawi were given only very limited access to the U.S. market. Highly dependent on the free world market, these countries had to remain competitive to export. Despite depressed world prices, these countries increased their exports during the 1980s.

When foreign competition is reduced (as occurred in those exporting countries with large quotas), local industries tend to become uncompetitive and resist the changes adopted in other countries (Kindleberger 1973). Fry (1982) has argued that having restricted access to protected sugar markets, such as in the United States, has caused producers, such as those in the Caribbean, to change from being low-cost to high-cost producers. Provision of rents from a market creates a need for governmental intervention of some kind in the recipient countries to control the distribution of those rents. When rents are distributed via the pricing mechanism, economic distortions will be introduced to an industry. Through time, the intervention and the distortions it creates can have costly, unintended side effects. Fry argues, for example, that in some countries, like the Dominican Republic and the Philippines, high returns to sugar have caused prices for such factors as labor and fertilizer to be bid up and have induced the development of inefficient growing and milling practices.

Although the costs imposed on exporting countries have been very large, the costs the policy imposes on the U.S. economy have been much greater. Sturgiss, Field, and Young estimate that between 1982 and 1988 the costs to U.S. consumers and stockholders exceeded the transfers to U.S. sugar and HFCS manufacturers by nearly $800 million per year on average. The income transfer to sugar and HFCS producers is estimated on average at roughly $1 billion each per year between 1982 and 1988. The estimated costs to consumers over the period are on the order of $2.5 billion annually. Costs and transfers of a similar order of magnitude have been estimated in several other studies on U.S. sugar policy.[4]

The losses to the U.S. economy arise from efficiency losses and the income transfer from U.S. consumers to foreign suppliers of sugar in the form of quota rents. U.S. sugar policy encourages industry to use resources in the production of sweeteners at a cost higher than the international value of such products, and on imports the U.S. economy pays more for its sweeteners than their international value. Because of the benefits U.S. policy confers to some countries, such as cheaper sugar imports for the former Soviet Union, Japan, and China, the net losses to the world economy are less than those to the U.S. economy itself. For the period 1982–88, the annual loss to the world economy is estimated to have averaged between $300 million and $500 million (Sturgiss, Field, and Young 1990). However, Sturgiss, Field, and Young note that there are many reasons for believing they have underestimated the costs of U.S. policy. Principally, they have not taken into account the impact of the policy on all other sectors of the economy. Rendleman and Hertel (1989), who look at the effects of the program on 17 producing sectors, conclude that the losses to the U.S. economy could be as much as double the estimates of most other studies.

The European Community

In the European Community, domestic sugar prices are maintained at levels well above the world price. The amount of production receiving this price is limited by quotas, and imports are subject to a system of variable levies that effectively excludes all imports except those that enter under the Lomé Agreement, which allows certain African, Caribbean, and Pacific Island (ACP) countries access to the high-priced EC market.

The EC intervention price established in the Common Agricultural Policy (CAP) serves as a floor price, since intervention agencies are required to purchase any sugar (up to the quota amount) offered to them at this price. In 1988/89 this price was 0.54 ecu/kg for refined and 0.45 ecu/kg for raw sugar.[5] In fact, producers do not usually receive the full intervention price, because their receipts are levied to help finance the losses incurred by the Community on exports when, as is generally the case, the world price is lower than the supported domestic price at which traders must buy. The Community pays an export "restitution" to the trader to cover the difference.

The EC identifies three categories of sugar—*A*, *B*, and *C*. The first two are limited by quota and receive supported prices, while the third is unlimited and must be exported at the world price. In any year when restitutions are made, a "coresponsibility" levy of two percent is placed on both *A* and *B* sugar. If the funds from the coresponsibility levy do not cover the cost of restitutions, an additional levy of either 30 percent or 37.5 percent is applied on *B* quota sugar only. On occasions when this levy is still not enough, a further levy of 5 percent has been imposed on *A* sugar and the total levy on *B* sugar has been raised to around 50 percent. However, even under these conditions the effective *B*-quota price exceeds the world price by one-half of the difference between the intervention price and the world price.

Thus, *A* quota sugar receives nearly the full intervention price. The bulk of sugar produced is *A* quota sugar. In 1988/89, for example, total sugar output in the Community was 14.1 million tons (refined), and the *A* quota was 10.3 million tons. The intervention price is high enough relative to costs to ensure that all *A* quotas are filled except where weather or disease outbreaks make it impossible. The *B* quota is much smaller. In 1988/89 it was set at 2.2 million tons. The beet producer price is also regulated, a "minimum" price being set on the basis of the sugar intervention price. In fact, this "intervention beet price" received by beet growers is reduced in proportion to the levies paid by the sugar producers. This reduction is significant for beets used in *B* quota production.

Although *C* sugar production must be sold on the world market without governmental support, the support provided to *A* and *B* quota production can indirectly assist producers of *C* sugar. In some countries, the *A*, *B*, and *C* returns are pooled (BAE 1985), which can have the effect that producers receive a price higher than the world price for an unlimited quantity. Even in countries where this does not occur, the assistance given to the production of *A* and *B* quota sugar covers the fixed costs of production, so that it is worthwhile to produce additional *C* sugar whenever the world price covers marginal costs. Furthermore, in some cases *C* sugar may be produced only to ensure sufficient sugar is produced to meet a grower's *A* and *B* quota obligations, and not because it is economical by itself.

Quotas are allocated to individual EC countries and then to individual beet-sugar factories, and are non-transferable. Thus, shortfalls in quota production cannot be met by other factories or countries and it is possible for the Community as a whole to have *B* quota sugar without having a full *A* quota, due to production difficulties in particular localities.

To protect the market from imports, a threshold price is established that determines levies on imports. It is based on a target price, which in 1988/89 was 0.57 ecu/kg for raw and 0.66 ecu/kg for refined sugar. When the world price is lower than the threshold price, imports are subject to a levy equal to the difference between the world and threshold prices. The levy removes the incentives to import sugar. Conversely, import subsidies and export taxes (in addition to the producer levies used to finance export restitutions) are used when the world price is higher than the threshold price. The effect is to ensure stable prices in the domestic market.

In essence, the effects of EC policy are to exclude imports (except for those allowed under the Lomé Agreement), raise domestic producer and consumer prices above the world price, raise production, lower consumption, and increase exports. Overall, the policy greatly adds to the structural surpluses that regularly overhang the world sugar market.

The long-term price-depressing effects of EC policy on the world market have been estimated at between 5 and 12 percent of equilibrium price (Tyers and Anderson 1989; BAE 1985; Koester and Schmitz 1982). The Australian

Bureau of Agricultural Economics (BAE 1985) estimated that EC production was between 1.3 and 2.3 million tons higher and exports 1.6 to 2.5 million tons greater than they otherwise would have been if these support arrangements had not existed. However, the nature of intervention in the EC sugar market so distorts supply it is very difficult to model accurately how producers would respond if they were exposed to the world price. Nonetheless, because the intervention price is usually several multiples of the world price, it seems reasonable to assume that a substantial reduction in EC supply would occur.

Our own work suggests that EC policies have the potential to have caused an even greater impact on the world market than that identified by the earlier studies. Using the model of Wong, Sturgiss, and Borrell (1989), a simulation was conducted in which it was assumed that the sum of A and B quota production was reduced to the level of EC consumption, C sugar only was traded, and all export restitution payments ceased, though subsidies were still paid on the reduced A and B quota production. The underlying assumption was that, in the absence of export restitutions, current producers of A and B quota sugar would not supply sugar to the world market, though producers of C sugar would do so and could even increase supply. This assumption does not seem unreasonable considering that it was not until after support prices were raised and A and B quotas were increased to a level well above 100 percent self-sufficiency in 1975/76 that the European Community became a net exporter at all. Even with considerable subsidies before 1975/76, the EC was not an exporter. Although changes in technology since 1975/76 have increased productivity in the industry, it appears that the large boost in subsidies granted the industry since 1975/76 has been a major factor sustaining the export of A and B quota sugar. The study by BAE (1985) concludes that the support arrangements for quota sugar enable substantial quantities of sugar to be produced in parts of the Community where cost structures would otherwise prevent them for producing any or much sugar at all.

The results of our work indicate that EC dumping of A and B quota sugar on the world market alone may have lowered the world price by 17.5 percent on average over the long term and by at least 30 percent during the low-price phases of the world price cycle. For 1982/83, Sudaryanto (1987) estimates that EC policies in total lowered the world price by 35 percent. Dumping of A and B quota sugar on the world market is not the only way EC policy depresses the world price. Because EC consumer prices are also set above the world price, EC consumption is depressed to some extent as well. The effect of this on the world price is not included in our own measurement, although it is in Sudaryanto's. Nonetheless, taking our estimate as a broad indication of the impact of EC policies on the world market, some indication of the welfare effects on exporting countries can be made. The policy is estimated to have cost Australia and Brazil up to $160 million each, annually between 1982 and 1988 (in 1984 dollar values), Thailand up to $72 million, the Philippines and South Africa up to about $50 million each, the Dominican Republic $23 million, and Colombia and Guatemala around $13 million each.

For the ACP countries with access to the high-priced EC market under the Lomé Convention, the net effect of the policy, after allowing for the price-depressing effects on the world market, is estimated to be positive for most between 1982 and 1988. These benefits are summarized in table 2. Among the larger exporters of this group, Mauritius appears to have been a clear beneficiary of the policy between 1982 and 1988, while for Zimbabwe, Swaziland, and Fiji the benefits have been considerably less, especially when measured on a unit export basis as shown in table 3. Over 75 percent of Mauritian exports have access to the EC market, while such access is less than 33 percent in the case of the other three ACP countries. Koester and Schmitz (1982) estimated the welfare effects of EC policy on the ACP countries for 1978/79, and also found wide disparities in the net benefits conferred on recipient countries. They pointed out that although the preferential access granted ACP countries is regarded as a form of aid for these countries, there is no correlation between the net benefit conferred and the GDP of those countries: the welfare effects are arbitrary and do not correspond to any obvious objective of EC development policy.

Like the estimates made by Sturgiss, Field, and Young (1990) for the effects of U.S. policy on Caribbean countries, the estimates given in tables 2 and 3 exclude the economic effects associated with resource misallocations arising from distortions to trade. Therefore, the benefits are likely to be less than reported. Zimbabwe and Swaziland, in particular, increased their exports to the world market during the 1980s despite the depressed world price. If world prices had not been so depressed by the EC policy, exports from these countries might have expanded even more quickly. If such effects could have been factored into the calculations, the estimated net benefits would be less than reported. Furthermore, the gross benefits are those arising during a period of very low world prices and are therefore near their maximum. At other stages of the world price cycle, the gross benefits would be less and even negative. Presently, the gross benefits from access to the high-priced EC market are less than those experienced between 1982 and 1988 because the world price is considerably higher than it was then. Meanwhile, the EC policy still exerts a price-depressing effect on the world market. The net benefits shown in table 2 should not, therefore, be regarded as indicators of the long-term annualized benefit of the policy for these countries.

For countries such as the Dominican Republic and the Philippines, the costs of the policy also may be considerably greater than those estimated. As pointed out in our discussion of the effects of U.S. policy, these countries

TABLE 2. Net Benefits to ACP Countries from EC Sugar Policy (in 1984 values, U.S. $ millions)

	1982	1983	1984	1985	1986	1987	1988
Barbados	6.73	11.20	9.93	11.06	9.41	16.80	13.72
Belize	3.41	6.80	6.77	7.73	6.74	12.67	9.97
Congo	2.34	2.45	1.82	2.56	2.01	3.30	2.63
Cote d'Ivoire	-1.21	0.09	1.78	2.40	2.24	3.83	3.00
Fiji	14.88	33.58	29.38	31.14	30.35	49.29	39.02
Guyana	22.07	34.31	33.64	35.76	31.67	54.97	46.19
Jamaica	21.58	29.33	27.63	28.15	25.56	42.84	34.16
Madagascar	1.95	2.39	2.18	2.24	2.63	3.85	2.89
Malawi	0.45	2.33	2.31	1.00	2.35	4.28	3.27
Mauritius	78.56	112.43	107.23	114.75	97.98	166.30	133.64
St. Christopher Nevis	1.57	3.21	2.90	3.26	2.89	5.03	4.10
Swaziland	7.94	18.91	16.80	19.61	13.89	31.20	24.33
Tanzania	1.77	2.00	2.20	2.33	2.07	3.53	2.83
Trinidad and Tobago	8.88	11.51	12.78	10.87	9.56	16.17	12.96
Zimbabwe	-6.10	-0.11	-0.30	1.17	-0.58	3.62	4.66

TABLE 3. Net Benefits to ACP Countries per Ton of Exports, (in 1984 Values, U.S. $)

	1982	1983	1984	1985	1986	1987	1988
Barbados	77.37	153.41	115.48	141.75	106.95	221.08	201.81
Belize	32.82	58.63	66.41	80.56	68.76	150.88	117.26
Congo	n/a	272.19	82.59	512.35	154.94	194.17	154.84
Cote d'Ivoire	-19.52	1.23	77.46	239.64	448.70	3829.93	499.33
Fiji	35.86	101.45	77.31	74.32	96.36	112.79	94.24
Guyana	83.30	128.49	156.48	155.46	144.63	281.91	332.33
Jamaica	203.58	308.70	328.97	230.70	280.84	516.13	319.21
Madagascar	177.05	132.84	114.84	97.36	n/a	321.04	151.87
Malawi	5.78	24.78	25.91	6.98	25.24	36.86	31.43
Mauritius	124.10	174.58	190.80	200.96	148.01	239.29	193.12
St. Christopher Nevis	46.08	123.31	103.63	130.56	120.52	218.87	195.10
Swaziland	23.07	50.69	42.98	51.61	27.90	71.72	60.23
Tanzania	177.05	95.24	200.45	194.19	188.32	353.23	257.33
Trinidad and Tobago	355.17	575.66	327.81	319.85	289.58	646.82	392.85
Zimbabwe	-26.02	-0.48	-1.31	5.52	-2.14	15.02	31.25

Source for tables 2 and 3: estimates based on the model of Wong, Sturgiss, and Borrell (1989).

have suffered reduced total exports over the 1980s. With the loss of access to the U.S. market, along with highly depressed world prices (due in large part to the U.S., EC, and Japanese sugar policies), these countries found themselves uncompetitive on the world market and were forced to decrease production. If higher world prices had prevailed, these countries might not have had to decrease production and exports by as much.

Although the available estimates of welfare effects of EC policy are not as comprehensive as those calculated for the United States, many of the broad effects are likely to be similar. For instance, the depressing effects on the world price confer a benefit on importing countries, the main beneficiaries being the former Soviet Union, China, and Japan. However, overall there is a reduction in world welfare because the patterns of production, consumption, and trade are distorted (see Koester and Schmitz 1982). Further, Roberts and Whish-Wilson (1991) recently estimated that EC sugar policy imposed a net cost on the EC itself of between 0.370 billion and 0.800 billion ecu per year over 1979–89, and a cost to EC consumers of 3.030 billion ecu (one ecu equalled U.S. $1.26 in mid-1991). These costs are large in comparison with EC sugar production worth 4.625 billion ecu per year, valued at world prices.

Japan

Although Japan is the world's second-largest importer of sugar, its sugar consumption per person is less than in any other developed nation. Moreover, its consumption has been declining, and in recent years sugar has lost market share to alternative sweeteners. In particular, HFCS consumption rose from virtually nil in the period prior to the 1974/75 world sugar price peak to 20 percent of the sweetener market by 1986/87. The decline in sugar consumption has been accompanied by a decline in sugar imports. One of the main driving forces behind these developments is the maintenance of high consumer prices under Japan's sugar policy.

The key policy instrument is a system of fixed and variable levies on imported raw sugar. A stabilization agency trades in both domestically-produced and imported sugar. Japanese consumer and producer prices are both maintained well above the world price. Consumer prices are kept above the world price (five times as high in 1985/86) by subjecting imported raw sugar to high tariffs and a complex system of variable levies, surcharges, and rebates. Producer prices are kept above world prices (eight times as high in 1985/86) through the payment of subsidies to growers. The high prices are intended to encourage domestic production, and are set broadly in line with millers', processors', and growers' costs of production.

The very high consumer price for sugar not only reduces sugar demand directly, but also allows HFCS to be priced below sugar. Consumption of HFCS is subject to a small tax, but maize, its major raw material, can be imported duty free. The unequal treatment of sugar and HFCS has encouraged the production and use of the syrup in place of sugar.

Sturgiss, Tobler, and Connell (1988) estimated that Japanese sugar import demand may be as much as 54 percent lower than it would be in the absence of governmental intervention. They also estimate that because of Japanese sugar policy the world price is on average lower by 2–5 percent over the long term and by up to 14 percent during the depressed phase of the world price cycle. The price is also 11 percent more variable. In 1986 the price-depressing effects of Japanese policy are estimated to have cost Australia between $41 million and $50 million (1984 U.S. dollar values); Brazil between $38 million and $46 million; and Thailand and the Philippines between $33 million and $40 million each. Within Japan, the policy is estimated to have provided HFCS producers an effective subsidy of more than $700 million in the three years up to 1987. Over the same period, sugar millers, processors, and growers together received an estimated subsidy of about $2 billion. Meanwhile, the cost to Japanese consumers over the period was an estimated $7 billion. In pointing out the sheer inefficiency of Japanese policy, Sturgiss, Tobler, and Connell noted that for every dollar transferred to Japanese sugar producers in 1987, the cost to Japanese consumers was an estimated $2.27, and to producers elsewhere in the world it was between $2.50 and $3.40.

3.2 Joint Effects: United States, European Community, Japan

The joint effects of the U.S., EC, and Japanese policies are not simply the addition of the separate effects. To estimate the joint effects, we ran the model of Wong, Sturgiss, and Borrell (1989) assuming no intervention in the Japanese and U.S. sugar markets and only minimal intervention in the European Community. EC consumers were assumed to be exposed to world prices, and A and B quota sugar production was assumed to be restricted to current levels of consumption. (Complete removal of intervention cannot be easily simulated with the model due to the separate modeling of A, B, and C sugar.) It was assumed that HFCS consumption grew in line with population in Japan and the United States.

The long-run, price-depressing effect of the policies jointly was estimated to be 33 percent. The policies were also estimated to increase world price variability by 28 percent and to increase the probability of receiving very low world prices.

3.3 Effects of Policies of Other Countries

Although the interventions of the United States, the European Community, and Japan have a large depressing effect on the world price, other large producing and consuming countries may be contributing to the problem. In particular, the former Soviet Union, China, and India heavily insulate their producers and consumers from the world price, and the Soviet Union also provided considerable support to the Cuban industry. Studies of the separate effects of the intervention of these countries, however, are not available.

Australia and Brazil also insulate their producers and consumers from the world market to some degree. However, the main effect of intervention in these countries appears to be to restrict production and exports below their optimal levels. By limiting production, Brazilian and Australian intervention may place some upward pressure on the world price, albeit at a cost to the economies of both countries. These policies also probably add to instability in the world price.

Australia

Though Australia is not a large producer of sugar by world standards, it is one of the leading exporters because its domestic market is small (0.8 million tons). In 1988/89 it exported about 2.8 million tons. The smallness of the Australian domestic market makes it impossible to provide high levels of support through the price system. Over the past two decades protection has on average been low or negative (Connell 1989). A greater proportion of Australian production is exposed to the world price than in any other country except possibly Thailand.

The major policy instruments are quotas on area and production, and the pooling of returns from domestic and export markets. An administratively determined domestic price operated before July 1989. However, since that time market forces have determined domestic prices, although imported sugar is subject to an import duty. All sugar produced in Queensland (95 percent of the Australian total) is compulsorily acquired by the Queensland state government.

Quotas on area, known as "land assignments," restrict production. It is not illegal to grow sugarcane on unassigned land, but sugar produced from such cane is compulsorily acquired by the Queensland government at A$1/ton; this price is so low that in effect land assignments are binding. Because of this tight restriction on area, increases in production are limited to what is possible by more intensive use of the assigned land.

Australia is a low-cost producer with considerable potential to produce more sugar even at low world prices, but regulatory provisions allow certain small groups who perceive some advantage from production controls to resist calls to eliminate them (see Borrell and Wong 1986). In the absence of intervention, output could expand considerably. The work of Sturgiss, Connell, and Tobler (1990) indicates that each 1 percent expansion of supply could lower the world price by up to 0.2 percent over the long term, given the existing structure of the world market. The cost to the Australian economy of maintaining its intervention is estimated conservatively at A$28.4 million (U.S.$22.0 million at 1990 exchange rates) per year for each 5 percent expansion potential foregone.

Brazil

Brazil is by far the largest sugarcane producer, producing well over 200 million tons of cane annually. However, only about one-third of the cane grown is used to produce sugar. The majority is used to produce ethanol, a substitute automobile fuel. Even so, Brazil is the fourth-largest sugar producer after the European Community, India, and the Commonwealth of Independent States. If all of its cane were used to produce sugar, Brazil's sugar output would rise from around 8 million tons annually to over 20 million tons. Currently, about 105 million tons of sugar are produced globally each year.

A tight net of institutional controls and interventions have long been features of the Brazilian industry, and have strictly limited the industry's ability to switch cane between ethanol and sugar production. Nonetheless, the economic incentives for the Brazilian economy as a whole to divert cane away from ethanol to sugar are great. With a border price of gasoline at about $24/barrel ($18/barrel Saudi crude) the shadow price of ethanol as a fuel substitute, measured in sugar equivalents, is only about 4–5¢/lb. Compared to the current world price for sugar of about 15¢/lb, the high marginal opportunity cost of not switching back to sugar is clear.

The Brazilian government indirectly determines the structure and behavior of the sugarcane, sugar, and ethanol industries. Annual production quotas allocated to farms, mills, and distilleries regulate the location, size, and distribution of the sugarcane crop. Domestic sugarcane, sugar, and ethanol prices are fixed and exports are controlled. Overall, intervention and controls isolate producers and consumers from changes in world market conditions. Changes in world sugar or fuel prices, therefore, have no direct effect on the production or consumption of sugarcane or its derivatives.

Sugarcane, sugar, and ethanol prices for producers are fixed high enough relative to costs to ensure all available production quotas are filled. By world standards, Brazilian sugarcane and sugar producers are very low cost. Ethanol is not cost competitive with imported oil, but ethanol prices to producers are set sufficiently high to ensure that distilleries have incentives to fulfill their quotas. Also, concessional credit is provided for investment in distilleries. Quotas, however, are the main determinants of production. Any switching that occurs between the production of sugar and ethanol occurs as the direct result of changes in quotas only. The empirical evidence (see Wong, Sturgiss, and Borrell 1989) is that Brazil's capacity to switch cane between sugar and ethanol in response to even large changes in oil and sugar prices is greatly limited under current policies.

Like Australia, Brazil is a low-cost producer with a clear advantage and considerable potential to produce more sugar even at low world prices. In the absence of intervention, output could expand considerably. Using the model of Wong, Sturgiss, and Borrell (1989), we estimate that for each 1 percent expansion of exports from Brazil, the world price could be lowered by up to 0.3 percent over the long term.

3.4 Overall Impact of Policy Intervention on the Sugar Market

Because it is difficult to determine accurately how much supply might increase from countries like Australia and Brazil in the absence of intervention, estimates of the total effects of intervention on the world market provide only partial insights, but insights nonetheless. Most studies have examined the impacts on the sugar market in a generalized, static, multicommodity framework. Only the work of Wong, Sturgiss, and Borrell (1989) has specifically examined sugar using a dynamic framework.

The Ministerial Trade Mandate model developed by the Organization for Economic Cooperation and Development (OECD 1987) has 11 regions and 14 commodities. The study indicates that a 10 percent reduction in assistance to sugar producers from 1979–81 levels would lead to a 0.93 percent increase in the world sugar price in those years.

Webb, Roningen, and Dixit (1987) use the Static World Policy Simulation model developed within the U.S. Department of Agriculture, with 8 regions and 12 commodities. Their study indicates that under complete trade liberalization the 1984 world sugar price would have been 53 percent higher.

Anderson and Tyers (1986) use a model in which 30 countries and 7 commodity groups are represented. Protection is measured at average 1980–82 levels. They estimate that, under full trade liberalization by Western European and East Asian countries, the world sugar price (taken at its 1987 level) would have been 10 percent higher and price variations would have been 22 percent lower. Western Europe and East Asia would have increased their net imports by 3.5 million tons, this increase being mainly supplied from developing countries.

Zietz and Valdés (1986) analyze the effects on 56 developing countries of a hypothetical removal of trade barriers by 17 industrial countries in a multicommodity context. They estimate that for 1983 the world sugar price would have been 13 to 30 percent higher in the absence of trade barriers. These results, plus results from earlier work by Valdés and Zietz (1980), imply that the estimated gains in sugar export revenues to developing countries would have been up to $5 billion in 1980 dollar values, among the highest for all agricultural commodities.

The results of these studies are not strictly comparable. The crucial factor affecting the results is the choice of the base period. Because world sugar prices were relatively high in 1979–82, the measured levels of producer assistance in various countries are generally relatively low. The results obtained by OECD (1987) and Anderson and Tyers (1986) can therefore be treated as only conservative estimates of the effects of protectionist policies on the world price of sugar over the longer term.

Using their dynamic sugar model, Wong, Sturgiss, and Borrell (1989) study the market adjustments over time in response to a variety of policy changes. A long period (1985 to 2004) is simulated under 60 different market scenarios, so that their results are less sensitive to the choice of base period. They find that significant reductions in the variability of world prices and sizable increases in the average price could be expected even from partial (though well-targeted) multilateral trade reforms.

In particular, they find that by making a small volume of production (up to 2.5 percent of world production) in low-cost producing countries like Brazil and Australia responsive to the world price, while also charging consumers in OECD countries world sugar prices, sugar consumption in OECD countries would increase and the average world price would be 7.6 percent higher than in the absence of policy reform. Their measure of variability of world prices was 33 percent lower; price peaks were lower, but prices were higher in trough periods.

The lower price peaks resulted from low-cost producers responding quickly and more directly to rising world prices, and from contractions in consumption in OECD countries in times of high world prices. Lower price peaks reduce the incentives for high-cost producers in other countries to expand production in the years following a price peak. There was still an expansion in production around the world in response to the price peak, but it was lessened. As a result, the consequent price trough was less severe. Given such results the benefits to efficient exporting countries would be sizable. For instance, Australia was estimated to benefit by as much as U.S. $294 million per year, including the gains to producers of receiving more stable prices.

Although the impact of policy intervention in all countries on the level of world sugar prices remains open to some conjecture, the impact of intervention on the variability of prices definitely seems to have been adverse and large. Moreover, there is little doubt that the policies of the United States, the European Community, and Japan have, separately and jointly, greatly lowered world prices. At the same time they have ensured a sustained misallocation of resources in the production and consumption of sweeteners worldwide, not only imposing high costs on their own economies but on those of efficient exporting countries as well.

4. Prospects for Reform

Wong, Sturgiss, and Borrell (1989) argue that, for durable reform to be achieved, measures must be adopted that alter the incentives that affect the policy formation process. In particular, the world price cycle must be changed so as to remove much of the price variability (perhaps, as a side-effect, even altering the period of the cycle). In order to accomplish these changes, marginal production, at least, should be exposed to the world price.

In a growing market like that for sugar, it may be possible to make producers in several lower-cost countries more responsive to the world price without imposing significant adjustment costs on producers, consumers, or taxpayers in those countries. The world sugar market is expanding by about 2 percent each year, despite inroads being made into it by some (generally protected) alternative sweeteners. World production must increase in some fashion to meet this increased demand. If lower-cost producers were not constrained by supply-control policies, they would respond more rapidly to rising world prices by producing extra sugar. In the past they have collectively responded some time after each world price peak. In an unconstrained situation producers would have incentives to anticipate growth in demand and to match their expansion more closely to emerging market opportunities than is possible at present. Smaller, gradual increases in production would then be likely, rather than the large, widely separated jumps in production that have occurred in the past. If oversupply occurred and the world price fell, marginal production would contract, so that long periods of a low world price would become less likely.

In a rising world market, producers in low-cost exporting countries have an incentive to support, either unilaterally or multilaterally, policy changes that would allow them to respond directly to the world price. Multilaterally, a group of countries may be able to influence substantially the variability of the world price. The results reported by Wong, Sturgiss, and Borrell (1989) suggest that a small amount of price-responsive production can substantially stabilize the world price. Interventions currently applying to existing volumes of sugar should be strictly limited to those volumes and reduced where possible.

Some developments in recent years may contribute to the introduction of reform in the sugar trading system. First, there may be growing appreciation for the advantages of multilateral liberalization. A multilateral approach is most promising because it could significantly ease the burden of adjustment to freer trade for individual countries. Under multilateral reform, the chances of long periods of depressed world prices would be reduced to a much greater extent than could be achieved by policy liberalization in only one or two economies. Further, the world price would be less variable, reducing the average costs to government and consumers of agricultural support programs and also reducing the costs imposed on producers by price risk.

Second, there is a growing public awareness of the cost of current policies and the advantages of freer trade. This trend may in some countries act to change the political balance in favor of reform.

In addition to the political factors that have traditionally favored agricultural producers, however, there are other factors working against reform. For one, multilateral, multicommodity negotiations involve a large number of groups. The larger is the number of groups, the more difficult it is to obtain agreement. In addition, the presently buoyant world sugar price may reduce concerns in producing countries about the adverse effects of the current trading system, and thus reduce interest in lowering the support levels to producers in high-protection countries.

4.1 Issues in Particular Countries

Agricultural trade reforms are presently under discussion in the "Uruguay Round" of multilateral trade negotiations taking place under the GATT. The contracting parties to the Uruguay Round have agreed that there is an urgent need to overcome the policy-induced distortions of agricultural trade. The most ambitious targets established were those of the United States and the Cairns Group.[6] In their opening position statements, both called for multilateral elimination of protectionist agricultural policies within ten years. The position statements of other participant groups, including that of the European Community, called for less restraint on the operation of market forces in agricultural markets. Complete free trade, however, was not considered a feasible option.

Following trilateral talks between the United States, the European Community, and the Cairns Group, agreement was finally reached in April 1989 on a framework for negotiations on agricultural reform during the balance of the Uruguay Round. The agreement encompassed both short-term and long-term reform measures. In the short term, participants in the Uruguay Round have agreed to freeze agricultural support at current levels. They also committed themselves in 1990 to reducing support and protection levels. For the longer term, participants have agreed on a negotiating framework designed to provide for substantial progressive reductions in agricultural support and protection over an agreed time period, in order to help overcome restrictions and distortions in world agricultural markets. Of course, while this agreement on a negotiating framework is encouraging, it remains to be seen whether the major agricultural trading blocks have the political will to act upon their proposals and deliver major trade reforms.

In the remainder of this section, we consider some of the options for unilateral sugar policy reform in the countries that have played prominent roles in sugar markets, as well as some of the specific obstacles to reform.

United States

The U.S. delegation to the GATT proposed that implementing trade-neutral policies using direct income payments be a goal for all countries in the GATT round. Sturgiss, Field, and Young (1990) argue that the United States itself could adopt various trade-neutral support policies for sugar that would be considerably less costly to the U.S. economy over the next five years than a continuation of existing policies. Such policies would also practically elimi-nate the costs imposed on other countries by the U.S. sugar program. Conflicts between U.S. domestic and foreign policy objectives would then be resolved.

Eight potential policy options for the United States were evaluated by Sturgiss, Field, and Young. The policies ranged from maintaining the current program to eliminating all producer assistance, with various forms of direct income supports, deficiency payments, and partial reductions in price supports considered as intermediate measures. Among this range of options,, the potential net gains to the U.S. economy were largest from a combination of free imports and deficiency payments to sugar producers that maintain a constant real assistance level, though this policy would be costly to the government in budgetary terms.

While such reform seems desirable, the political difficulties in securing it cannot be denied. In retrospect, the United States missed an excellent opportunity for mounting the political will for policy change in 1990. Prior to the U.S. farm bill debates of 1990, Sturgiss, Field, and Young (1990, page 4) noted:

> The coincidence of the timing of the Uruguay Round, the GATT panel finding on the inconsistency of current U.S. sugar import quotas with the GATT, and the forthcoming 1990 farm bill may provide an impetus for U.S. reform that was missing from the farm bill debates in 1981 and 1985, and a unique opportunity both for reform of the U.S. sugar program and participation by the United States in wider-ranging multilateral reforms.

That such reform was not forthcoming in 1990 is testament to the strong political constraints that limit possibilities for program revision. Three such constraints stand out. First, the U.S. program is designed to operate at no budgetary cost to the federal government. In the present era of budgetary stringency, it is most unlikely that the government would simultaneously make the costs of sugar support more visible to taxpayers and consumers and more costly to itself. Second, sugar is an important crop in many areas of the United States, lending a strong regional basis to legislative opposition to liberalization. Third, because the sugar program continues to provide an attractive market for corn output and a profitable niche for HFCS producers, its political support is far wider than it would have been on the basis of sugar production alone. Indeed, the simulations in Sturgiss, Field, and Young indicate that HFCS producers would be the largest losers from sugar-policy liberalization in the United States.

That reform has not taken hold suggests that the United States might impose ever-larger distortions on the world sugar market. As Sturgiss, Field, and Young (1990, page 66) concluded:

> There is a danger that U.S. policies, if not reformed unilaterally or as part of multilateral trade negotiations, could follow the path taken earlier by EC sugar policies. The United States, with the development of new corn- and chemically-based sweeteners, could become a large exporter of [subsidized] sweeteners. This would raise the costs of the program and would also create a new set of unintended beneficiaries with a stake in seeing policies maintained. The tendency to perpetuate current inefficient policies would thus be increased.

The European Community

Because the EC sugar regime is largely self-financing and thereby does not impose excessive costs on the Community budget, it is regarded within the Community as being one of the less problematic aspects of the Common Agricultural Policy. However, as long as EC policy encourages the sugar industry to use resources well past the point at which their cost exceeds the international value of sugar, the policy will impose a large cost on the EC economy.

In the past the European Community expanded quotas and/or prices following booms in the world price. If prices boom some time in the next few seasons, pressures may arise again to raise these support mechanisms. For instance, a period of high world prices may provide the impetus and apparent political justification within the EC to raise sugar quotas in a united Germany. Ensuring that current production quota limits and/or subsidized prices are not increased in response to high world prices may be an important policy challenge in the 1990s. Any reforms that achieve a reduction in production quota levels would represent a major increase in efficiency.

Continuation of existing EC policy has the potential not only to impose high costs on the Community itself, but also on many exporters, including some ACP exporters and the world economy more generally. As the exports from efficient ACP exporters grow through time, their quota access to the high-priced EC market will decline as a proportion of total exports. The world price-depressing effects of the EC policy could then tend to outweigh the benefits deriving from the quota sales to the EC itself. Simulations by Wong, Sturgiss, and Borrell (1989) suggest that a continuation of the EC program on current terms would impose net costs on the majority of ACP countries by the year 2002.

Japan

Many of the benefits from Japan moving to free trade could be achieved by reducing consumer prices and making them more responsive to world prices. Protection to producers could be continued through the use of well-targeted direct payments from government. Sturgiss, Tobler, and Connell (1988) conclude that direct income supplements to farmers in Japan would provide a more efficient and equitable means of assistance than is currently provided under unit subsidies. Targeting assistance to help inefficient farmers leave the industry or providing incentives to establish alternative industries may be more efficient ways of providing support to various regions than by distorting prices.

In 1988, Japan introduced a number of reforms to its agricultural sector. Forces within Japan as well as pressure from the United States may have precipitated these changes. While this may be an indication of a desire by the Japanese to reduce intervention affecting some agricultural products, reforms to the sugar industry may be of lower priority. To date the reforms have mostly involved products exported by the United States.

As in the United States, failure to reform the sugar industry could lead to the establishment of larger groups with a stake in retaining existing supports. The further technical development and market penetration of alternative sweeteners would ultimately increase the proportion of the sweetener market being met from subsidized domestic sources.

The Cairns Group

The sugar exporters of the Cairns Group constitute the majority of the world's low-cost producers. Production in these countries is currently highly regulated, though lightly protected. Collectively, this group has the potential to reduce the volatility of the world price. To do this, they would have to implement policy changes that would leave their producers free to make their own marginal production decisions based on expected world prices.

The Cairns Group exporters have a common interest in reducing price volatility and in supplying more sugar to the growing world market. In a buoyant market such as is likely to prevail over the next few seasons, concerted action by members of this group may improve the trading environment of each member.

As pointed out by Wong, Sturgiss, and Borrell (1989), a Cairns Group initiative designed to prevent boom prices on the world market could be undertaken by low-protection nations independently of the reform problems of high-protection countries. Such an initiative would be consistent with the Cairns Group's first aim of heading off a buildup in global protection by removing the incentive for new demands by vested interests in higher-cost countries. At the same time, such an initiative is not likely to jeopardize other moves by the Group toward a more open trading system. Indeed, it may strengthen the position of the group. By reducing the probability of low prices it would lessen the perceived need for policies such as those operated in the United States and the European Community. The more substantial and widespread the reforms undertaken, and the greater the proportions of production and consumption that are exposed to the world price, the less variable the price will become. Despite the incentives for low-cost countries to free up their markets, political constraints remain that make such countries cautious to change.

Of the Cairns Group members, Australia and Brazil are the two countries with the greatest potential to influence world price variability if reforms are introduced. While there has been some relaxation of production controls in Australia in recent times, they have been small, and controls still greatly restrict the responsiveness of Australian supply. In Brazil in the past two years, instead of increasing sugar production, sugar quotas have been reduced to allow for the expansion of ethanol output. Although pressure has been exerted by Brazilian producers for relaxation of production controls on sugar, it has not yet resulted in any significant liberalization.

5. Conclusion

Without concerted action by low-cost exporting countries immediately to reform their policies in ways that allow their producers to respond directly to world prices, supply shortfalls and an 18–month to two-year price boom are likely to occur sometime before 1995. The attention given to the disruptive policies of the United States, the European Community, and Japan in recent years, and agreements already reached through GATT, may create enough pressure to hold absolute levels of support in check in these countries over the 1990s. The prospects for durable and worthwhile reform of these policies, however, remain very much in doubt, given the vested interests already established. Nonetheless, any reforms in these countries that increase the exposure of their producers and consumers to the world price would allow for significant gains from trade to be achieved.

NOTES

The authors wish to acknowledge the valuable contributions made to the development of many ideas expressed in this paper, through earlier work conducted at the Australian Bureau of Agricultural and Resource Economics by Robert Sturgiss and Gordon Wong.

1. To this point, we have relied on the notion of self-interested groups to explain the existence of policies that benefit growers and processors at the expense of others. As Robert M. Stern observed in his comments on an earlier version of this paper, however, the framework could be augmented to take other influences on policy makers into account. For example, important aspects of support for sugar farmers may be better understood in terms of Corden's (1974) "conservative social welfare function," which suggests that governments will often undertake policies to prevent economic changes from making important groups significantly worse off compared to their initial level of economic welfare. In this view, there could be relatively large numbers of producers affected by such intervention, rather than a small concentration of producer interests, and the intervention could be condoned by those who foot the bill. Moreover, there may be important foreign policy objectives at stake in carrying out sugar policies. This is evident in the manner in which U.S. policies have been administered, with quotas being reallocated from less friendly to more friendly nations. In the EC, sugar imports are limited to the Lomé Convention signatories, which are primarily former colonies of Britain and France.

2. See Michael Tracy, "The Political Economy of Agriculture in the European Community," in Michelmann, Stabler, and Storey (1990). For further discussion of agricultural political economy in the industrial countries, see the contributions in Sanderson (1990).

3. Robert M. Stern notes that partial-equilibrium models may not fully capture the effects of interactions among markets. One alternative approach is to construct multicommodity models, as represented by the Jabara-Valdés paper in this volume. Given the interrelationships among different types of agricultural commodities in production and consumption, there is great interest in developing models that can capture the multicommodity effects of specific distortions and their removal. Unfortunately, as more commodities are included in such efforts, it is inevitable that the amount of institutional detail that can be treated will be reduced. A final alternative would be to build general-equilibrium models that determine how agricultural markets interact with markets for other goods and services. General equilibrium interactions do matter, both within and between countries, the more so the larger and more geographically dispersed are the changes being considered. Future efforts need to be made to embed the detailed

partial-equilibrium models in a general-equilibrium framework in order to determine the intersectoral effects of changes in policies.
4. For a review of estimates from partial equilibrium studies on the U.S. sugar program, see Rendleman and Hertel (1989).
5. In comparison, the world raw sugar price was about 0.22 ecu/kg, CIF Rotterdam.
6. The Cairns Group consists of Argentina, Australia, Brazil, Canada, Chile, Colombia, Fiji, Hungary, Indonesia, Malaysia, the Philippines, New Zealand, Thailand, and Uruguay.

REFERENCES

ABARE (Australian Bureau of Agricultural and Resource Economics). 1988. *Japanese Agricultural Policies: A Time of Change*. Policy Monograph No. 3. Canberra: Australian Government Publishing Service.
Anderson, Kym, and Rodney Tyers. 1986. "Agricultural Policies of Industrial Countries and their Effects on Traditional Food Exporters." *Economic Record* 179: 385–99.
Anderson, Kym, and Rodney Tyers. 1989. *Global Effects of Liberalizing Trade in Farm Products*. Thames Essay No. 55. London: Trade Policy Research Centre.
BAE (Bureau of Agricultural Economics). 1985. *Agricultural Policies in the European Community: Their Origins, Nature and Effects on Production and Trade*. Policy Monograph No. 2. Canberra: Australian Government Publishing Service.
Ballinger, Roy A. 1971. *A History of Sugar Marketing*. U.S. Department of Agriculture, Economic Research Service. Agricultural Economic Report No. 197.
Borrell, Brent, and Gordon Wong. 1986. *Efficiency of Transport, Milling, and Handling in the Sugar Industry*. BAE Occasional Paper No. 96. Canberra: Australian Government Publishing Service.
———, Robert Sturgiss, and Gordon Wong. 1987. *Global Effects of the U.S. Sugar Policy*. BAE Discussion Paper No. 87.3. Canberra: Australian Government Publishing Service.
———, Gordon Wong, and Robert Sturgiss. 1989. "Growth in World Sugar Consumption." ABARE paper presented at the National Agricultural Outlook Conference. Canberra. 17–19 January.
Commission of the European Communities. 1988. *The Agricultural Situation in the Community: 1988 Report* (and previous issues). Brussels.
Connell, Peter. 1989. "Effects of the New Domestic Sugar Marketing Arrangement." *Agricultural and Resources Quarterly* 1: 59–70. Canberra: Australian Government Publishing Service.
Corden, W. Max. 1974. *Trade Policy and Economic Welfare*. Oxford: Oxford University Press.
Fry, James. 1982. "The Costs of Production of Sugar and HFCS." In *F.O. Licht 1982 Yearbook*. Ratzeburg, Federal Republic of Germany.
Kindleberger, Charles P. 1973. *International Economics*. Homewood, IL: Richard D. Irwin.
Koester, Ulrich, and Peter Michael Schmitz. 1982. "The EC Sugar Market Policy and Developing Countries." *European Review of Agricultural Economics* 9: 183–204.

Michelmann, Hans J., Jack C. Stabler, and Gary G. Storey. 1990. *The Political Economy of Agricultural Trade and Policy: Toward a New Order for Europe and North America.* Boulder, CO: Westview Press.

Moyer, H. Wayne, and Timothy E. Josling. 1990. *Agricultural Policy Reform: Politics and Process in the EC and the USA.* Ames: Iowa State University Press.

Olsen, Mancur. 1982. *The Rise and Decline of Nations.* New Haven: Yale University Press.

Organization for Economic Cooperation and Development. 1987. *National Policies and Agricultural Trade.* Paris: OECD.

Rendleman, M., and Thomas W. Hertel. 1989. "Economy-wide Effects of the Sugar Program," Selected paper. American Agricultural Economics Association. Baton Rouge, Louisiana. August.

Roberts, I. M., and P. Whish-Wilson. 1991. *Domestic and World Market Effects of EC Sugar Policies.* ABARE Discussion Paper 91.1. Canberra: Australian Government Publishing Service.

Sanderson, Fred H., ed. 1990. *Agricultural Protectionism in the Industrialized World.* Washington, DC: Resources for the Future.

Sturgiss, Robert, Peter Tobler, and Peter Connell. 1988. *Japanese Sugar Policy and its Effects on World Markets.* ABARE Occasional Paper No. 104. Canberra: Australian Government Publishing Service.

———, Peter Connell, and Peter Tobler. 1990. "Australia's Influence on World Sugar Prices." *Agricultural and Resources Quarterly* 2: 47–55. Canberra: Australian Government Publishing Service.

———, Heather Field, and Linda Young. 1990. *1990 and U.S. Sugar Policy Reform.* ABARE Discussion Paper No. 90.4. Canberra: Australian Government Publishing Service.

Sudaryanto, T. 1987. "The Potential Impacts of Liberalized Trade Policies in the United States and the European Economic Community in International Markets for Sugar." Ph.D. dissertation. Graduate Faculty of North Carolina State University, Raleigh.

Valdés, Alberto, and Joachim Zietz. 1980. *Agricultural Protection in OECD Countries: Its Costs to Less-Developed Countries.* International Food Policy Research Institute. Washington, DC. Research Report 21.

Webb, Alan T., Vernon O. Roningen, and Praveen Dixit. 1987. "Analyzing Agricultural Trade Liberalization for the Pacific Basin." Paper presented at the Livestock and Feedgrains Working Group of the Pacific Economic Cooperation Conference. Napier, New Zealand. 20–22 October.

Wong, Gordon C., Robert Sturgiss, and Brent Borrell. 1989. *The Economic Consequences of International Sugar Trade Reform.* ABARE Discussion Paper No. 89.7. Canberra: Australian Government Publishing Service.

Zietz, Joachim, and Alberto Valdés. 1986. *The Costs of Protectionism to Developing Countries: An Analysis for Selected Agricultural Products.* World Bank. Staff Working Paper 769.

CHAPTER 3

The Economics and Politics of U.S. Sugar Policy

Andrew Schmitz and Douglas Christian

1. Introduction

The U.S. sugar program is arguably the most criticized of all U.S. farm programs, the dairy program being the only possible exception. Criticism of the sugar program centers on its high net domestic cost and its increasingly deleterious effects on third-world exporters. In this paper, we examine a variety of conceptual and empirical issues that suggest that recent estimates of both the domestic and foreign effects of the program must be treated with caution. We also examine the regional basis for political support of the program.

We first survey the long history of U.S. government intervention in sugar markets, and then examine the current U.S. sugar policies in detail. While we do not try to justify U.S. sugar policies, we do point out the sensitivity of estimated costs and benefits to the underlying assumptions. The factors we examine include the elasticities of sugar supply and demand in the U.S. sugar market, the extent of consumer substitution into lower-cost corn sweeteners, the difference between the supported U.S. price and the world price at a point in time, and the extent to which liberalization of U.S. sugar policy would cause the world price to increase. One of our specific conclusions is that the net-cost estimates prepared in conjunction with the debate on the Food Security Act of 1985, based on the uncharacteristically low world prices of the period, tend to overstate current net costs of the program. Moreover, although the extent of the role of the U.S. sugar program in the development of the U.S. high fructose corn syrup (HFCS) industry cannot be determined with certainty, the benefits derived from the availability of that sugar substitute nevertheless tend to be overlooked.

We also consider the U.S. sugar program in its world trading context—in which the world sugar price is distorted by the policies of many nations and is depressed downward relative to the free-trade equilibrium price: we point out that *multilateral* sugar policy reform and trade liberalization would not necessarily have substantial effects on U.S. sugar trade, prices, production, or consumption. In other words, if viewed as a response to the policies of other industrial market economies that depress the world sugar price, the U.S.

49

import-quota program may actually *restore* the market price that would prevail in the United States under free trade.

Finally, even though the sugar program appears to impose a net economic cost on the United States overall, its impact varies substantially by region, and regions within the United States that are net sugar exporters can gain from the program. We argue on this basis that the geographical distribution of sugar production and processing, in conjunction with that of corn production and HFCS processing, will likely provide broad regional support for sugar in the future. As a simple test of the argument, we examine the regional pattern of support for the sugar program in votes in the U.S. Senate and House of Representatives during deliberations on the 1990 Farm Bill.

2. U.S. Sugar Policy

Because the United States is a net sugar importer, the means by which the government supports U.S. sugar producers have typically differed significantly from the support measures used for other farm commodities, most of which are exportables. The government has been directly involved in the sugar market as part of national policy as far back as 1789 (Bates and Schmitz 1969). Since that time, a variety of mechanisms have been used as instruments of U.S. sugar policy. These include foreign import quotas, import tariffs, domestic acreage restrictions, support prices, subsidies, and special loan and purchase programs.

The history of U.S. sugar policy consists of three major periods (Messina 1989). From 1789 to 1890, tariffs were imposed on sugar, among other imported commodities, as a means to generate governmental revenue. There was initially little or no domestic production to be protected (Langley and Zellner 1986). Domestic production grew over the years, and in 1890 the U.S. Treasury removed the tariffs, which resulted in a large inflow of low-priced world sugar. Because of the influx of sugar, U.S. refiners and processors were given a bounty of two cents per pound on sugar produced. In 1894 a tariff of 40 percent was imposed on sugar imports in lieu of the bounty.

The third stage of U.S. sugar policy began in the early 1930s and was in response to a rapid expansion of world sugar production that drove prices to extremely low levels. The ad valorem tariff rate established in 1894 was no longer sufficient to support the industry. In 1934, the Jones-Costigan Act (also known as the Sugar Act) was passed, establishing the basic sugar policy instruments of import quotas and marketing allotments to restrict supply and support domestic prices. Jones-Costigan was followed by the Sugar Act of 1937, which was extended in 1940, 1941, 1944, 1946, and 1947. The Sugar Act of 1948 represented a refinement of policies set out by the previous acts, revising the quota allocation process primarily to provide preferential treatment for Cuba. Although sugar imports from Cuba were terminated in 1960, the 1948 Act was extended, with minor amendments, in 1951, 1962, 1965, and 1971.

In 1974, shortages in the world market resulted in an approximate tripling of sugar prices. Thus, when the Sugar Act of 1948 came up for renewal in 1974, it was allowed to expire as Congress no longer deemed it necessary. However, because of the large production response to the price increases and the resulting decline in world prices, in May of 1977 the President instituted a temporary price-support program under the authority of the Agriculture Act of 1949 until new sugar legislation could be enacted. The Food and Agriculture Act of 1977 subsequently established special purchase and loan provisions for the 1977 and 1978 sugar crops. Under these provisions, the Commodity Credit Corporation (CCC) of the U.S. government lent to sugar processors an amount equal to a specified loan rate for each pound of sugar in storage. Processors had the option of repaying the loan (with interest) and marketing the sugar, or defaulting and forfeiting the sugar to the CCC. Processors, in turn, agreed to pay a minimum price for sugarcane and sugarbeets. Thus, the loan rate established a minimum price for sugar in a manner similar to that of the wheat and feed grain programs. Import duties and fees were imposed under Section 22 of the Agricultural Adjustment Act of 1933, in order to support the domestic price at a level that would discourage forfeiture to the CCC.

The price supports and loan program were maintained for the 1979 crop under discretionary presidential authority, but the world price spike of 1980 obviated the need for price supports in 1980 and most of 1981 (Barry et al. 1990). As world sugar prices turned downward, however, the Agriculture and Food Act of 1981 formally established a loan-purchase program including domestic price supports for the years 1982 through 1985. Sugarcane loan rates were graduated from 16.75 cents per pound for raw sugar in 1981 to 18 cents per pound in 1985. To minimize the risk of the CCC acquiring sugar, the U.S. Department of Agriculture (USDA) introduced the market stabilization price (MSP) as its policy price objective. The MSP represents the minimum raw sugar price for which commercial sales are more profitable than forfeiture of sugar used as collateral for CCC loans. In addition to the loan rate, it includes interest on the loan, estimated freight and marketing costs, and an incentive factor.

As world prices continued to drop, the statutorily limited tariffs and fees became insufficient to support the MSP, and the Reagan administration chose to reintroduce import quotas in 1982 under the President's authority in the headnote to the Tariff Schedule of the United States. The quotas have remained in effect to this day. The total quota level is set on the basis of

USDA estimates of U.S. domestic consumption and production with the MSP as the market price. Quotas were allocated initially to 41 countries, based on their shares of the U.S. market during 1975–81, when imports were relatively unrestricted. Duties have played only a minor role since that time, and were only 0.625 cents per pound in 1989.[1] Unlike the quota programs in effect prior to 1974, the sugar program since 1982 has not included domestic production controls. Thus, domestic producers presumably can increase their output at will. In section 5.1, we examine why domestic production has *not* increased substantially in recent years, despite the comparatively high returns per acre to sugar crops.

The Food Security Act of 1985 provided protection for the 1986 through 1990 crops. It specified a minimum national nonrecourse loan rate of 18 cents per pound for raw cane sugar, while sugarbeets were to be supported at a level (21.54 cents per pound) consistent with the historical relationship between beet and cane sugar prices. For fiscal 1990, the MSP was 21.95 cents per pound.

In 1985, the U.S. government announcement of unexpectedly large import quotas for the 1985–86 market year resulted in sugar forfeitures to the CCC (Maskus 1989). This affected negotiations on the 1985 Farm Bill, and was responsible for the inclusion of the Dole Amendment, which required the sugar program to be conducted at no net cost to the federal government. This provision effectively eliminated the possibility of further CCC forfeitures, thus forcing the use of the import quota mechanism in order to support high domestic sugar prices.

Amendments to the 1990 Farm Bill that would have lowered the sugar loan rate were defeated in both houses of Congress, and the nominal loan rate remains at 18 cents per pound today. In real terms, however, the loan rate has clearly eroded since 1985.

3. The Domestic Effects of the U.S. Sugar Program

Considerable controversy surrounds the extent to which U.S. sugar import quotas impose net costs on the U.S. economy. As we will show, the net costs of these quotas were estimated to be as high as several billion dollars per year in the mid-1980s, with consumer costs far in excess of producer gains.

3.1 Assumptions on which the Analyses Hinge

In estimation of the effects of the U.S. sugar program, the assumptions made about several critical factors can significantly affect the results obtained. This section surveys four sets of such factors: supply and demand elasticities, substitution into HFCS, the relevant world sugar price, and the effect of the U.S. sugar policy on the world price of sugar. We then show how recent calculations of the net costs of the sugar program have varied as a function of the assumptions made about these factors.

Supply and Demand Elasticities

The conclusions of any study of the costs and benefits associated with the sugar program depend on the price elasticities of demand and supply used in the analysis, among other factors. A wide range of supply elasticities have been used in empirical work. Lopez (1989) estimated the price elasticities of supply for cane and beet sugar to be 0.231 and 0.479 in the short run, and 0.579 and 1.201 in the long run. For beet sugar, his short-run elasticity was comparable to the 0.40 estimate of Jesse (1977). Gemmill (1976) estimated a U.S. cane supply elasticity of 1.57 and a beet supply elasticity of 1.74. Jesse and Zepp (1977) implicitly found a total U.S. supply elasticity of 0.20 for cane and 1.65–2.15 for beets. Leu, Schmitz, and Knutson (1987) assumed aggregate supply elasticities of 1.5 for cane and 2.0 for beet. For foreign supply, Gemmill found the foreign cane sugar supply elasticity to range from 0.3 to 1.0, while the excess supply curve of quota-holding countries was estimated by Lopez to have an elasticity of 0.05. Such disparate measures of the sugar supply response have inevitably led to a wide range of cost and benefit estimates.

Demand elasticities also vary by study, but generally the aggregate demand for both sugar and corn sweeteners is price inelastic.[2] However, considerable substitution exists between the two sweeteners. For example, Leu et al. found a statistically significant substitution relationship between sugar demand and corn sweetener demand.

Substitution

It is crucial to take into account the degree of substitution that has occurred between sugar and corn sweeteners. The greater is the degree of substitution, the more price elastic is the demand for sugar. The elasticity of demand then bears on the consumer costs estimated for the program.[3]

Over the years, there has been a significant increase in both U.S. corn sweetener production and use.[4] Figure 1 shows U.S. domestic deliveries of imported sugar, domestic sugar, and high fructose corn syrup (HFCS) between 1975 and 1989 (Barry et al. 1990, table 10). As the figure shows, the corn-sweetener share of the market has increased significantly: HFCS had only 5 percent of the market in 1975, but 44 percent in 1989. Since 1986, however, the per capita consumption of both sugar and corn sweeteners has been stable, which perhaps suggests that HFCS has completed its displacement of liquid sugar (Ives and Hurley 1988).

Annual U.S. net imports of raw sugar in the early 1970s were roughly 5

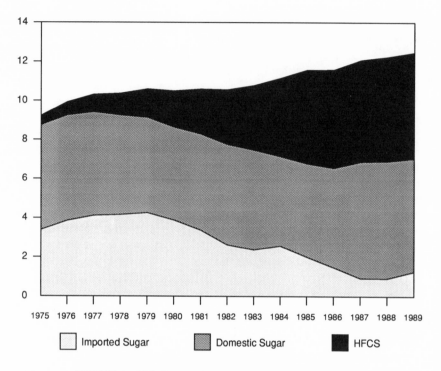

FIGURE 1. U.S. Domestic Deliveries of Sugar and HFCS, 1975–89 (millions of metric tons, refined dry basis)

million metric tons. Beginning in 1982, the year that quotas were reimposed, imports fell sharply, reaching a low of roughly 1 million metric tons in 1987 before recovering slightly in 1989 to 1.2 million metric tons, 24 percent above the low two years earlier. Figure 1 suggests that the imports were displaced primarily by increased U.S. use of corn sweeteners: the increase in HFCS production in the United States (from 1 million metric tons in 1977 to 5.3 million in 1989) is roughly equivalent to the decrease in sugar imports over the same period. Increases in domestic sugar production had a much smaller impact.

The competitiveness of corn sweeteners depends on the relationship between the prices of domestic sugar and corn sweeteners, and the extent to which consumer tastes and the production technologies for food and beverages allow for substitution between sugar and corn sweeteners. As the internal price of sugar rose due to the imposition of import quotas, consumers were induced to switch from sugar to corn sweeteners. This outward shift in the demand for corn sweeteners caused the quantity demanded and price of corn sweeteners to rise, but the realization of dynamic scale economies and technological progress in corn sweetener production over time shifted out the supply of corn sweeteners, driving down their price. This lower price then induced further substitution from sugar into corn sweeteners. It follows that the greater is the degree of substitution between sugar and corn sweeteners, the lesser will be the impact of sugar quotas on U.S. consumers.

World Sugar Price

The third important consideration in estimating the effects of the U.S. sugar program is the import price, which is often referred to as the "world sugar price." The lower the import price, the greater will be the opportunity cost of a given level of sugar quotas to U.S. consumers, and the higher will be the benefit implied for U.S. sweetener producers, all else equal. Figure 2 shows that the world price of sugar has varied considerably since 1950. It also shows the extent to which the U.S. price has been supported above the world price; the gap between the two has closed only during major world price spikes. When analyses were carried out for the 1985 U.S. Farm Bill (from

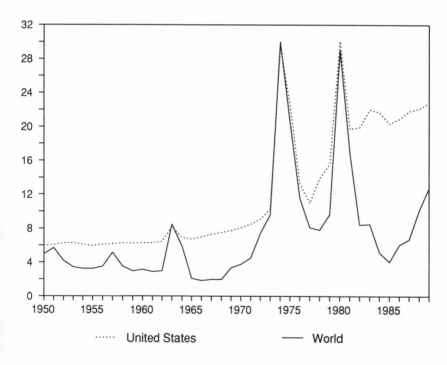

FIGURE 2.   Raw Sugar Prices, 1950–89 (cents per pound)

which the highest sugar program costs are reported), world sugar prices were essentially at an all-time low in real terms, and the U.S. price premium at its all-time high. Therefore, in using 1985 data, one gets a much higher estimate of the cost to U.S. consumers and to the U.S. economy overall from quotas than if one uses 1989 data, which reflect a considerably higher world market price for sugar.

Price Effects

The costs and benefits calculated for the U.S. sugar program also depend on the extent to which the program influences world sugar prices. Should one use a "large-country" or "small-country" assumption for the United States? The large-country assumption is that the level of U.S. imports affects the world price of sugar. In this case, elimination of the sugar program would cause the world price to rise, yielding a smaller savings to U.S. consumers than if the world price had remained unchanged. However, under the small-country assumption, world prices would not change, and the internal price rise due to the quota would simply be added to the existing world price of sugar.

The data show that the United States has been at times a large importer of sugar. For example, during 1983–85, U.S. imports exceeded 10 percent of world sugar imports even in the presence of quotas, as shown in table 1. It is reasonable to assume, based on empirical estimates, that changes in the U.S. sugar import quota have had an impact on the world price of sugar (Lopez 1989). The effect depends on the price elasticity of aggregate foreign export supply. If one uses the highly inelastic estimates of Lopez (0.05) or Gemmill (0.3 to 1.0), the price effect is much greater than if one uses the Hammig et al. (1982) estimate of 2.37.

3.2 Sugar Program Costs

Table 2 gives a summary of one set of results of the effects of the U.S. sugar program in 1983, estimated by Leu, Schmitz, and Knutson (1987) in connection with the debate on the 1985 Farm Bill. Leu et al. constructed a model using a general equilibrium demand schedule for domestic sugar. This approach allows for the substitution into corn sweeteners due to increases in the price of sugar, and takes into account the effects of the sugar program on the corn sweetener market. The results highlight some of the points brought out in section 3.1. In particular, we show that the estimates depend critically on the world price of sugar, the degree of substitution into corn sweeteners, and the price elasticity of aggregate foreign export supply. Specifically, the calculations are shown for quota price premiums over the world price of 7.49,

10.70, and 16.05 cents per pound. (In 1983 the U.S. price premium was 13.55 cents per pound. The premium rose to more than 16 cents per pound in 1984 and 1985, but was only slightly above 8 cents per pound in early 1990.) Likewise, price elasticities of excess sugar supply from the rest of the world of 2.37 and infinity are used.

Combined in various scenarios, these alternative assumptions can lead to a wide range of estimates on the cost of the U.S. sugar program. In table 2, if one assumes that the quota price premium is 16.05 cents per pound, the United States is a small country (so that the elasticity of excess supply in the rest of the world is infinite), and there is no substitution into corn sweeteners, then the estimated net cost of the program is $3.2 billion annually. Under this scenario, sugar producers gain more than $800 million, while consumers lose more than $4 billion. However, with a quota price premium of 7.49 cents per pound, the large-country assumption that the excess supply

TABLE 1.   Net EC and U.S. Sugar Imports Relative to Total World Imports (all types, raw value, fiscal years)

Year	EC	U.S.	World	EC Share	U.S. Share
	thousands of metric tons			percent	
1970/71	1,806	4,821	17,352	10.4	27.8
1971/72	969	4,973	17,813	5.4	27.9
1972/73	1,456	5,099	19,590	7.4	26.0
1973/74	1,644	5,346	23,112	7.1	23.1
1974/75	2,769	3,690	22,877	12.1	16.1
1975/76	1,339	4,157	23,439	5.7	17.7
1976/77	490	4,737	25,967	1.9	18.2
1977/78	-1,505	4,629	26,476	-5.7	17.5
1978/79	-1,161	4,562	26,762	-4.3	17.0
1979/80	-2,020	3,892	29,277	-6.9	13.3
1980/81	-2,945	2,828	27,785	-10.6	10.2
1981/82	-3,631	3,840	31,606	-11.5	12.1
1982/83	-3,980	3,024	29,955	-13.3	10.1
1983/84	-2,451	3,091	29,015	-8.4	10.7
1984/85	-2,064	2,989	29,055	-7.1	10.3
1985/86	-2,601	1,940	28,876	-9.0	6.7
1986/87	-2,971	912	27,326	-10.9	3.3
1987/88	-2,656	786	28,050	-9.5	2.8
1988/89	-2,855	1,290	29,084	-9.8	4.4
1989/90	-3,579	1,705	28,589	-12.5	6.0

Source: U.S. Department of Agriculture, Economic Research Service, Commodity Economics Division, *Sugar and Sweeteners: Situation and Outlook Report*, various issues. (Updated through December 1990.)

TABLE 2. U.S. Costs and Benefits of the Sugar Program, 1983

Quota Price Premium	Elasticity of Foreign Excess Supply	Consumer Cost Substitution:		Producer Gain	Net Societal Cost Substitution:	
		Without	With		Without	With
cents per pound				millions of 1983 dollars		
7.49	2.37	423	372	169	253	203
	∞	1,856	1,636	598	1,258	1,038
10.70	2.37	926	815	345	580	470
	∞	2,661	2,347	742	1,919	1,605
16.05	2.37	1,769	1,559	578	1,191	981
	∞	4,017	3,546	833	3,184	2,713

Source: Leu, Schmitz, and Knutson (1987).

elasticity is 2.37, and substitution into corn sweeteners, the net societal cost of the program drops to only $203 million. Under this scenario, producers gain only $169 million, while consumers lose only $372 million.

Table 3 compares the implications of this model with estimates from other studies—one by the U.S. Department of Agriculture (1984) and one by Schmitz, Allen, and Leu (1987). The USDA used a forecast of a quota price premium of 12.50 cents per pound for 1983 in its welfare calculations, while Schmitz et al. assumed a quota price premium of 9.76 cents per pound for 1983 in their welfare calculations. Both studies made the small-country assumption. For purposes of comparison, the model of Leu et al. (with substitution into corn sweeteners assumed) was used to calculate welfare effects for each of these quota premiums, under both the small-country and large-country assumptions. In addition, the net revenue gains to the U.S. government from sugar import duties and fees are included in the calculations.

The USDA estimated the annual cost of the program to be $2.3 billion to consumers, with producers gaining $1.5 billion. The implied net-cost estimate of $0.7 billion is substantially below the comparable $1.9 billion estimate in table 3 based on the model of Leu et al. Schmitz et al. estimated smaller consumer costs than Leu et al., but also estimated smaller producer gains. However, their estimate of the net cost to society was $1.3 billion, nearly identical to the comparable estimate of Leu et al. Finally, in a seminal piece, Maskus (1989) estimated the net national cost of the U.S. sugar program to be between $460 million and $1.3 billion, using data prior to 1985. These are among the lowest estimates reported on the effects of the U.S. sugar quotas.

Of the four studies—by the USDA, Schmitz et al., Maskus, and Leu et al.—the findings of Leu et al. reported in table 2 are by far the highest net cost estimates for the U.S. sugar program. Therefore, although the net cost of the U.S. sugar program has been estimated to be as high as $3.2 billion, other credible estimates are much lower. If 1989–90 data were used, the net costs would be well below $1 billion, based on the model of Leu et al.

Part of the reason for the wide discrepancy in results on the effect of quotas is due to the lack of data on how much they benefit the corn sweetener industry. In the work by Leu et al., the effects of quotas on the corn sweetener market were quantified by allowing for consumer substitution between sugar and HFCS. However, the dynamics of the supply side of the HFCS industry were not explicitly modeled. Because of the positive impact of the U.S. sugar policy on the corn sweetener industry, the net-cost estimates of Leu et al. are overstated. Specifically, over time the costs of HFCS production have decreased significantly because new technologies have markedly increased the rate of extraction of sweetener from corn.

TABLE 3. A Comparison of Estimates of U.S. Costs and Benefits of the Sugar Program, 1983

Quota Price Premium	Study[a]	Elasticity of Foreign Excess Supply	Consumer Cost	Producer Gain	Government Revenue[b]	Net Societal Cost
			millions of 1983 dollars			
cents per pound						
9.76	Schmitz, et al.	∞	1,740	326	67	1,347
9.76	Leu, et al.	2.37	685	296	67	322
		∞	2,138	707	67	1,364
12.50	USDA	∞	2,292	1,500	67	725
12.50	Leu et al.	2.37	1,065	432	67	566
		∞	2,749	794	67	1,888

Sources: Leu, Schmitz, and Knutson (1987); Schmitz, Allen, and Leu (1987); and U.S. Department of Agriculture (1984).

[a] A quota price premium of 9.76 cents per pound was assumed for 1983 in the welfare calculations made by Schmitz, et al. A forecast of a quota price premium of 12.50 cents per pound for 1983 was used in the welfare calculations by the USDA. The model of Leu et al. was used to calculate welfare effects for each of these price premiums for purposes of comparison.

[b] Government revenue includes import fees and duties, calculated at 1983 levels, and used to adjust the net societal cost of the sugar program in 1983.

A study undertaken by the U.S. Department of Commerce on U.S. sugar policy (Ives and Hurley 1988) suggests that the HFCS industry experienced a very favorable climate for growth under the sugar program. It estimated that during 1981–85 corn refiners received a net revenue gain from the program of more than $2.3 billion, based on the difference between the actual U.S. price of HFCS and an assumed world price of 15 cents per pound.

There is not enough data to determine the extent to which the emergence of the corn-sweetener industry was triggered by the sugar quotas, though it is certainly the case that the price umbrella provided under the sugar program facilitated the development of the industry. Clearly, further analysis is needed on the benefits accruing to the corn producers and processors from the program.

3.3 Additional Caveats

There are several additional reasons to view the conclusions of recent analyses of the U.S. sugar program with caution.

(1) The analyses to this point do not consider whether the world price of sugar is truly a free market price. However, both casual empiricism and the formal studies considered in the next section suggest that the world price is a "distorted" price that is depressed by the policies of many countries, such as U.S. import quotas and European export policies. Given that the true free market price is above the existing world price, a movement toward multilateral free trade in sugar will not necessarily harm U.S. producers, nor benefit U.S. consumers. In other words, the impact of multilateral trade liberalization in the sugar market is a much different issue from that of unilateral elimination of U.S. sugar quotas. Section 4 examines these issues in detail.

(2) These analyses do not take into account the role of U.S. quotas in the reduction of producer risk. To the extent that producers are risk averse, quotas result in both an increase in producer price and a shift to the right of the U.S. supply curve for sugar. The latter is a benefit of the U.S. sugar program—one that has not been measured to this point. Studies by Just (1972) and others suggest that risk reduction is important for efficiently allocating resources. Also, given the decreased ratio of stocks to consumption in the world sugar market (for example, 17.9 percent in 1989–90 versus 31.2 percent in 1982–83), the degree of instability and uncertainty in the world market has increased.[5]

(3) These analyses assume that, if a drop in sugar prices occurred due to removal of the U.S. program, consumers would be the beneficiaries. This assumption has not been empirically tested, however. To the extent that the industrial users of sugar exercise market power in their output markets, not all of a sugar price decrease would be passed on to consumers.

4. The U.S. Sugar Program in a World Trading Context

It is clear from the discussion in previous sections that the costs and benefits of the U.S. sugar program depend critically on the level of world prices. The lower is the world price relative to the internal support price, the larger is the opportunity cost from the U.S. sugar program. However, there remains the question of the appropriate border price, which in turn depends on whether the analysis is of unilateral or multilateral sugar policy reform and trade liberalization. In other words, is the appropriate border price the present distorted price, or the price that would exist under multilateral free trade as proposed in Uruguay Round of the GATT?

The importance of this question is made clear in figure 3, which draws upon Schmitz, Schmitz, and Vercammen (1991). S is the supply curve and D is the demand curve for sugar in the United States. ES_{OLC} is the excess supply curve of another large country, and ES_{ROW} is the excess supply curve of the major exporters of the rest of the world. In a free-trade regime, price P_s prevails. The United States imports $Q_2 - Q_1$, while the other large country imports Q_4. Both are supplied by exports of Q_3 from the rest of the world.[6]

Now suppose that the other large country subsidizes its sugar production at price P_e. Rather than importing sugar, it now exports Q_5. The price in the rest of the world, including the United States, is driven down to P_u, causing U.S. imports to rise. If the United States responds to the imposition of the foreign subsidies with a quota of $Q_2 - Q_1$, the price in the United States rises back to P_s, while the price in the rest of the world falls to P_w. Foreign exporters to the United States obtain a quota rent of *cabd*.

What is the net cost to the United States from the imposition of sugar quotas? If the United States is assumed to be a small country, the costs are given by area *c'abd'*. If the large-country assumption is used and correctly incorporated so that price P_u rather than P_w is used, the quota costs are given by the shaded area. Use of the small-country assumption is incorrect, and grossly overstates costs. Equally important, however, is the free-trade result: when compared to a free-trade regime in which other countries do not subsidize sugar production, the net cost to the United States from the imposition of sugar quotas is zero, since the quotas have merely reestablished for the United States a status equivalent to free trade. Therefore, if a return to free trade in sugar were achieved (through the GATT, for example), there might be no impact on the United States in terms of either the quantity traded or prices to producers or consumers. That is, a quota need not be trade distorting for a nation when measured against the free-trade solution, even though it is clearly distorting if measured against a distorted world price. It is true that the U.S. quota, as illustrated, is inefficient for the United States given the present distorted world price. However, it does not follow that a

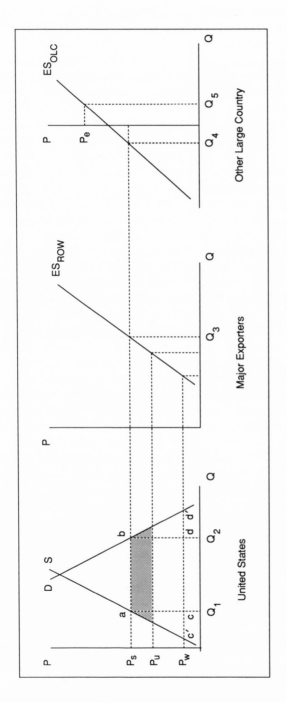

FIGURE 3. U.S. Sugar Quotas in a World Trading Context

free-trade solution, which is globally efficient, would alter U.S. sugar production, prices, or imports, or make the United States any better off on net.

Several recent studies have analyzed the effects of moving to freer trade in sugar. Some of the studies include those by Brown (1987), Zietz and Valdés (1986), Tyers and Anderson (1987), Johnson et al. (1988), Kirby et al. (1988), Roningen and Dixit (1989), and Wong, Sturgiss, and Borrell (1989). Virtually all of the studies found that the world sugar price rises following trade liberalization. However, the degree of price increase varies with the model used.

Brown (1987) simulated the effects of full trade liberalization by the industrial market economies (IMEs). He found that liberalization by the EC would raise the world sugar price by 3 percent, and the gain would be 1 percent if either the United States or Japan liberalized trade. Tyers and Anderson (1987) found that the world price would increase by as much as 22 percent if all IMEs liberalized. Zietz and Valdés (1986) reported price gains of roughly 65 percent.[7] Roningen and Dixit (1989) found a price increase in the neighborhood of 50 to 55 percent. They also found that, among the IMEs, the policies of the EC had the most depressing effect upon the world price.[8]

One problem in interpreting these results is that the conclusions depend on the base-year price. For example, the implications are far different if one applies these price increases to early 1990 rather than 1984–85, when world prices were significantly lower. If world prices had increased by 50 or 60 percent above their levels in early 1990, then the U.S. border price would have equaled or even exceeded U.S. producer prices at the time. This outcome is consistent with the scenario pictured in figure 3—that the distortionary effects of sugar policies around the world have driven the world price to P_w from P_s, while U.S. sugar policy maintains P_s for domestic producers. Thus, there is evidence that in recent years the U.S. import quotas have merely protected U.S. producers from a downwardly distorted world sugar price. If so, even if trade liberalization were achieved in sugar, it does not follow that there would be any major effect on the U.S. sugar industry. In fact, Schmitz, Schmitz, and Vercammen (1991) use the USDA SWOPSIM model to show empirically that free trade in sugar may not result in a lower sugar price for U.S. producers.

Regardless of the domestic effects, though, the primary losers from the sugar policies of the IMEs appear to be the sugar exporters. On the positive side, some countries with access to preferential arrangements may gain. The EC subsidizes the production of some Third World sugar producers through the Lomé Convention, while the U.S. quota rents similarly go to exporters. Thus, it is an empirical question whether foreign holders of U.S. quotas gain or lose from the U.S. program, though non-quota holding exporters obviously lose.

Maskus (1989) assumes a world price of 12 cents per pound, and estimates that the U.S. sugar program benefited quota holders in 1982–83, increasing their foreign-exchange earnings by $166 million. He estimates that by 1986–87 the program cost quota holders nearly $800 million, however. Consistent with these findings, Leu (1990) observes that quota-holding countries switched their support from more restrictive to less restrictive U.S. sugar import policies in lobbying activities related to the 1985 Farm Bill. Ives and Hurley (1988) estimate that total export earnings of quota-holding countries would have been $2.8 billion higher for the period 1983–87 had the U.S. loan rate been set at 12 cents per pound instead of 18 cents per pound. These estimates, like the earlier ones on the effect of free trade, depend on the size of supply and demand elasticities and on the size of the distortions caused by non-U.S. exporters and importers.

A negative effect of the U.S. sugar program, and a more specific concern for U.S. foreign policy, is its impact on the Caribbean. Roughly 35 percent of U.S. sugar imports come from the Caribbean region. The largest exporter is the Dominican Republic, which exported approximately 204,000 metric tons to the United States in 1989. This area has long been of special interest, not only because it is the source of a substantial proportion of U.S. sugar imports, but also because of its political and strategic value to the United States.

Messina (1989) and Messina and Seale (1990) have studied the impact of quota allocations to the Caribbean. The latter study finds that the Caribbean would benefit from a larger quota allocation despite the fall in the U.S. sugar price that would ensue. Specifically, it finds that raising the quota from 1.24 million to 1.935 million short tons raw value would provide an annual net gain to Caribbean exporters of $134.6 million.[9]

5. The U.S. Sugar Program in a Regional Context

From the perspective of national economic welfare, the U.S. sugar import quota system is one of the most economically inefficient ways to support domestic sugar producers. Leu et al. (1987) examine some alternatives.[10] Even relative to other U.S. farm programs, the sugar program does have some important political advantages, however. The program does not require federal budgetary resources, so it does not have to compete against other expenditures or deficit reduction. Moreover, it buys acquiescence or even support from some countries, since the quota rents go to countries that export sugar to the United States.

In analyses of the effects of U.S. sugar quotas, the focus has generally been on U.S. producers and consumers in the aggregate, though a few estimates have been made of the effects on processors of sugarbeets, sugarcane, and corn. Seldom does one see any analysis of the effect of the sugar program by region, however, even though the effects can differ substantially on that basis. For example, import quotas will generally have a greater impact on producer rent in cane-growing regions than in beet-growing regions, because the price elasticity of supply for beets generally exceeds that for cane.[11] These sorts of regional economic differences can have important political implications.

5.1 Net Returns per Acre by Crop and Region

It is generally argued that U.S. farm policy favors sugarcane and sugarbeet producers much more than growers of other program-supported crops. Table 4 supports this assertion for a variety of regions and crops. The table shows the average value of output per acre planted, plus direct payments from government, net of variable costs.[12] The value of output per acre reflects governmental intervention through the price mechanism, while direct payments reflect other kinds of governmental support. Fixed costs are omitted because the returns to assets used in production of a crop will depend on the value of the crop: a policy that drives up the market price of a crop will tend to drive up the rents for the land on which that crop is grown, or the quasi-rents for the capital equipment used to produce it.

Table 4 shows two-year averages for 1983–84 and 1986–87, along with the percentage changes between these periods, for the sugarcane and sugarbeet growing regions in the United States. The data are shown for the two periods in order to reflect the systematic effects of the Food Security Act of 1985, which cut federal supports for most farm commodities, by an average of 10 percent, but left the sugar program intact. It should be emphasized, however, that this is not the only factor that could cause differences between the two periods: weather problems, systematic cost changes, and market-driven price changes could also be at work. Moreover, there are important alternative farm products not subject to governmental support, for which data are not available, such as vegetables in California and Florida. Finally, one has to take risk into consideration. For example, even though the returns to wheat in California have been roughly half those of sugarbeets, sugarbeet acreage has declined while wheat acreage has increased. One general explanation is that beet production is riskier than wheat production.

Given these qualifications, table 4 shows, for both periods and in every region, that sugarbeets and sugarcane had higher returns net of variable cost per acre than all of the alternative crops that were supported by the federal

TABLE 4. Gross Return Less Variable Cost per Acre for Sugarbeets and Sugarcane versus Alternative Crops (dollars per acre, two-year averages)

Sugarbeet States	Crops	1983-84	1986-87	% change
Michigan and Ohio	sugarbeets	428.31	359.75	-16.01
	corn	218.38	176.85	-19.02
	oats	71.59	61.51	-14.09
	soybeans	156.97	131.55	-16.20
	wheat	181.29	265.93	46.69
Minnesota and	sugarbeets	398.84	551.61	38.30
eastern North Dakota	barley	57.16	43.53	-23.85
	corn	209.16	180.77	-13.57
	oats	38.96	35.76	-8.20
	wheat	124.44	131.18	5.41
SE Wyoming, Nebraska,	sugarbeets	222.14	462.78	108.33
and NE Colorado	corn	209.16	180.77	-13.57
	grain sorghum	118.29	90.18	-23.76
	soybeans	156.97	131.55	-16.20
	wheat	122.73	87.66	-28.57
Montana, NW Wyoming,	sugarbeets	374.03	579.43	54.92
and NW North Dakota	barley	57.16	43.53	-23.85
	oats	38.96	35.76	-8.20
Texas and New Mexico	sugarbeets	264.16	138.08	-47.73
	barley	73.73	77.48	5.09
	cotton	66.98	95.00	41.84
	grain sorghum	122.53	74.13	-39.50
	wheat	83.42	21.93	-73.71
Eastern Idaho	sugarbeets	503.47	621.92	23.53
	barley	57.16	43.53	-23.85
	wheat	106.73	90.20	-15.49
Oregon and western Idaho	sugarbeets	643.31	653.70	1.62
	barley	100.34	116.18	15.79
	wheat	204.47	170.09	-16.81
California	sugarbeets	386.00	450.15	16.62
	barley	83.48	40.42	-51.58
	corn	246.11	211.45	-14.08
	cotton	372.47	353.24	-5.16
	wheat	163.02	238.91	46.55
Sugarcane States	Crops	1983-84	1986-87	% change
Florida	sugarcane	303.22	324.90	7.15
Louisiana	sugarcane	336.86	455.29	35.16
	cotton	180.30	157.26	-12.78
	soybeans	96.58	56.51	-41.49
Texas	sugarcane	30.50	355.55	1,065.70
Hawaii	sugarcane	572.25	630.73	10.22

government. For example, in Minnesota and North Dakota, two of the top beet-producing states, the return over variable costs for sugar beets in 1986–87 was $552 per acre. The closest competing crop was corn at $181 per acre, but the return for sugarbeets was more than three times that for corn. In Eastern Idaho, the closest competition to sugar beets was white wheat, but sugarbeets generated more than six times the return of white wheat. The comparisons are similar but less dramatic for the other regions in which sugar crops are grown. Only in California were the returns over variable costs per acre for some program crops—cotton in particular—close to those for sugarbeets.

In all regions except Michigan/Ohio and Texas/New Mexico, the return per acre to sugarbeets increased between the two periods, while only six of the 26 alternative crops in the eight sugarbeet regions enjoyed increases. Likewise, returns per acre increased for sugarcane in all four states in which it is produced, but decreased for the alternative supported crops in Louisiana. National-average data on returns net of variable costs per acre for 1983–84 and 1986–87 show that returns increased for sugarbeets by 27.5 percent and for sugarcane by 20 percent, while returns for all of the major alternative crops decreased.[13] Therefore, it is evident that sugar producers in the United States have enjoyed high returns compared to producers of other crops, even after direct payments from government to the latter are considered, and that the differences between returns to sugar crops versus alternative crops have typically increased in recent years. Because sugarbeets are typically grown in rotations of three to five years with many of these competing crops, the sugar program may in effect provide a means to cross-subsidize production of these other crops.

Despite the support given sugar producers, U.S. sugar production has not increased substantially in the 1980s, particularly if compared to earlier decades. This conclusion is illustrated in figure 4 for beet sugar in the upper graph and for cane sugar in the lower one. Each graph shows crop acreage harvested (in millions of acres) and sugar produced (in millions of metric tons).[14] (Because the quantities of sugar from U.S. beet and cane are roughly equal, the figures are drawn with the same scale.) The ratio of the two is the yield per acre, which has varied considerably due to weather, and has increased over the long run due to technological advances. Several factors can explain the stability of sugar production in the 1980s—apart from weather problems toward the end of the decade. First, sugar cane acreage has almost reached the capacity afforded by climate and soil. Second, although sugar beet acreage has expanded in some areas—most notably in the Red River Valley of Minnesota and North Dakota—in other regions the costs of production are so high that other crops can be competitive. This appears to be the case in California, where high costs and recent disease problems have caused beet acreage to decline.

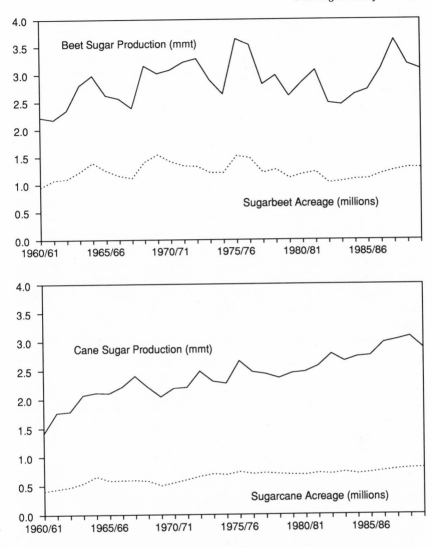

**FIGURE 4.   U.S. Sugar from Domestic Beet and Cane, and
U.S. Beet and Cane Acreage Harvested, 1960/61–89/90**

A third important reason may be the reluctance of sugarbeet processors to build new processing factories or expand existing ones, given the policy risks created by uncertainty over the future of the sugar program. Although plants in some locations are operating at capacity, it is apparently felt that the high prices presently supporting sugar production are not certain enough into the future to justify the investment in new plants.[15]

5.2 Political Support and Net Regional Benefits

A regional analysis of the sugar market is also important in that it may help explain why political support has generally been available for the U.S. sugar industry. In particular, even though the U.S. sugar program imposes a cost on consumers that in the aggregate outweighs the benefit to producers, its effects on a given region can be significantly different. For example, if the sugar program results in an increase in internal U.S. prices because of quota restrictions, then local producers and processors can gain more than local consumers lose if the region is a net exporter of sugar.

To illustrate how the sugar program can provide positive net benefits to a region, table 5 presents data on average sugar production, consumption, and exports for California and Hawaii over 1987–89. The two states together are large net exporters of sugar. The sugar from California beets nearly met the state's consumption of 15 million hundredweight. In addition, of the 17.2 million hundredweight of production in Hawaii, a large percentage was refined in California, adding to that state's income from sugar. Total refined sugar production in California and Hawaii averaged 31.8 million hundredweight; of this, roughly 15.8 million hundredweight was exported to other destinations.

Now suppose that the sugar program raises internal prices by 4 cents per pound on a refined basis. In California and Hawaii, the cost to consumers would be roughly $64 million, but this cost would be far outweighed by the $127 million gain to producers and processors. Thus, the effect of the U.S. sugar program on California and Hawaii is of a totally different dimension from that reported for the United States in the aggregate. Even California alone is a net beneficiary of the sugar program, since it earns substantial income from the processing of raw Hawaiian cane sugar.

In short, that the sugar program causes a net loss to the United States as a whole does not imply that every region in the United States experiences a net

TABLE 5.   Production, Consumption, and Exports of Refined Sugar, California and Hawaii (million hundredweight[a])

	Production[b]	Consumption	Exports
California	14.6	15.0	-0.4
Hawaii	17.2	1.0	16.2
Total	31.8	16.0	15.8

Source: Calculations by authors from state population figures and data appearing in U.S. Department of Agriculture, *Sugar and Sweetener Outlook and Situation Report*, various issues.

[a] One hundredweight equals one hundred pounds.

[b] Based on an average of 1987–89 production years.

loss. Moreover, casual observation confirms that political support will generally be positive for programs providing net gains to a region. With regard to the sugar program, in a region in which the loss to consumers from sugar quotas is less than the gain to producers and processors, a program will generally have the support of politicians from that region.[16]

Political support for the U.S. sugar program comes first of all from areas that produce sugar crops. Sugarbeets are grown or processed in California, Colorado, Idaho, Michigan, Minnesota, Montana, Nebraska, New Mexico, North Dakota, Ohio, Oregon, Texas, Washington, and Wyoming. Sugarcane is grown and milled in Florida, Hawaii, Louisiana, and Texas. These 17 states command more than one-third of the votes in the U.S. Senate. On the other hand, the farm areas in which sugar crops are grown are typically sparsely populated, and span at most 48 districts of the U.S. House of Representatives. However, the support of cane refiners in California, Texas, Georgia, Maryland, and New York typically can be added to that of the sugar producers and processors.[17] This brings the total to 20 states and 54 congressional districts involved in sugar production or processing. Moreover, HFCS refiners perceive a clear gain from sugar quotas, and thus support the program as well. Since corn is the primary input in the manufacture of HFCS, corn producers also gain. If areas that produce or refine corn are added to the sugar-producing areas, the basis for congressional support for the sugar program grows considerably.

Table 6 shows cross-tabulations of sweetener production by district and state with the 1990 U.S. House and Senate votes to maintain producer support levels under the sugar program.[18] The table divides members of Congress into three categories: those who have *sugar* production or refining in their state or district; those who do not have sugar production or refining, but do have substantial *corn* production or refining; and *other* members.[19] Voting on the sugar program is classified as *pro* for those who voted to maintain the support level, *con* for those who voted to reduce the level, and *n/v* if the member did not vote or the seat was vacant.[20] Table 6(a) shows the breakdown for individual House districts. Of the 54 members of the House in *sugar* districts, 51 voted in favor of the sugar program, and only 2 opposed it. Of the 116 members in *corn* districts, 72 voted in favor of the program, and 43 opposed it. The support rates in these two sets of districts were both well above those in *other* districts. The chi-square statistic of 31.55 with four degrees of freedom (df) indicates that we can strongly reject the hypothesis that voting behavior is independent of the presence of sweetener production in the district.[21]

Table 6(b) shows the breakdown for the House by state delegations. For example, members were taken to be in *sugar* states if any district(s) in their state had sugar production or refining. Notice that full representation from the *sugar* states accounts for a majority of the membership of the House. If *corn* states are added in, the potential coalition includes 362 of the 435 seats. More than two-thirds of the votes in *sugar* states were in favor of the program, as were nearly two-thirds of the votes in *corn* states. In *other* states, well below half of the votes were in favor of the program. The chi-square statistic of 26.59 implies that voting behavior is significantly associated with the presence of these farm activities in the state.

Finally, table 6(c) shows the breakdown for the Senate. In this case, we see a weaker relationship between voting behavior and farm activity than in table 6(a). This is to be expected, as the political clout of sugar and corn interests would tend to be more diluted for states overall than for individual districts. Nevertheless, three-fourths of the senators from *sugar* states voted in favor of the program, while the support in *corn* states was marginally stronger than that in *other* states. The chi-square statistic of 10.30 is significant at the 5 percent level.

Table 6 provides a clear picture of the core of the coalition supporting the sugar program in the 1990 farm legislation in Congress. We do not imply that a regional analysis of this sort can entirely explain the existence of the

TABLE 6. Cross-Tabulations of Sweetener Production by District or State with 1990 U.S. House and Senate Votes on the Sugar Program

(a) U.S. House Voting by Individual District: chi–square (4 df) = 31.55

	sugar	corn	other	total
pro	51	72	148	271
con	2	43	105	150
n/v	1	1	12	14
total	54	116	265	435

(b) U.S. House Voting by State Delegation: chi–square (4 df) = 26.59

	sugar	corn	other	total
pro	160	84	27	271
con	64	45	41	150
n/v	7	2	5	14
total	231	131	73	435

(c) U.S. Senate Voting by State: chi–square (4 df) = 10.30

	sugar	corn	other	total
pro	29	14	11	54
con	11	15	18	44
n/v	0	1	1	2
total	40	30	30	100

U.S. sugar program. For example, we recognize that many other commodities receive federal support in the absence of a "regional majority" in Congress. In particular, it is widely believed that vote-trading in Congress occurs on behalf of a number of farm programs. In a recent study of farm legislation in 1985–86 in the U.S. House of Representatives, Abler (1989) finds evidence of a coalition among tobacco, sugar, peanut, and dairy interests, as well as the poor, who stood to benefit from the food-stamp and school-lunch provisions included in the legislation.

On the other hand, the regional benefit-cost approach does help to explain the form of the present program. For example, it suggests that import quotas will likely remain, though imports might not be allowed to fall below a specified minimum, in order to retain the support of refiners of imported cane. Moreover, if a minimum-quota provision is introduced, then the program will not entail a budgetary outlay as sugar will not become an export commodity.[22] The point is that broad regional support for a sugar program is likely to continue in the 1990s.

6. Conclusion

The potential for a multilateral movement toward free trade in the 1990s presents the prospect of radical change in the U.S. sugar program. As we have pointed out, however, restoration of free trade may not be as beneficial to consumers nor as costly to sugar producers and processors as is generally believed. When proper account is taken of substitution into HFCS, the large-country role played by the United States, and the recovery of world prices over the last five years, estimates of the net U.S. costs of the sugar program derived in conjunction with the 1985 Farm Bill debate appear unreasonably large. Furthermore, these estimates neglect the distortions reflected in the current world price, which is depressed relative to its free-trade level by sugar policies around the world.

Finally, cost-benefit analyses of the sugar program for the entire United States have neglected important regional differences that bear heavily on the pattern of political support for the program. The geographical dispersion of sugar production and processing, in conjunction with that of corn production and HFCS processors, will likely provide broad regional backing for sugar supports well into the future.

NOTES

We thank Stephen Marks and Keith Maskus for their many helpful comments and suggestions on earlier drafts.
1. However, in October 1990 the President replaced the absolute import quotas with tariff-rate quotas that had an identical effect: an amount of sugar imports up to the

quota level set by USDA was allowed into the United States subject to the usual nominal tariff. Amounts in excess of the quota level were subject to a duty of 16 cents per pound, raw basis. For all but the lowest world sugar prices, this duty would be prohibitive. The spur for the change came from a GATT panel decision in 1990 that the U.S. sugar program was in violation of the GATT. The case against the U.S. program had been brought to the GATT by Australia in 1989. For details, see U.S. Department of Agriculture, Economic Research Service, *Sugar and Sweeteners: Situation and Outlook Report*, December 1990; and General Agreement on Tariffs and Trade, *United States: Restrictions on Imports of Sugar*, Report of the Panel, 1989.

2. Lopez (1989) found the price elasticity of demand to be -0.111 in the short run and -0.597 in the long run. Carman and Thor (1979) estimated the demand elasticities for all sweeteners to be -0.05 and -0.27 in the short and long run, respectively. Lopez and Sepulveda (1985) estimated non-industrial demand for all sweeteners to be -0.16, and industrial demand to be -0.15 before the introduction of HFCS-55, and -0.04 afterwards. Gemmill (1976) found the own-price demand elasticity of sugar to be -0.07, while George and King (1971) found it to be -0.24.

3. For a general exposition of the principles involved, see Just, Hueth, and Schmitz (1982).

4. Unlike the United States, the European Community (EC) maintains strict production controls on HFCS (Maskus 1989).

5. On the other hand, neither have the effects of increased risk on LDC exporters been taken into account. In his comments on an earlier version of this paper, Keith Maskus noted that the U.S. sugar program has the effect of transferring risk from efficient U.S. markets for risk to areas in which risk cannot be handled as efficiently.

6. The diagrams are drawn to the same scale, making it easy to determine that the world market clears at price P_s.

7. They use the 1979–81 period as a basis for comparison. It is difficult to comprehend a significant effect of U.S. quotas when, essentially, U.S. quotas were not binding in that period.

8. In 1975, the EC raised its sugar intervention price and domestic quotas in response to the worldwide shortage of the early 1970s. Prior to that time, the EC had been a net importer of sugar. Since 1977, however, the EC has exported sugar, as shown in table 1, and it is presently the world's largest net exporter of sugar. EC net exports peaked in 1982 at 3.97 million metric tons raw value. In 1981, the costs of subsidizing these exports forced the EC to tighten internal production quotas and impose levies on EC producers. Since that time, net exports have been fairly stable at 2.5 to 3 million metric tons. However, the annual excess demand of the EC has declined approximately by 4.5 million metric tons over the period. By comparison, annual U.S. imports have declined by 3 to 3.5 million metric tons in the 1980s.

9. In his comments on an earlier version of this paper, James Seale compared the findings of Seale and Messina (1990) with those of an earlier study of the effects of U.S. enactment of the Caribbean Basin Economic Recovery Act (CBERA)

(Pelzman and Schoepfle 1988): access to the U.S. sugar market for Caribbean sugar producers at the level of their sugar imports prior to the CBERA would have provided larger benefits to the region as a whole than all of the benefits accruing from the CBERA in 1983 if the CBERA had been implemented in that year. The effect of this expanded sugar-market access on the U.S. sugar price would have been small.

10. For a more general discussion of the principles of efficient farm policy design, see "Toward Agricultural Policy Reform," chapter 5 of the *Economic Report of the President, together with the Annual Report of the Council of Economic Advisers,* January 1987, Washington, DC: U.S. Government Printing Office.

11. Unfortunately, there is little agreement on the shutdown prices for sugarbeet and sugarcane production. Since costs vary widely by region and commodity, this makes economic assessment difficult when large price changes are involved. For example, California beet growers suffered losses in 1989 but this did not appear to be the case for the United States in aggregate.

12. All of the data used in this analysis are from studies done at the U.S. Department of Agriculture. The information on major alternative crops for sugarbeets is from Jesse (1977), and for sugarcane from Zepp (1977). The data on the average value of output and variable expenses per acre are from McElroy, et al. (1989), while the data on direct payments by government are from Webb, et al. (1990).

13. The percentage rates of decrease were 17.7 for barley, 20.5 for corn, 1.3 for cotton, 30.1 for grain sorghum, 12.6 for oats, 16.1 for rice, 11.8 for soybeans, and 26.0 for wheat.

14. The data are from U.S. Department of Agriculture, *Agricultural Statistics,* Washington, DC: U.S. Government Printing Office, various issues.

15. The debate in Minnesota between sugar beet growers and non-growers partly relates to this issue. It is alleged that enormous profits are made by beet growers in Minnesota relative to farmers who do not grow beets because they are not members of a beet-processing cooperative. At the same time, these profits have bid up the price of farmland making it difficult for non-beet growers to compete. Since there are no governmental production controls, acreage ought to expand if beets are such a lucrative crop. In addition to the uncertainties over future policy, the cooperatives themselves limit the number of acres that their members may harvest: it was recently reported that cooperatives in the Red River Valley charged a one-time fee of $900 per acre for additional acreage to be harvested by their members. See Bruce Ingersoll, "Range War: Small Minnesota Town is Divided by Rancor over Sugar Policies," *Wall Street Journal,* June 26, 1990.

16. Using this argument, different welfare weights need not be attached to various groups to explain political support for the program. To the extent that producers carry a heavier weight than consumers in the political process, regional support for the program would be strengthened further.

17. For the 1990 Farm Bill, for example, support came from eastern states that have sugar refineries. These refineries appeared to be supporting the program provided that the United States agreed to import at least 1.25 million metric tons annually. In the past, only those refiners with access to a domestic supply of sugar have supported the quota program.

18. These votes were held on amendments that would have reduced the sugar loan rate by 10 percent—from 18.0 to 16.2 cents per pound.
19. The basic data source is a 1990 data map of the geographical distribution of the U.S. sweetener industry by county, from the American Sugar Alliance, Washington, DC. Counties were matched to congressional districts by means of the *Congressional District Atlas: Districts of the 100th Congress*, U.S. Bureau of the Census, Washington, DC: U.S. Government Printing Office, 1985. A state or district is defined to have "substantial" corn production if it contains counties that produce at least two million bushels of corn per year, or that have corn refining facilities.
20. Data on the House and Senate votes come from the *Congressional Quarterly Weekly Report*, July 28, 1990, 2449–53.
21. With a 5 percent level of significance, the chi-square cutoff value for the hypothesis is 9.49; with a 1 percent level of significance, it is 13.28.
22. This provision would be enforced through the use of marketing quotas in the United States.

REFERENCES

Abler, David G. 1989. "Vote Trading on Farm Legislation in the U.S. House." *American Journal of Agricultural Economics* 71: 583–91.

Barry, Robert D., Luigi Angelo, Peter J. Buzzanell, and Fred Gray. 1990. *Sugar: Background for 1990 Farm Legislation*. U.S. Department of Agriculture, Economic Research Service, Commodity Economics Division. Staff Report No. AGES 9006.

Bates, Thomas H. and Andrew Schmitz. 1969. *A Spatial Equilibrium Analysis of the World Sugar Market*. University of California, Berkeley. Giannini Foundation Monograph No. 23.

Brown, James G. 1987. *The International Sugar Industry: Developments and Prospects*. World Bank. Staff Commodity Working Paper Number 18.

Carman, Harold F., and Peter K. Thor. 1979. *High Fructose Corn Sweeteners: Economic Aspects of a Sugar Substitute*. University of California, Berkeley, Giannini Foundation of Agricultural Economics. Information Series No. 79–2.

Gemmill, Gordon. 1976. *The World Sugar Economy: An Econometric Analysis of Production and Policies*. Michigan State University. Agricultural Economics Report No. 313.

George, Poykayil, and Gordon King. 1971. *Consumer Demand for Food Commodities in the United States with Projections for 1980*. University of California, Berkeley. Giannini Foundation Monograph No. 26.

Hammig, Michael, Roger Conway, Hosein Shapouri, and John Yanagida. 1982. "The Effects of Shifts in Supply on the World Sugar Market." *Agricultural Economics Research* 34: 12–18.

Ives, Ralph, and John Hurley. 1988. *United States Sugar Policy: An Analysis*. U.S. Department of Commerce, International Trade Administration. Washington, DC: U.S. Government Printing Office.

Jesse, Edward V. 1977. *Beet Sugar Supply Response in the United States.* U.S. Department of Agriculture, Economics Research Service, Commodity Economics Division. Agricultural Economic Report No. 371.

Jesse, Edward V., and Glenn A. Zepp. 1977. *Sugar Policy Options for the United States.* U.S. Department of Agriculture. Agricultural Economics Report No. 351.

Johnson, Brian, Barry Krissoff, Vernon Roningen, John Sullivan, and John Wainio. 1988. "Economic Effects of Agricultural Trade Liberalization on Developing Countries: A Partial Equilibrium Approach." Unpublished paper. U.S. Department of Agriculture, Economic Research Service.

Just, Richard E. 1972. *Econometric Analysis of Production Decisions with Government Intervention: The Case of the California Field Crops.* Ph.D. dissertation, University of California, Berkeley.

Just, Richard E., Darrell L. Hueth, and Andrew Schmitz. 1982. *Applied Welfare Economics and Public Policy.* Englewood Cliffs, NJ: Prentice-Hall.

Kirby, Michael G., Henry Hazler, David T. Parsons, and Michael G. Adams. 1988. *Early Action on Agricultural Trade Reform.* Australian Bureau of Agricultural and Resource Economics. Discussion Paper 88.3. Canberra: Australian Government Publishing Service.

Langley, Suchada V., and James A. Zellner. 1986. "Government Intervention and Technological Change in the Sweetener Industry: A Welfare Analysis." Unpublished paper presented at the Annual Meeting of the Southern Agricultural Economics Association, February.

Leu, Gwo-Jiun M. 1990. *Multimarket Welfare Analysis of U.S. Sugar Policy.* Ph.D. Dissertation, University of California, Berkeley.

————, Andrew Schmitz, and Donald D. Knutson. 1987. "Gains and Losses of Sugar Program Policy Options." *American Journal of Agricultural Economics* 69: 591–602.

Lopez, Rigoberto A., and J. S. Sepulveda. 1985. "Changes in the Demand for Sugar and Implications for Import Policies." *Northeastern Journal of Agricultural and Resource Economics* 14: 177–182.

Lopez, Rigoberto A. 1989. "Political Economy of U.S. Sugar Policies." *American Journal of Agricultural Economics* 71: 20–31.

Maskus, Keith E. 1989. "Large Costs and Small Benefits of the American Sugar Programme." *World Economy* 12: 85–104.

McElroy, Robert, Mir Ali, Robert Dismukes, and Annette Clauson. 1989. *Costs of Production for Major U.S. Crops, 1975–87.* U.S. Department of Agriculture, Economic Research Services, Agriculture and Rural Economy Division. Staff Report No. AGES 89–22.

Messina, William A., Jr. 1989. "U.S. Sugar Policy: A Welfare Analysis of Policy Options Under Pending Caribbean Basin Expansion Act Legislation." M.S. thesis, University of Florida.

Messina, William A., Jr., and James L. Seale, Jr. 1990. *U.S. Sugar Policy: A Welfare Analysis of Policy Options Under Pending Caribbean Basin Expansion Act Legislation.* University of Florida, Food and Resource Economics Department, Institute of Food and Agricultural Sciences. Staff Paper 382.

Pelzman, Joseph, and Gregory K. Schoepfle. 1988. "The Impact of the Caribbean

Basin Economic Recovery Act on Caribbean Nations' Exports and Development."
Economic Development and Cultural Change 36: 753–796.
Roningen, Vernon O., and Praveen M. Dixit. 1989. Economic Implications of
Agricultural Policy Reforms in Industrial Market Economies. U.S. Department of
Agriculture, Economic Research Service. Staff Report No. AGES 89–36.
Schmitz, Andrew, Roy Allen, and Gwo-Jiun M. Leu. 1987. "The U.S. Sugar Program
and Its Effects." In *Alternative Agricultural and Food Policies and the 1985 Farm
Bill*, ed. Gordon C. Rausser and K. R. Farrell. Washington, DC: National Center
for Food and Agricultural Policy, Resources for the Future.
Schmitz, Andrew, Troy G. Schmitz, and James Vercammen. 1991. "Endogenous
Policy Response and Free Trade: A Case Study from Agriculture." University of
California, Berkeley, Giannini Foundation Working Paper No. 581.
Tyers, Rod, and Kym Anderson. 1987. *Liberalizing OECD Policies in the Uruguay
Round: Effects on Trade and Welfare*. Australian National University. Working
Papers in Trade and Development No. 87/10.
U.S. Department of Agriculture. 1984. *Sugar: Background for 1985 Farm
Legislation*. Economic Research Service. Agriculture Information Bulletin No.
478.
Webb, Alan J., Michael Lopez, and Renata Penn. 1990. *Estimates of Producer and
Consumer Subsidy Equivalents: Government Intervention in Agriculture,
1982–87*. U.S. Department of Agriculture, Economic Research Service,
Agriculture and Trade Analysis Division. USDA Statistical Bulletin No. 803.
Wong, Gordon, Robert Sturgiss, and Brent Borrell. 1989. *The Economic
Consequences of International Sugar Trade Reform*. Australian Bureau of
Agricultural and Resource Economics, Discussion Paper 89.7. Canberra:
Australian Government Publishing Service.
Zepp, Glenn A. 1977. *Cane Sugar Supply Response in the United States*. U.S.
Department of Agriculture, Economic Research Service, Commodity Economics
Division. Agricultural Economic Report No. 370.
Zietz, Joachim, and Alberto Valdés. 1986. "The Potential Benefit to LDCs of Trade
Liberalization in Beef and Sugar by Industrialized Countries." *Weltwirtschaft-
liches Archiv* 122 (no. 1): 93–111.

CHAPTER 4

A Reassessment of Empirical Evidence
on the U.S. Sugar Program

Stephen V. Marks

1. Introduction

As one of the most controversial of U.S. farm programs, the U.S. sugar program has long attracted the attention of scholars and policy analysts. A variety of studies of the program have been completed in recent years, each with particular strengths and weaknesses. In the context of that body of work, this chapter assesses the U.S. sugar program on the basis of an alternative empirical model of sugar and sweetener markets in the United States and the rest of the world. The goal is to develop a parsimonious partial-equilibrium model that will permit measurement of the long-run, static welfare effects of alternative U.S. sugar policies.[1]

Two policy evaluations are conducted on this basis. First, I estimate the overall economic impact of the U.S. sugar program for crop years (September through August) 1984/85 to 1988/89: its long-run effects on prices in the United States and the rest of the world, the economic welfare of U.S. and foreign consumers and producers, and U.S. government revenues. Second, I examine the effects of a marginal reform of the program—a permanent 10 percent real reduction in the U.S. sugar loan rate, the basic U.S. support price for sugar. This analysis is intended to approximate the provisions of proposed amendments to the 1990 farm bills of the U.S. Senate and House of Representatives. The amendments would have cut the nominal U.S. sugar loan rate by 10 percent for the five-year duration of the farm bill.[2]

Current political realities weigh against unilateral reform of the sugar program, especially given the recent signs of progress toward a multilateral agricultural agreement under the General Agreement on Tariffs and Trade. Nonetheless, this analysis yields valuable insights on both economic modeling and sugar policy. Though my treatment of the rest of the world is highly aggregative, for example, it allows a simple but defensible means of calculation of domestic and foreign welfare effects of U.S. sugar policy, which can inform both unilateral and multilateral policy reform initiatives. Moreover, I estimate standard deviations for the welfare effects in order to present confidence intervals for the estimates. The widths of these intervals reflect the statistical uncertainties inherent in the welfare calculations, information not provided by most empirical studies in the past.

Section 2 outlines the basic approach in the context of previous literature on the U.S. sugar program, and section 3 lays out the empirical model. Section 4 establishes a rationale for the welfare analysis, and presents the estimates of the domestic and foreign price and welfare effects of the sugar program. Section 5 offers conclusions.

2. The Basic Approach and Earlier Literature

The empirical approach adopted in this paper differs in two fundamental ways from much of the previous literature on the U.S. sugar program: in the modeling of U.S. sweetener demand and foreign sugar export supply.

The modeling of U.S. sweetener markets has been complicated by the emergence of high fructose corn syrup (HFCS) as an alternative to sugar in recent years. Specifically, between 1975 and 1988, industrial sweetener users systematically turned to HFCS instead of liquid sugar. HFCS now commands 44 percent of the market that was once the exclusive domain of beet and cane sugar. However, most observers feel that the substitution of HFCS for liquid sugar is now complete. Crystalline forms of HFCS exist, but so far have not gained widespread acceptance as alternatives to cane or beet sugar.

Leu, Schmitz, and Knutson (1987) and Lopez (1989) have modeled the substitutability between sugar and HFCS explicitly by including the price of HFCS as a determinant of sugar demand. With the displacement of liquid sugar by HFCS at its technological limits, however, the nature of this substitution relationship may be very different in the future than in the past. Moreover, there is a serious data problem with this approach: because HFCS prices have been available only since 1975, these studies have used a composite price of corn sweeteners—glucose and dextrose, as well as HFCS—in order to generate a longer time series (back to 1955, for example). Because glucose and dextrose are much less substitutable for sugar than is HFCS, the composite-commodity assumption is questionable.

More generally, the pattern of substitution of HFCS for sugar is a function not only of the demand for sweeteners, but also of supply behavior. For example, few industry observers would argue that a reversal of the time path of real U.S. sugar prices would yield the same substitution pattern in reverse, now that the HFCS industry is in place with hundreds of millions of dollars of sunk costs to protect and the advantages of learning by doing and other scale economies.[3]

Though there is no ideal way to handle these problems in empirical analysis, I concluded that it was better to be less dependent on estimation of the problematic substitution relationship. Instead, I estimate total demand for refined sugar *plus* HFCS as functions of their prices. The prices of refined sugar and HFCS in turn are modeled as functions of the U.S. raw sugar price, the variable targeted by policy makers. For purposes of policy analysis, I assume that the market shares of refined sugar and HFCS will remain fixed at their current levels.

The approach is not without drawbacks. In particular, substantial changes in sweetener prices could invalidate the assumption of fixed market shares as well as the estimated functions for the prices of refined sugar and HFCS. To handle these problems, I impose additional constraints on HFCS price adjustment based on economic theory, as described in section 3.

For the rest of the world (ROW), I estimate equations for aggregate sugar demand and supply. These estimates can be used to infer a price elasticity of ROW export supply. The price elasticity of foreign exports is important because it determines the degree to which changes in U.S. imports will affect the world free-market sugar price: with a higher price elasticity, changes in U.S. imports will tend to have a smaller effect on the world price.

Leu, Schmitz, and Knutson (1987) derive a constant elasticity of ROW export supply of 2.37, based on previous estimates of ROW supply and demand relationships by Hammig et al. (1982). The estimated supply and demand elasticities of Hammig et al. are comparable to my own.[4] Even if the price elasticities of ROW supply and demand are constant, however, the elasticity of ROW *export* supply will vary as the levels of ROW production, consumption, and net exports change. In particular, the lower is the ratio of net exports to production, the higher will be the elasticity of export supply.[5] The estimate of 2.37 is actually very low for the 1980s: with foreign output growing, but net ROW exports shrinking due to cuts in U.S. sugar import quotas, the elasticity of export supply increased considerably. My own ROW supply and demand elasticity estimates yield an average long-run ROW export supply elasticity of 13.12 for the 1980s, while those of Hammig et al. yield a nearly identical 13.21.

Maskus (1989) focuses on the international effects of the U.S. sugar program, and calculates quota rents and net dollar gains to U.S. quota-holding countries for crop years 1982/83 and 1986/87 under the assumption that the world price would be 12 cents per pound if the U.S. sugar program were ended. A problem with the assumption that the world price would equal a particular value in the absence of the program is that it imputes a greater burden to the program in years in which the actual world price is lower. Consistent with this observation, Maskus calculates that quota-holding countries derived a net gain of $166.3 million in current dollars from the U.S. program in 1982/83—in which the world price averaged 7.58 cents per pound—but a net loss of $796.8 million in 1986/87—in which it averaged 6.19 cents per pound.

3. Empirical Model

All of the empirical relationships are specified in terms of real or relative prices. Demand and supply relationships are estimated in double-logarithmic, constant-elasticity form, and are specified as partial-adjustment processes, so that a lagged dependent variable is included as an explanatory variable in each.[6] Time trends were included in all equations, but were dropped from the ones in which time did not appear significant. The Ljung-Box (1978) statistic is used to test for serial correlation. I calculated the statistic from six autocorrelations of the residuals, so that it is distributed chi-square with six degrees of freedom under the null hypothesis that the error terms are not serially correlated. (At a 5 percent level of significance, values of the statistic greater than 12.59 indicate the presence of serial correlation.) The sample consists of annual data for crop years 1960/61 to 1988/89, though data limitations preclude estimation of all relationships over the entire period.

In all that follows, t indexes the time period. In parentheses below the estimated coefficients are t-statistics. Natural logarithms are denoted by $\ln(\ )$, and predicted values by a bar over the variable. In square brackets beneath the price and income coefficients in the demand and supply functions are the implied long-run elasticities. For each equation, the method of estimation, sample period, R^2, and Ljung-Box statistic (LB_6) are shown. All but a few of the equations were estimated by ordinary least squares (OLS); details for the others are provided as needed. Sources for the data are given in an appendix.

3.1 Empirical Model for the United States

As indicated in section 2, the basic approach is to model U.S. sweetener demand as a function of the prices of refined sugar and HFCS, and in turn to estimate equilibrium values for these prices as functions of the price of raw sugar, which is taken to be exogenously determined by policy.[7]

First, the quantities of refined sugar and HFCS are added to obtain the total quantity of caloric sweeteners consumed:

Quantity per Capita of Caloric Sweeteners

$$(1)\ Q_t\ =\ Q_{S,t}\ +\ Q_{F,t}$$

Q_S = consumption per capita of refined sugar, pounds
Q_F = consumption per capita of HFCS, pounds dry value

Next, a price index for sweeteners is formed as a weighted average of the prices of refined sugar and HFCS:

Real Price of Caloric Sweeteners

$$(2) \quad P_t = \theta_t \cdot P_{S,t} + (1 - \theta_t) \cdot P_{F,t}$$

P_S = wholesale price of refined sugar, Chicago, cents per pound, deflated by the consumer price index

P_F = wholesale price of HFCS, Midwest, cents per pound, deflated by the consumer price index

θ = (Q_S/Q), the market share for refined sugar; $(1 - \theta) = (Q_F/Q)$, the market share for HFCS

For purposes of estimation of sweetener demand, the historical annual market shares of refined sugar and HFCS were used as the weights in this price index. However, to estimate the effects of future policy changes, given that the substitution of HFCS for liquid refined sugar is now complete, the current market shares of 56 percent for refined sugar and 44 percent for HFCS are assumed to prevail.

Equation (1) suggests that refined sugar and HFCS are perfect substitutes on a pound-for-pound basis, while equation (2) is the appropriate price index if refined sugar and HFCS are demanded in fixed proportions.[8] One way to reconcile these two implications is to envision a representative consumer of caloric sweeteners whose indifference map between refined sugar and HFCS is pictured in figure 1 (time subscripts omitted). At a given point in time, HFCS cannot be used for all sweetener applications. For those for which it can be used, however, it is a perfect substitute for refined sugar. Over the range of perfect substitutability, then, the indifference curves have a slope of negative one. However, there is a kink in the indifference curves along a ray from the origin, $(Q_F) = (\theta/(1 - \theta)) \, Q_S$, which indicates the maximum feasible market share of HFCS at the given point in time: the indifference curves turn vertical at this ray, as additional quantities of HFCS provide no additional utility. As long as the price of HFCS is lower than the price of sugar, the optimal consumption points will be along this ray from the origin, and price index (2) is appropriate.

In perhaps more intuitive terms, part of the market can use only refined sugar, so that its demand for caloric sweeteners will be a function of the price of refined sugar. The rest of the market treats HFCS and refined sugar as perfect substitutes, but as long as the price of HFCS remains lower than the price of refined sugar, that part of the market will demand only HFCS, so that its demand for caloric sweeteners will be a function of the price of HFCS.

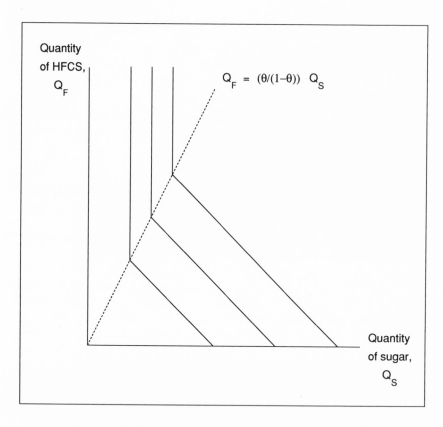

FIGURE 1.   Indifference Map between Refined Sugar and HFCS

Therefore, the price $P_{S,t}$ will be relevant to a share θ_t of the market, while the price $P_{F,t}$ will be relevant to a share $(1 - \theta_t)$ of the market. The market shares of sugar and HFCS are taken to be exogenously determined over time by technological change, though a more complete demand specification would include estimation of a dynamic demand system in which the market shares evolved endogenously.

Next, the price and quantity terms defined in equations (1) and (2) are embedded into a demand function in which the share of expenditures on caloric sweeteners overall is constant. For caloric sweetener demand, ordinary least squares and two-stage least squares (with the prices of refined sugar and HFCS endogenized as functions of the raw sugar price and other factors, as in equations (4) and (5) that follow) yield virtually identical results, so OLS is used for simplicity.

Caloric Sweetener Demand

$$(3)\ \overline{\ln(Q_t)} = \underset{(4.906)}{1.836} - \underset{\substack{(-6.348) \\ [-0.126]}}{0.061 \cdot \ln(P_t)} + \underset{\substack{(2.830) \\ [0.139]}}{0.068 \cdot \ln(Y_t)}$$

$$+ \underset{(4.874)}{0.513 \cdot \ln(Q_{t-1})}$$

OLS   1961–88 $R^2 = 0.90$ $LB_6 = 4.44$

Q = consumption per capita of refined sugar and HFCS, pounds dry value
P = index of wholesale prices of refined sugar and HFCS, cents per pound, deflated by the consumer price index
Y = disposable personal income per capita, current dollars, deflated by the consumer price index

The estimates of the price and income elasticities of sweetener demand are generally consistent with those of other recent studies. Lin and Novick (1988), for example, estimate the short-run sweetener-demand price elasticity for the United States to be -0.054 and the income elasticity to be 0.056, compared to my estimates of -0.061 and 0.068. However, their long-run price and income elasticities of -0.179 and 0.172 exceed in absolute value my estimates of -0.126 and 0.139.[9]

The next two equations are used to predict changes in the prices of refined sugar and HFCS in response to the policy changes examined. For the price of refined sugar, an iterative feasible generalized least squares (FGLS) procedure is used to correct for serial correlation.[10]

Real Price of Refined Sugar

$$(4)\ \overline{P_{S,t}} = \underset{(5.734)}{8.203} + \underset{(28.68)}{1.028 \cdot P_{R,t}} - \underset{(-2.535)}{0.164 \cdot t}$$

FGLS   1961–88 $R^2 = 0.96$ $LB_6 = 1.30$

P_R = wholesale price of raw cane sugar, New York, cents per pound, deflated by the consumer price index

Since the estimated coefficient for the price of raw sugar is within one standard deviation (0.036) of unity, one cannot reject the hypothesis that the coefficient is equal to one—that refined sugar prices increase cent-for-cent with raw cane sugar prices. However, the negative time trend indicates a significant decrease over time in the markup of the real price of refined sugar over that of raw sugar.

The HFCS price equation is consistent with the notion that an increase in the U.S. price of raw sugar, supported by adjustments in sugar imports quotas, extends the umbrella of protection over the corn sweetener market and allows an increase in the equilibrium price of HFCS:

Real Price of HFCS

$$(5) \ \overline{P_{F,t}} \ = \ \underset{(3.132)}{16.429} \ + \ \underset{(4.824)}{0.622 \cdot P_{R,t}} \ - \ \underset{(-2.713)}{0.424 \cdot t}$$

$$\text{OLS} \qquad 1976\text{--}88 \qquad R^2 = 0.81 \qquad LB_6 = 2.39$$

The equation indicates that a one-cent increase in the real price of raw sugar causes the HFCS price to increase by 0.62 cents, and that over time there has been a significant downward trend in the real price of HFCS, given the price of raw sugar. In a prior version of (5), I included as an additional independent variable the net cost of corn starch, the primary raw material used in the manufacture of HFCS. It was likely that causality ran both ways between the price of HFCS and the net cost of corn starch, so I used two-stage least squares to correct for simultaneity bias. Because the net cost of corn starch had a positive but statistically insignificant effect on the price of HFCS, I did not include it in the final version of (5).[11]

Two comments are in order. First, some supporters of the sugar program argue that the program raises the price of corn, and therefore lowers the budgetary costs to the federal government of supports for corn growers. For the limited sample period available, however, my reduced-form estimation showed that the price of raw sugar had positive but small and statistically insignificant effects on both the net cost of corn starch and the price of corn itself. On the other hand, as corn is subject to price supports of its own, the sugar program *could* be lowering federal outlays for corn price supports by reducing the corn surplus directly.

Second, relationship (5) could break down under market liberalization, especially if the HFCS price were forced down to the level of HFCS variable costs per unit, or if the refined sugar price were to undercut the HFCS price. To account for these problems, my welfare calculations assume that HFCS producers will reduce the HFCS price below their variable costs per unit only if the HFCS price would otherwise be undercut by the price of refined sugar, which itself adjusts via (4). In this case, I assume that HFCS producers match the refined sugar price.[12]

The analysis of sugar supply relationships follows that of Lopez (1989), who included two expected relative price terms, one for the price of sugar relative to inputs, and one for the prices of alternative outputs relative to inputs. In contrast to Lopez, I use beet and cane sugar output as my dependent variables, rather than acreage harvested. A problem with acreage is that, as production expands onto marginal land, yield per acre is expected to decline, so that the change in acreage harvested may not be the ideal predictor of changes in sugar output. A related consideration is that Lopez assumed that the prices of inputs are known at the time of harvesting, but that the prices of sugar and other farm outputs are not known. Since acreage planting decisions are made early in the year, however, and have a major impact on the ultimate level of output, I found it more appropriate to treat the prices of inputs, as well as the prices of sugar and alternative outputs, as uncertain. Finally, I use the price of refined sugar rather than raw cane sugar, since sugarbeets are processed directly into refined sugar. I assume that the two relative price expectations (each denoted by a superscript e) are formed from univariate autoregressive processes (not shown).[13]

Beet Sugar Supply

$$(6)\ \ln(R_{B,t}) = \underset{(4.309)}{4.901} + \underset{\underset{[1.762]}{(3.833)}}{0.793 \cdot \ln((P_S/P_I)_t^e)} - \underset{\underset{[-0.913]}{(-1.429)}}{0.411 \cdot \ln((P_O/P_I)_t^e)}$$

$$+ \underset{(3.699)}{0.550 \cdot \ln(R_{B,t-1})} + \underset{(0.619)}{0.003 \cdot t}$$

$$\text{OLS} \qquad 1962\text{--}88 \qquad R^2 = 0.53 \qquad LB_6 = 2.68$$

R_B = production of beet sugar, thousands of short tons, raw value
P_I = index of prices paid by farmers for all commodities, interest, wages, and utilities; deflated by the consumer price index
P_O = index of prices received by farmers for all farm products, deflated by the consumer price index

Cane Sugar Supply

$$(7)\ \ln(R_{C,t}) = \underset{(3.926)}{5.477} + \underset{\underset{[0.294]}{(1.762)}}{0.198 \cdot \ln((P_S/P_I)_t^e)} - \underset{\underset{[-0.188]}{(-0.807)}}{0.126 \cdot \ln((P_O/P_I)_t^e)}$$

$$+ \underset{(1.776)}{0.327 \cdot \ln(R_{C,t-1})} + \underset{(2.732)}{0.010 \cdot t}$$

$$\text{OLS} \qquad 1962\text{--}88 \qquad R^2 = 0.87 \qquad LB_6 = 3.98$$

R_C = production of cane sugar, thousands of short tons, raw value

For both supply functions the elasticity of supply with respect to input prices is negative, as is expected. In the short run, for beet sugar it is $(0.411 - 0.793) = -0.382$, and for cane sugar it is $(0.126 - 0.198) = -0.072$. The own-price elasticity is much higher for beet sugar than for cane sugar, which is plausible given that cane is more constrained than beet by land and climate.

I find a larger difference between the price elasticities of beet and cane sugar than did Lopez, who estimated long-run elasticities of 1.20 for beet and 0.58 for cane. However, it turns out that my long-run own-price elasticities closely match the elasticities posited in earlier USDA studies of costs of production and supply responses for U.S. cane and beet sugar in various regions of the country—studies based on a totally different methodology. Implicit in the supply schedules adopted by Jesse and Zepp (1977) on the basis of these studies are an elasticity of supply of beet sugar of between 1.65 and 2.15 (compared to my long-run estimate of 1.76) and a constant elasticity of supply of cane sugar of 0.20 (compared to my 0.29).[14]

The model for the U.S. sector is closed with a long-run sugar market clearing condition, in which refined sugar demand per capita, Q_S, is multiplied by U.S. population, N, and converted to its raw sugar equivalent.

Sugar Market Clearing

$$(8) \quad R_{B,t} + R_{C,t} + Q_{I,t} = Q_{S,t} \cdot N_t \cdot X$$

Q_I = net quantity of U.S. imports, thousands of short tons, raw value
X = pounds of raw sugar per pound of refined sugar (roughly 1.07)

Given that the market price of raw sugar is constrained by policy to equal the federal support price, constraint (8) determines the level of imports that will yield an equilibrium at that price.

3.2 Empirical Model for the Rest of the World

The rest of the world is characterized via aggregate sugar demand and supply functions and a market clearing condition. The "world" price of raw sugar is taken to be the Caribbean free-market price. The earlier notation applies, but asterisks appear on all variables. In general, I find that quantity demanded and supplied are not very responsive to the free-market price, consistent with the observation by Wong, Sturgiss, and Borrell (1989) that the policies of many nations have tended to insulate their sugar producers and consumers from external price changes.

The ROW demand function is estimated by two-stage least squares (2SLS) to correct for simultaneous equations bias, given the endogeneity of the world free-market price.

Sugar Demand

$$(9)\ \ln(Q^*_{S,t}) = \begin{array}{c} -2.374 \\ (-2.125) \end{array} \quad - \quad \begin{array}{c} 0.015 \cdot \ln(P^*_{S,t}) \\ (-1.859) \\ [-0.064] \end{array} \quad + \quad \begin{array}{c} 0.511 \cdot \ln(Y^*_{S,t}) \\ (2.318) \\ [2.132] \end{array}$$

$$+ \quad \begin{array}{c} 0.760 \cdot \ln(Q^*_{S,t-1}) \\ (8.326) \end{array}$$

| 2SLS | 1961–86 | $R^2 = 0.97$ | $LB_6 = 5.54$ |

Q^*_S = demand per capita for centrifugal sugar, pounds raw value, rest of world

P^*_S = wholesale price of raw cane sugar, Caribbean, cents per pound, deflated by an index of world consumer prices

Y^*_S = real gross national product per capita, rest of world

The price elasticity of demand is small and marginally significant. On the other hand, the estimated income elasticity of demand for sugar is higher than in the United States. Given that roughly three-fourths of sugar consumption in the rest of the world is outside of the high-income OECD countries, this finding is consistent with the general observation that income elasticities of demand for food products tend to be higher in lower-income countries.

For sugar supply, I use a functional form similar to that for the U.S. supply functions. The equation does not include farm input prices, which are difficult to identify for the rest of the world overall. It does include the expected price of sugar relative to a price index for all farm commodities worldwide, however, derived from an autoregressive process.

Sugar Supply

$$(10)\ \ln(R^*_{S,t}) = \begin{array}{c} 6.583 \\ (3.583) \end{array} \quad + \quad \begin{array}{c} 0.110 \cdot \ln((P^*_S/P^*_F)^e_t) \\ (2.983) \\ [0.174] \end{array} \quad + \quad \begin{array}{c} 0.369 \cdot \ln(R^*_{S,t-1}) \\ (2.166) \end{array}$$

$$+ \quad \begin{array}{c} 0.018 \cdot t \\ (3.492) \end{array}$$

| OLS | 1961–86 | $R^2 = 0.97$ | $LB_6 = 6.09$ |

R_S^* = supply of centrifugal sugar, rest of world, thousands of short tons, raw value

P_F^* = index of world food commodity prices, deflated by an index of world consumer prices

The price elasticity of ROW supply is small but significant, and over time there has been a significant expansion of supply.

The ROW model is closed with a market-clearing condition, in which per capita demand, Q_S^*, is multiplied by the total population, N^*, to obtain total ROW demand:

Sugar Market Clearing

$$(11) \quad R_{S,t}^* = Q_{S,t}^* \cdot N_t^* + Q_{I,t}$$

Conditions (8) and (11) are linked by U.S. imports, Q_I, and together imply global market clearing.

4. Quantitative Evaluation of the U.S. Sugar Program

This section evaluates the static, long-run implications of the U.S. sugar program for domestic and foreign welfare through two policy analyses. The first estimates the overall effects of the program. The second estimates the effects of a permanent 10 percent real reduction in the U.S. sugar loan rate.

The welfare calculations for domestic and foreign sugar consumers and producers apply the standard measures of consumer surplus and producer surplus to the aggregate demand and supply curves given in section 3, and also account for the quota rents earned by foreigners able to sell under quota in the U.S. market. The welfare effects for domestic HFCS producers are calculated on the basis of the estimated changes in the price of HFCS net of costs per unit (see note 12) multiplied by the quantity produced.

These welfare analyses entail estimation of the effects of the U.S. sugar program on the equilibrium U.S. and world sugar prices, based on an iterative procedure that uses the long-run elasticities of demand and supply presented in section 3. In addition, changes in the U.S. raw sugar price are linked to changes in the U.S. prices of refined sugar and HFCS via the parameters of equations (4) and (5).

The estimated price effects are not at issue in conceptual terms. However, because the world sugar market is distorted by the policies of many countries, the appropriate welfare calculations for the rest of the world could in principle be very complicated. Therefore, an important preliminary task is to provide a rationale for the simple welfare calculations made in this paper.

4.1 Rationale for the Foreign Welfare Calculations

As Schmitz and Christian emphasize in this volume, the U.S. sugar quotas could have a corrective effect on the level of U.S. sugar imports, given the presence of other distortions in the world sugar market. For example, if other countries subsidize their sugar exports, and the U.S. import quotas reduce the level of subsidized exports, then these quotas could in principle make the world market more efficient. In any case, the proper welfare calculations would take into account not only the effects on consumers and producers in the United States and abroad, but also of the reduction in export subsidies paid by foreign governments.

On the other hand, consider the sugar supply-demand diagrams in figure 2, in which the world is divided into the United States, the European Community (EC), and other countries (OC). The figure is intended to roughly reflect the conditions of the world sugar market and the policies of its two most important players. The United States has demand D_u and supply S_u in figure 2.a, the EC has net export supply X_e in figure 2.b, and other countries have net export supply X_r in figure 2.c.[15] At the free-trade equilibrium price, P^*, U.S. imports $(c - b)$ plus EC net imports (e) are equal to OC net exports (g). Suppose now that the EC imposes an export subsidy (as well as prohibitive import restraints) in order to support a higher domestic target price, P_1. Absent further policy changes, this will drive the world market price to a lower equilibrium level, P_2, at which U.S. imports $(d - a)$ equal EC net exports (f) plus OC net exports (h). The total EC export subsidy is $f \cdot (P_1 - P_2)$.

Suppose next that the United States responds to the EC export subsidy by imposing an import quota that (for simplicity) restores U.S. imports to the free-trade level and the U.S. price to P^*, but that the EC holds its net exports fixed (and thus fully insulates its domestic market from the U.S. policy change) by boosting its export subsidy. At the new world equilibrium price, P_3, U.S. imports $(c - b)$ equal EC net exports (f) plus OC net exports (i).[16] The welfare gains and losses can be identified in figure 2. The United States loses the shaded area in figure 2.a because it now pays a higher price for imported sugar. The EC incurs a loss of $f \cdot (P_2 - P_3)$ in figure 2.b due to the higher export subsidy it now pays. Other countries lose as net exporters whose export price has fallen (the loss shown by the shaded area in figure 2.c), but gain as recipients of quota rents of $(c - b)(P^* - P_3)$ in figure 2.a for their exports to the U.S. market (the EC does not hold any of the U.S. import quota).

The aggregate welfare calculations made in this paper for the rest of the world amount to the sum of the effects for the EC and other countries shown in figure 2 (including the quota rents). In other words, the welfare effects for

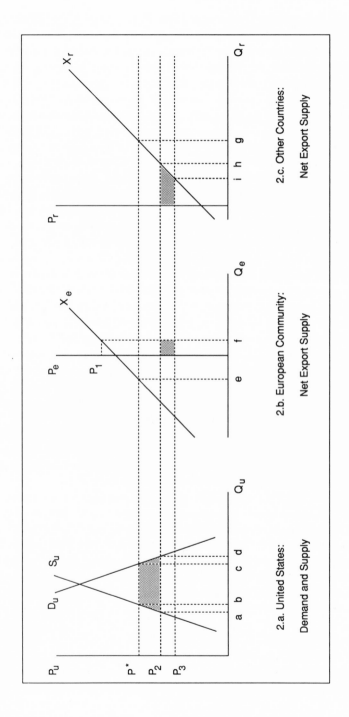

FIGURE 2. Welfare Effects of Unilateral U.S. Policy Reform

the ROW are inferred directly from the initial ROW quantities supplied and demanded, and from the extent to which these quantities change in response to changes in the world price. A sufficient condition for these calculations to be correct is that there be no *indirect* efficiency gains or losses due to changes in other sugar policies around the world. In particular, (1) the countries that target their domestic producer prices (or consumer prices) via *price* instruments (like subsidies or tariffs) adjust these instruments so as to hold domestic producer prices (or consumer prices) constant, and (2) the countries that impose binding *quantity* limits (like production, consumption, or import quotas) do not vary the quantities that are subject to restriction. In short, it is sufficient that the governments that intervene in sugar markets *fully* insulate their targeted domestic groups (consumers, producers, or both) from changes in the world free-market sugar price. Thus, the welfare measurements given in this paper can be viewed as applying to a *unilateral* sugar market liberalization by the United States subject to this condition.

As a first approximation, however, sugar market interventions have been consistent with this condition.[17] The EC, the largest sugar exporter, does insulate its domestic market from shifts in the world price. The price to consumers is fixed, and most of production is under binding quotas. Additional sugar production is allowed, but only for export without governmental support at the margin.[18] Japan, which is second only to the Commonwealth of Independent States as a sugar importer, virtually fully insulates its domestic market from world price changes through variable import levies and other measures. Wong, Sturgiss, and Borrell (1989) report that other countries with large sugar markets—like the former Soviet Union, China, and India—heavily insulate their producers and consumers from fluctuations in the world price. In addition, the policy interventions by major sugar exporters like Australia and Brazil have essentially taken the form of production quotas, though these quotas have been adjusted occasionally in response to changes in the world price.

Not only do the governments that are major players in the world sugar market tend to insulate their domestic sugar markets from changes in the world price, their departures from this behavior are not easily predicted. Additional empirical investigation of the sugar policies of other countries clearly is in order. On the other hand, to develop a complete and accurate representation of the sugar policies of *all* other countries, especially the nonmarket economies, would be very difficult. As a first cut, this paper will adopt the most aggregative perspective on the rest of the world.

4.2 Overall Effects of the U.S. Sugar Program

To get the most comprehensive picture of the effects of the U.S. sugar program, it is useful to evaluate the program across years in which the domestic-foreign price differential varied widely. Crop years 1984/85 to 1988/89 are ideal in these terms. For these years, table 1 shows the actual U.S. and world sugar prices, and the long-run equilibrium world price that would have obtained absent all U.S. sugar price supports and import restrictions, including both the import quotas and some minor import duties and fees.[19] (In this case, the U.S. and world sugar prices differ only by transportation costs of 1.5 cents per pound.) The U.S. program's depressive effect on the world price is estimated at close to 16 percent in the global sugar slump of 1984/85, but at less than 9 percent in 1988/89.

The results presented in table 2 support the intuition that the distortive effect of the U.S. sugar program is large when the wedge between the U.S. and world free-market sugar prices is large. For 1984/85, when the differential between the U.S. and world prices averaged 16.38 cents per pound, the program exacted its heaviest toll on U.S. consumers, estimated at 3.922 billion 1988 dollars. Likewise, the benefits to U.S. sugar and HFCS producers of being shielded from the world price were greatest in that year, and are estimated at $2.799 billion. By 1988/89, however, the wedge between the U.S. and world prices averaged only 10.66 cents per pound, and these welfare effects were both roughly 50 percent smaller—a $1.694 billion consumer loss and a $1.429 billion producer gain.

The last column of table 2 shows the five-year averages of the estimated welfare effects, and the average bounds for the 95 percent confidence intervals for these effects. (Calculation of the quota rents and tariff revenues did not require estimated parameters, and so was not subject to statistical error.) The bounds are equal to ±1.96 times the estimated standard error of each of the welfare estimates. Given the nonlinearities of the model, these standard errors were derived by drawing 1000 sets of the relevant supply, demand, and price-markup parameters from normal probability distributions, with means and standard deviations taken from the estimates in section 3, and

TABLE 1.   U.S. and World Free-Market Raw Sugar Prices with and without U.S. Import Restrictions, 1984/85 to 1988/89 (U.S. cents per pound)

	1984/85	1985/86	1986/87	1987/88	1988/89
U.S. Raw Sugar Price	20.80	20.75	21.53	22.02	22.58
World Free-Market Price	4.42	5.38	6.49	9.02	11.92
World Price in Absence of U.S Import Restrictions	5.23	6.34	7.70	10.36	13.05
Effect of U.S. Restrictions on World Price (percent)	-15.5	-15.1	-15.7	-12.9	-8.7

TABLE 2. Estimated Welfare Effects of U.S. Sugar Import Restrictions, 1984/85 to 1988/89 (billions of 1988 dollars)

	1984/85	1985/86	1986/87	1987/88	1988/89	1984/5-1988/89 Average Confidence Interval
United States						
Consumer Surplus:	-3.922	-3.374	-2.939	-2.026	-1.694	-2.791 ± 0.421
Producer Surplus:	2.799	2.474	2.245	1.670	1.429	2.123 ± 0.415
Beet Sugar Producers:	0.519	0.495	0.578	0.543	0.413	0.510 ± 0.204
Cane Sugar Producers:	0.838	0.790	0.783	0.655	0.505	0.714 ± 0.132
HFCS Producers:	1.442	1.190	0.883	0.472	0.511	0.900 ± 0.221
Government Revenue:	0.018	0.015	0.010	0.007	0.010	0.012
Net U.S. Welfare:	-1.122	-0.900	-0.695	-0.356	-0.265	-0.667 ± 0.219
Rest of World						
Consumer Surplus:	1.711	1.947	2.484	2.654	2.193	2.198 ± 2.768
Producer Welfare:	-1.080	-1.487	-2.230	-2.526	-2.014	-1.867 ± 2.858
Quota Rents:	0.707	0.539	0.339	0.197	0.234	0.403
Producer Surplus:	-1.787	-2.026	-2.568	-2.723	-2.248	-2.271 ± 2.858
Net Foreign Welfare:	0.631	0.460	0.254	0.128	0.180	0.331 ± 0.093
Net Global Welfare:	-0.491	-0.440	-0.440	-0.228	-0.085	-0.337 ± 0.238

then obtaining a distribution for each of the various welfare effects from the 1000 sets of parameters.[20]   Although the bounds indicate considerable uncertainty, especially in the estimates of ROW consumer and producer effects, the *net* effects on the domestic, foreign, and global economies are relatively reliably estimated.

For 1984/85 to 1988/89, the average U.S. consumer loss was $2.791 billion, while the average U.S. producer gain was $2.123 billion. Over these years, the U.S. government gained an average of $0.012 billion in revenue from raw sugar duties of 0.625 cents per pound on imports from some countries. With all these factors taken into account, I estimate that the U.S. sugar program cost the U.S. economy overall an average of $0.667 billion annually over 1984/85 to 1988/89.

The domestic welfare implications of the U.S. sugar program can be put in perspective in several ways. The program appears rather innocuous on the basis of cost per consumer, which averaged $11.52 per person in 1988 dollars over 1984/85 to 1988/89. On the other hand, in crop year 1988/89 there were 9,893 sugarbeet farms and 1,038 sugarcane farms in the United States. One can estimate the annual average return per farm from the program to be $51,892 for the beet sugar sector and $567,230 for the cane sugar sector over the five years. Moreover, the two largest cane sugar producers in Florida, one a corporation and the other a family, control more than 25 percent of total cane sugar production in the United States.[21]   This puts their average combined benefits from the program at $179 million over the five-year period. Finally, the four largest HFCS producers, with their market share of roughly 86 percent, averaged a collective annual gain from the sugar program of $772 million over 1984/85 to 1988/89.

The estimates of the effects of the U.S. sugar program on the rest of the world appear paradoxical: the program benefited the rest of the world in the aggregate over 1984/85 to 1988/89, by an average of $0.331 billion. The program depressed the world raw sugar price, and cost foreign sugar producers an annual average of $1.867 billion, but these costs were outweighed by $2.198 billion in gains to foreign consumers. The paradox is resolved by recognition of the role of the rents created by the U.S. sugar import quotas. These rents went to foreign quota holders, who profited from the price differential between the United States and the rest of the world.[22]   The amount of the transfer averaged $0.403 billion net of U.S. import duties, though it clearly shrunk as U.S. quota imports shrunk—from 2.193 million short tons in 1984/85 to 0.874 million in 1987/88. By 1988/89, U.S. quota imports had risen to 1.376 million short tons, but the closing of the differential between U.S. and foreign prices due to tightness in the world sugar market meant that the quota rents remained at a low level.

Global economic efficiency is clearly reduced by the U.S. sugar program. I estimate that the average global efficiency loss over 1984/85 to 1988/89 was $0.337 billion. However, efficiency is not the only concern. Specifically, the sugar program can be evaluated in terms of its effects on the distribution of economic welfare. On the foreign side, the gains tend to go to countries that are net sugar importers, the losses to countries that are net sugar exporters, particularly those without U.S. import quota rights.

Some rough estimates of the effects of the U.S. sugar program on U.S. sugar import quota-holding countries and other major sugar exporters and importers are shown in table 3. The first column shows the 1984/85 to 1988/89 quota shares for quota-holding countries.[23] The other five columns show the net economic gain to each country due to the sugar program in each of the five crop years. These economic effects are derived by assigning shares of the total estimated ROW quota rents, producer losses, and consumer gains on the basis of the quota shares of quota-holding countries, and the production and consumption shares of all countries.

These estimates should be viewed as rough because they assume that all countries in the rest of the world would exhibit identical consumption and production responses, which is patently false and is inconsistent with the assumption that some countries fully insulate their domestic sugar markets from world price changes, while others do not intervene at all. This approach may understate the losses to countries that would be better able to increase their supplies in order to take advantage of an increase in the world sugar price, and similarly may overstate the losses to others.

Thus, the approach involves a crude approximation of the distribution of welfare effects that are based on *changes* in quantities supplied and demanded for individual countries. On the other hand, it captures well the fundamental terms-of-trade effects and changes in quota rents that these countries will experience, given their *initial* levels of quantity supplied and demanded.

Even though the rest of the world is estimated to have gained on net from the program, table 3 suggests that there are some big losers, notably Australia and Thailand among the quota-holding countries. Some countries with large quota shares, like the Dominican Republic and the Philippines, remain net beneficiaries from the program, though their benefits in 1988/89 were only a fraction of their 1984/85 levels, due to the cutbacks in the amount of U.S. quota imports. Despite its large quota share, Brazil is estimated to have been hurt on net by the program in recent years, due to its high level of exports to countries other than the United States. The island nations of Fiji and Mauritius both were hurt by the program; both derive more than one-third of their merchandise export revenues from sugar.

Relative to gross national product, the biggest losers in 1988/89 among U.S. quota-holding countries were Swaziland (-0.37 percent), Fiji (-0.31), Mauritius (-0.21), and Thailand (-0.04). The biggest winners were the Dominican Republic (+0.18 percent), Panama (+0.08), El Salvador (+0.07), and Honduras (+0.06).[24] Among other sugar exporters, Cuba and the

TABLE 3. Estimated Net Welfare Effects of U.S. Sugar Program for Specific Countries, 1984/85 to 1988/89 (millions of 1988 dollars)

	Base Quota (percent)	1984/85	1985/86	1986/87	1987/88	1988/89
U.S. Quota Holders:	100.0	508.0	314.5	40.6	-110.1	-38.7
Argentina	4.3	22.2	20.6	12.8	5.2	3.0
Australia	8.3	5.3	-13.4	-42.7	-61.6	-46.9
Barbados	0.7	3.5	1.8	0.6	-0.4	0.3
Belize	1.1	6.3	4.2	1.7	0.1	0.8
Bolivia	0.8	5.2	3.6	1.7	0.9	1.8
Brazil	14.5	45.6	28.9	-10.6	-37.8	-16.0
Canada	1.1	27.1	28.3	29.9	26.9	23.2
Colombia	2.4	11.2	9.2	3.0	-0.6	-1.8
Costa Rica	2.1	14.0	10.3	5.6	2.8	4.0
Dominican Republic	17.6	110.7	80.5	45.8	18.0	27.3
Ecuador	1.1	8.0	6.4	4.2	2.5	4.1
El Salvador	3.0	19.9	13.8	7.4	5.1	6.9
Fiji	0.7	-3.2	-2.8	-9.9	-8.9	-7.7
Guatemala	4.8	29.2	19.1	7.3	-0.7	3.0
Guyana	1.2	4.7	2.0	-0.2	-1.4	0.1
Honduras	2.1	13.4	9.0	4.7	3.2	4.1
India	0.8	46.6	26.6	-2.2	-2.3	14.4
Jamaica	1.1	6.5	3.9	1.5	-1.0	0.5
Malawi	0.7	3.1	1.9	-0.1	-1.1	0.1
Mauritius	1.1	-2.7	-8.0	-15.0	-17.3	-11.7
Mozambique	1.3	9.6	7.6	5.7	3.4	3.8
Panama	2.9	20.1	14.8	8.9	4.6	6.4
Peru	4.1	28.0	25.2	21.7	14.6	11.2
Philippines	15.8	81.5	62.8	47.9	29.2	28.3
South Africa	0.0	-5.2	-8.1	-24.7	-23.9	-23.4
Swaziland	1.6	4.1	0.9	-7.9	-8.8	-5.7
Taiwan	1.2	4.9	4.9	3.8	-0.8	1.5
Thailand	1.4	-23.7	-32.9	-45.3	-51.3	-70.2
Trinidad and Tobago	0.7	4.7	3.5	1.8	0.7	0.8
Zimbabwe	1.2	4.2	1.0	-3.1	-3.1	-2.3
Other	0.3	3.0	-11.0	-14.0	-6.3	1.5
Major Exporters:						
Cuba	-	-139.5	-139.8	-171.3	-187.5	-166.6
EC	-	-48.8	-71.9	-90.0	-67.7	-65.1
Major Importers:						
Soviet Union	-	87.7	101.4	138.0	110.4	106.9
Japan	-	37.1	39.3	42.7	48.9	40.1
China	-	28.2	18.0	30.1	72.1	51.9
Rest-of-World Total:	-	631.3	460.3	254.4	127.9	179.6

European Community were hardest hit by the program, while the major sugar importers—the former Soviet Union, Japan, and China were the biggest winners.[25] These effects on particular countries will have to be weighed, along with the aggregate foreign and domestic effects, in future debates on the merits of the program.

The aggregate welfare effects estimated in this study may be readily compared to those of previous studies of the U.S. sugar program. Leu, Schmitz, and Knutson (1987) estimated the domestic welfare effects in 1983 under various assumptions about the domestic-foreign raw-sugar price differential, the elasticity of foreign sugar export supply, and the substitutability between HFCS and sucrose from cane and beet. Their estimates of the costs to consumers range from 0.372 to 4.017 billion 1983 dollars, while their estimates of the gains to sugar producers range from $0.169 to $0.833 billion. They do not assess the gains to producers of HFCS. Their estimates of the net welfare cost to the United States range from $0.203 to $3.184 billion, a much wider range than is admitted by my analysis for the years I examine.

On the other hand, in a study of the U.S. sugar program for the government of Australia, Borrell, Sturgiss, and Wong (1987) tend to find smaller domestic effects and larger foreign effects—despite some basic structural similarities between their model and my own.[26] The foreign effects are larger because the model generates a much stronger effect on the world price, ranging from 11 to 50 percent over the years examined and over low and high scenarios. The authors find moreover that the rest of the world is made worse off on net by the U.S. sugar program, in contrast to my conclusion that the rest of the world gains on net.[27]

Finally, in a later study for the government of Australia, Sturgiss, Field, and Young (1990) use the dynamic, multicountry sugar model developed by Wong, Sturgiss, and Borrell (1989) to estimate the domestic and foreign effects of the U.S. sugar program. The results of their dynamic simulations are remarkably consistent with my own static calculations: they estimate an average net cost to the U.S. economy of $776 to $785 million 1988 dollars over 1982–88, and an average net gain to the rest of the world of $277 to $467 million. The similarities to my own midpoint estimates—a $667 million net cost to the United States and a $331 million net gain to the rest of the world on average over 1984/85–88/89—suggest that the limitations of a static and highly aggregative model are not serious, at least for purposes of aggregate welfare calculations.

4.3 Effects of a Marginal Liberalization

The finding that the U.S. sugar program has made the rest of the world better off in the aggregate could be taken to suggest that further tightening of U.S.

import quotas would add even more to foreign welfare. My second policy experiment suggests that this is not the case: the U.S. quotas are already too tight to maximize foreign welfare.

Specifically, table 4 shows the effects on U.S. and ROW welfare of a permanent 10 percent reduction in the real U.S. sugar loan rate for the five crop years previously examined. This cutback would have allowed expansion of the U.S. sugar import quotas, reducing the wedge between domestic and foreign prices. The final column of the table shows the average estimate over the five-year period, as well as the 95 percent confidence bounds.

The estimated domestic welfare effects are relatively stable across the years shown, since the only major domestic variations were on the production side, and were largely due to weather changes. I find that the average gain to U.S. consumers would have been 436 million 1988 dollars, and the average loss to U.S. sweetener producers $389 million, with roughly equal shares for cane, beet, and corn sweetener producers. The U.S. government would have gained $5 million on average in tariff revenues due to the expansion of sugar imports implied by the reduction of the loan rate. The net gain to the U.S. economy would have averaged $47 million. The net gain to the rest of the world would have averaged $70 million; foreign producers would have enjoyed both increased quota rents and a higher sugar price. The net global gain would have averaged $117 million.

4.4 Additional Qualifications to the Analysis

Several qualifications to the welfare calculations should be emphasized. First, as the approach is partial equilibrium in nature, it is able to focus on important institutional details of U.S. sweetener markets and policies. This approach allows quota rents to be taken into account directly, for example, unlike multicommodity studies that typically model trade policies in terms of their ad-valorem tariff equivalents. On the other hand, a partial-equilibrium approach may miss interactions with related markets and policies. Second, I applied long-run supply and demand elasticities to actual market data for the years examined, even though these data in general do not represent long-run equilibria. This appeared to be the safest approach, since it made the calculations less susceptible to measurement errors in the data. Specifically, I calibrated the model to the data by forcing the U.S. and ROW supply curves through the initial quantities supplied at the initial prices, then determined implied levels of U.S. and ROW consumption by taking the corresponding production level and adding (for the United States) or subtracting (for the ROW) the level of U.S. quota imports. The effect was to lump any changes in inventories or statistical discrepancies into consumption.[28]

Third, my calculations of the effects of the sugar program assume that the

TABLE 4. Estimated Welfare Effects of a Permanent 10 Percent Cut in the Real U.S. Loan Rate, 1984/85 to 1988/89 (billions of 1988 dollars)

	1984/85	1985/86	1986/87	1987/88	1988/89	1984/5-1988/89 Average Confidence Interval
United States						
Consumer Surplus:	0.466	0.446	0.443	0.420	0.405	0.436 ± 0.069
Producer Surplus:	-0.386	-0.381	-0.406	-0.401	-0.371	-0.389 ± 0.061
Beet Sugar Producers:	-0.116	-0.116	-0.138	-0.139	-0.119	-0.125 ± 0.015
Cane Sugar Producers:	-0.123	-0.125	-0.129	-0.128	-0.122	-0.126 ± 0.009
HFCS Producers:	-0.146	-0.139	-0.139	-0.134	-0.129	-0.138 ± 0.057
Government Revenue:	0.005	0.005	0.005	0.005	0.004	0.005 ± 0.004
Net U.S. Welfare:	0.080	0.065	0.037	0.019	0.034	0.047 ± 0.017
Rest of World						
Consumer Surplus:	-0.223	-0.279	-0.385	-0.508	-0.519	-0.383 ± 0.940
Producer Welfare:	0.283	0.348	0.494	0.597	0.539	0.452 ± 0.999
Quota Rents:	0.055	0.062	0.104	0.083	0.012	0.063 ± 0.103
Producer Surplus:	0.228	0.285	0.391	0.515	0.527	0.389 ± 0.960
Net Foreign Welfare:	0.061	0.069	0.110	0.089	0.021	0.070 ± 0.111
Net Global Welfare:	0.141	0.134	0.146	0.108	0.055	0.117 ± 0.124

United States could increase its imports of raw cane sugar without any increase in the unit costs of processing that sugar. However, under the sugar program, U.S. cane refining capacity shrunk from 9.3 million tons in 1981 to only 5.5 million tons in 1988.[29] Given the capital costs required to restore refining capacity if the program were dismantled, the constant-unit-cost assumption clearly is problematic, though in principle these capital costs could be amortized over a great many years.

Fourth, my calculations do not reflect one especially important set of economic effects of the program: the increase in price volatility and risk to foreign sugar producers and consumers, and the decrease in price volatility and risk to domestic sweetener producers and consumers. As Borrell and Duncan have emphasized in this volume, there clearly are welfare consequences, though these effects are difficult to measure.

Fifth, the consumption losses in the United States are not all incurred by the ultimate consumers of sweeteners, who purchase for their shelves roughly 15 percent of U.S. sweetener sales. Part of these losses are instead incurred by the industries that use sweeteners in processed food and beverages. Sixth, the gains to cane and beet sugar producers are split between processors and growers. The processors actually receive the U.S. government loans based on the loan rate, then pay a share of their revenues to the growers, though in many cases the two operations are integrated.

Finally, as in virtually all other empirical policy studies, my welfare estimates do not account for problems like the dissipation of rents through wasteful rent-seeking activities.

5. Conclusions

I find that the U.S. sugar program has depressed the world sugar price by between 8 and 16 percent in recent years, and conclude that U.S. sugar policy has made the rest of the world better off in the aggregate, though it is harmful to the United States and to global economic welfare overall. My analysis of a marginal reform of the U.S. sugar program shows that U.S. sugar import quotas are already too tight to maximize welfare in the rest of the world: a 10 percent reduction in the real U.S. loan rate, and the attendant relaxation of import quotas, is found to lead to higher welfare in the aggregate in both the United States and the rest of the world.

The welfare analysis suggests that both the United States and European Community are heavily penalized by the U.S. sugar program. Other countries gain in the aggregate—both from an improvement in their terms of trade as net sugar importers overall, and from the quota rents created by the U.S. policy—though countries like Cuba, Thailand, Australia, and Brazil are big losers. Ironically, were it not for the U.S. sugar import quotas, the United

States overall would gain from the EC sugar regime, as its terms of trade as a net sugar importer would be improved by the EC policies that expand net EC sugar exports and drive down the world price. Of course, given the producer adjustment problems that unilateral U.S. reform would create, such reform will continue to meet heavy resistance from the sweetener sector and its representatives in Congress. These observations point, therefore, to the importance of the multilateral liberalization efforts that to this point remain in doubt in Geneva.

APPENDIX: DATA SOURCES

Data for the United States

Consumption per capita of refined sugar and HFCS, wholesale price of refined sugar, wholesale price of HFCS, wholesale price of raw cane sugar, net cost of corn starch, and net quantity of U.S. sugar imports: *Sugar and Sweetener Situation and Outlook Report*, U.S. Department of Agriculture, Economic Research Service, Commodity Economics Division, various issues.

Consumer price index (1982–84=100), disposable personal income per capita, population, and indexes of prices received and paid by farmers (1977=100): *Economic Report of the President, 1991*, Washington, DC: U.S. Government Printing Office.

Production of beet sugar, production of cane sugar: *U.S. Sugar Statistical Compendium*, U.S. Department of Agriculture, Economic Research Service, Commodity Economics Division, Statistical Bulletin No. 830, August 1991.

Data for the Rest of the World

World population and gross national product (1984 dollars): Ruth Leger Sivard, *World Military and Social Expenditures, 1991*, Washington, DC: World Priorities, 14th edition (and previous editions).

Indexes of world food commodity prices and world consumer prices (1980=100), and U.S. gross national product: *International Financial Statistics Yearbook, 1988*, Washington, DC: International Monetary Fund.

Wholesale price of raw sugar in the Caribbean: *Sugar and Sweetener Situation and Outlook Report*, U.S. Department of Agriculture, Economic Research Service, Commodity Economics Division, various issues.

Production and consumption of centrifugal sugar (world totals and by individual country): data files on world sugar production, supply, and distribution, from the U.S. Department of Agriculture, Economic Research Service.

U.S. import quota shares by country (from the Headnotes of Schedule 1, Part 10, Subpart A of the *Tariff Schedule of the United States*): John Nuttal, *Evolution of Sugar Import Policies and Programs, 1981–1988*, U.S. Department of Agriculture, Foreign Agricultural Service, International Trade Policy Division, FAS Staff Report No. 8, November 1988. This publication also includes information on U.S. sugar loan rates, duties, and other import fees.

NOTES

Earlier versions of this paper were written while the author was Visiting Economist, U.S. Department of State, Bureau of Economic and Business Affairs, Planning and Economic Analysis Staff. The views expressed in this paper are those of the author alone, and are not necessarily those of the Department of State or the U.S. government. The author is grateful to William Dewald, Steven Husted, David Kennett, Rigoberto Lopez, Keith Maskus, and seminar participants at the U.S. Department of Agriculture, Claremont McKenna College, and Princeton University for their helpful comments.

1. For surveys of recent multicommodity, multicountry analyses of agricultural policy liberalizations that include sugar, see Lord and Barry (1990) and the other chapters in this volume.

2. For details, see David S. Cloud, "House and Senate Resist Calls to Alter Course on Farm Bill," *Congressional Quarterly Weekly Report*, July 28, 1990, 2393–2396.

3. It can be argued that an HFCS supply curve per se does not exist, because the industry is imperfectly competitive: the four largest HFCS producers averaged 86 percent of production capacity in the industry over 1984/85 to 1988/89, and entry by newcomers would have required high levels of capital investment in an environment subject to considerable policy risk.

4. Their estimated long-run price elasticities are 0.15 for ROW supply and -0.09 for ROW demand. These are derived at mean data values from linear supply and demand functions, but do not differ substantially from my constant long-run elasticity estimates of roughly 0.17 and -0.06.

5. For example, ROW net exports to the United States were higher in the 1960s than in the 1980s. For the earlier period, the average ROW export supply elasticity is 3.09 based on Hammig et al., and 2.56 based on the present study. Formally, define e_s and e_d to be the (constant) ROW elasticities of supply and demand (the first positive, and the second negative), and let S, D, and X indicate ROW quantities supplied, demanded, and exported (on net). The ROW elasticity of export supply equals the change in exports divided by the initial level of exports, relative to the change in price divided by the initial price. After some manipulation, this can be written as $(e_s \cdot S - e_d \cdot D)/X = (e_s \cdot S - e_d \cdot (S - X))/X = (e_s - e_d) \cdot S/X + e_d$. Given that the last term in parentheses is positive, and that all the elasticities are constant, the result in the text follows directly (by taking the derivative of the last expression with respect to S/X).

6. An earlier version of this paper included estimates of sugar stock behavior in the

United States and the rest of the world. These estimates are not needed for the static long-run calculations presented, and so are not included in this paper. However, an important criterion for validation of a commodity market model is that it be dynamically stable. With the equations for sugar stocks included, the model met this test.

7. This assumption is not a problem for 1960/61 to 1973/74, and 1982/83 to 1988/89, when import quotas were in effect. From 1974/75 to 1981/82, the quotas were allowed to lapse. Though tariffs provided some protection to the industry, the U.S. price tended to move with the world price. Even so, I will take the price as exogenous over that period, on the grounds that the U.S. government could have reimposed import quotas, as it did in 1982, had it found the domestic raw sugar price inappropriate.

8. Specifically, this price index appears in the demand functions implied by constrained maximization of the utility function $U(Q_{S,\,t}, Q_{F,\,t}) = \min(\theta_t \cdot Q_{S,\,t}, (1 - \theta_t) \cdot Q_{F,\,t})$, in which θ_t and $(1 - \theta_t)$ are the fixed consumption shares of sugar and HFCS, respectively.

9. A variety of previous studies have estimated or assumed the sweetener demand elasticity to be -0.1, close to my long-run elasticity estimate. For a survey of previous estimates, see the chapter by Schmitz and Christian in this volume.

10. The estimated serial correlation coefficient is 0.534.

11. With two-stage least squares, the coefficient and t-statistic for the net cost of corn starch were 0.605 and 0.678, and for the price of raw sugar were 0.539 and 2.463. The variables used in the reduced form equation for the net cost of corn starch were the price of raw sugar, a price index for farm inputs (also used in equations (6) and (7)), the lagged corn price, an index of summer drought for corn-belt states, and a time trend. Complete details are available on request.

12. This situation could clearly create serious difficulties for the industry. There are considerable differences of opinion on the unit costs of production of HFCS, however. My estimates assume they are constant at all relevant output levels, and are based on Earley (1988), who links HFCS costs to the net cost of corn starch. I find the HFCS price to be forced *below* the estimated level of HFCS unit costs for 1984/85 through 1986/87, and *to* the level of unit costs for the final two years. Variations in the world sugar price over the period account for these differences.

13. These processes included time trends, and were taken to be of sufficiently high order that the residuals showed no evidence of autocorrelation.

14. The U.S. government enforced domestic sugar marketing controls from 1934 to 1974, and had no quota system at all from 1974 to 1981. There now exist other institutional restraints on sugar production, however, like restrictions on entry into beet processing cooperatives, or the threat that the government could impose production or marketing controls if sugar imports were to shrink too much. I have tested for structural change in the beet and cane supply equations, however, from 1960–74 to 1974–1988, and from 1960–82 to 1983–88, and find no evidence for it in any of the cases.

15. The prices and quantities in the diagrams are not scaled to actual data. For simplicity, HFCS and sucrose can be considered to be lumped together in the demand and supply curves for the United States.

16. In reality, excluding the EC, the rest of the world is currently a net sugar importer.
17. Lord and Barry (1990) provide a useful tabular summary of the sugar policies of many nations.
18. In this volume, Harris and Tangermann point out that variations in the world sugar price lead to variations in the EC producer price net of official levies for roughly one-fourth of quota sugar. However, as these quotas are consistently filled, it can be argued that the price changes merely represent transfers from EC sugar producers to the EC itself, without any effect on production decisions at the margin. On the other hand, the quota levels have in fact been adjusted from time to time in response to fluctuations in the world price.
19. These tariffs currently do not affect U.S. or world prices or quantities, because the import quotas are binding, but rather merely transfer part of the quota rents back to the United States.
20. The relevant estimates all came from different equations, and were assumed to be independent of each other.
21. Bruce Ingersoll, "Range War: Small Minnesota Town is Divided by Rancor over Sugar Policies," *Wall Street Journal*, June 26, 1990. The remainder of the data used to calculate benefits per producer come from Barry et al. (1990), tables 5 and 7, and appendix table 17.
22. The U.S. government leaves it to foreign governments to allocate their sugar quotas within their countries. A foreign government may retain the quota rents or transfer them to the private sector, depending on the method by which it allocates its quota. Some observers may be predisposed to view the quota rents as implicit U.S. foreign aid expenditure. If the foreign country would have been given this level of foreign aid in any case, then the quota rents could be more properly viewed as additions to U.S. welfare. On the other hand, Ron Lord of USDA notes that foreign aid is usually monitored to ensure that it reaches targeted groups, but that in some countries sugar quota rents may get no farther than governmental bureaucracies. Moreover, these rents will be dissipated to some extent by rent-seeking activities by the foreign government, or by private parties within the foreign country, though aid-seeking activities could lead to a similar dissipation of foreign aid.
23. These shares sum to 100 percent. The actual shares typically sum to more than 100 percent, however, due to the opportunity for the countries with small shares to ship minimum quota amounts. South Africa received a 2.3 percent share through 1985/86. The share was given to the Philippines starting in crop year 1986/87.
24. GNP data for 1988 were calculated in U.S. dollars on the basis of data presented by Robert Summers and Alan Heston, "The Penn World Table (Mark 5): An Expanded Set of International Comparisons, 1950–1988," *Quarterly Journal of Economics* 106: 327–368.
25. Preferential Soviet purchases of Cuban sugar offset the loss to Cuba and the gain to the Soviet Union to a considerable extent.
26. Their model is partial equilibrium, and splits the world into the United States and the rest of the world. Moreover, my approach to the modeling of U.S. sweetener demand is similar to theirs (as well as that of Wong, Sturgiss, and Borrell (1989)). Their modeling of the supply side in both the United States and the rest of the world is much different, however.

27. Their analysis covers crop years 1981/82 to 1985/86. To make their findings comparable to those of the present study, I have converted their 1984/85 crop-year estimates into billions of 1988 dollars using the U.S. consumer price index. Their midpoint estimates of the effects of U.S. sugar policy on U.S. consumers (-2.840), sugar producers (1.143), and HFCS producers (0.972) are smaller in magnitude than my own, as is their estimate of the net U.S. loss (0.725). Their estimate of the net foreign loss is 0.375.

28. Over the crop years for which I have done the calculations, the implied U.S. consumption level deviates from the published official estimate of that level by no more than ±2.4 percent, and by an average of +0.5 percent. The implied ROW consumption level deviates from the official estimate by no more than ±3.5 percent, and by an average of -0.75 percent. This implies that there may be on average a slight upward bias in my estimates of U.S. consumer losses, and a slight downward bias in my estimates of ROW consumer gains. However, these biases are not large enough to change my conclusions about the net domestic, foreign, and global welfare effects of the program.

29. These figures are from Amstar Sugar Corporation, Economic Research, May 15, 1990.

REFERENCES

Barry, Robert D., Luigi Angelo, Peter J. Buzzanell, and Fred Gray. 1990. *Sugar: Background for 1990 Farm Legislation.* U.S. Department of Agriculture, Economic Research Service, Commodity Economics Division. Staff Report No. AGES 9006.

Borrell, Brent, Robert Sturgiss, and Gordon Wong. 1987. *Global Effects of the US Sugar Policy.* Australian Bureau of Agricultural and Resource Economics. Discussion Paper 87.3. Canberra: Australian Government Publishing Service.

Earley, Thomas C. 1988. *The Corn Market: Effects of Reforming the Sugar Program.* Alexandria, VA: Abel, Daft & Earley.

Hammig, Michael, Roger Conway, Hosein Shapouri, and John Yanagida. 1982. "The Effects of Shifts in Supply on the World Sugar Market." *Agricultural Economics Research* 34: 12-18.

Jesse, Edward V., and Glenn A. Zepp. 1977. *Sugar Policy Options for the United States.* U.S. Department of Agriculture, Economic Research Service, Commodity Economics Division. Agricultural Economic Report No. 351.

Leu, Gwo-Jiun M., Andrew Schmitz, and Ronald D. Knutson. 1987. "Gains and Losses of Sugar Program Policy Options." *American Journal of Agricultural Economics* 69: 591-602.

Lin, William, and Andrew Novick. 1988. "Substitution of High Fructose Corn Syrup for Sugar: Trends and Outlook." *Sugar and Sweetener Situation and Outlook Report.* June. U.S. Department of Agriculture, Economic Research Service, Commodity Economics Division.

Ljung, G., and G. E. P. Box. 1978. "On a Measure of Lack of Fit in Time Series Models." *Biometrika* 65: 297-303.

108   World Sugar Policies

Lopez, Rigoberto A. 1989. "Political Economy of U.S. Sugar Policies." *American Journal of Agricultural Economics* 71: 20-31.

Lord, Ron, and Robert D. Barry. 1990. *The World Sugar Market: Government Intervention and Multilateral Policy Reform*. U.S. Department of Agriculture, Economic Research Service, Commodity Economics Division. Staff Report No. AGES 9062.

Maskus, Keith E. 1989. "Large Costs and Small Benefits of the American Sugar Programme." *The World Economy* 12: 85-104.

Sturgiss, Robert, Heather Field, and Linda Young. 1990. *1990 and US Sugar Policy Reform*. Australian Bureau of Agricultural and Resource Economics. Discussion Paper 90.4. Canberra: Australian Government Publishing Service.

Wong, Gordon, Robert Sturgiss, and Brent Borrell. 1989. *The Economic Consequences of International Sugar Trade Reform*. Australian Bureau of Agricultural and Resource Economics. Discussion Paper 89.7. Canberra: Australian Government Publishing Service.

CHAPTER 5

A Review of the EC Sugar Regime

Simon A. Harris and Stefan Tangermann

1. Introduction

Developed-country sugar policies can lead to apparently paradoxical results. Some sugar-exporting developing countries argue for the maintenance of high European Community (EC) support prices, for instance, while the biggest supporter of the U.S. sugar program is the U.S. corn sweetener industry. On the other hand, economic analysis clearly implies that both policies lower global and domestic welfare overall—with domestic consumers and most sugar exporters the losers, and domestic sweetener producers the winners.

Our objective in this paper is to describe the sugar regime of the European Community, to set it in an historical context, and to evaluate its effects on the EC economy as well as other countries. We first highlight the origins of the European beet sugar industry and of European sugar policy in the early nineteenth century. We then survey the much more recent history of the EC sugar regime. We discuss in detail the mechanics of the regime, which includes two quota categories for domestic sugar, as well as preferential import quotas established by the EC for the African, Caribbean, and Pacific (ACP) countries associated with it under the Lomé Convention. The regime also allows outside-quota production, although such production is not eligible for EC support. (Nevertheless, it can be argued this production is indirectly supported, as is the case with other major world sugar exporters whose internal prices are higher than world prices.)

We next examine a number of recent empirical studies on the effects of the EC sugar regime. We start with a number of recent empirical estimates of the world-market-price effects of multilateral and unilateral agricultural market liberalization by the industrial market economies. Based on the results of one of these studies, we calculate the implied effects of such liberalization for domestic economic welfare in the Community and for the ACP countries. To assess in very general terms the dynamic effects of the sugar regime, we examine the evolution of the performance of the Community beet sugar industry in recent years. Though it is difficult to establish a clear counterfactual case, we argue that price signals under the EC regime have been sufficiently flexible to promote rapid productivity increases in beet production and processing. Moreover, international cost comparisons in the early 1970s and in the late 1980s clearly indicate that EC sugar producers have held their own in international competition; the sugar of some Community members remains among the lowest-cost of all major producers in the world.

Finally, we offer a brief comparison of the EC sugar regime with the U.S. sugar program. The EC regime is arguably less distorting in important respects than the U.S. program—even though it is clearly more complex and involves direct intervention into domestic production. Among the differences between the regimes, two stand out. First, with its strict quotas on production of some cereal sweeteners (in particular, high fructose corn syrup, or, as it is termed in the EC, isoglucose), the EC regime has managed to prevent the emergence of a new set of domestic beneficiaries of the program. By contrast, the biggest supporter of the U.S. sugar program is the U.S. corn sweetener industry. Second, under the EC regime, domestic producer prices at the margin are considerably more sensitive to movements in world prices than are U.S. producer prices. This suggests that *at the margin* the EC regime contributes less to world sugar price volatility than does the U.S. program. Third, the EC's preferences for third countries supplying its market do not vary between years in volume, unlike those of the United States.

2. The EC Sugar Regime and the Market Situation

2.1 History

The European beet sugar industry dates back to the era of Napoleon. Heckscher (1922) reports that at the time the technology for extraction of sugar from beet was fairly advanced, but the availability of Caribbean cane sugar inhibited the emergence of domestic production. The British blockade of continental Europe in 1807, however, cut off continental imports of cane sugar from the Caribbean. The resulting high sugar prices on the Continent provided the necessary incentives for the European beet sugar industry to be developed. With a new opportunity for economic development at hand, as well as the prospect of a domestic source of supply independent of imports, Napoleon ordered extensive beet cultivation and the development of a system of imperial beet sugar factories. The industry experienced more than a decade of difficulties—not one of the original sugar factories survived the demise of the empire—but the imposition of a high duty on colonial sugar by France sent a rejuvenated industry on its way by 1830. Over the next several decades, continental European countries supported their beet sugar industries through competitive and costly export bounties in addition to import barriers, and their domestic sugar production surged.[1] With the aid of these measures, beet sugar by 1889 accounted for more than 60 percent of sugar output worldwide (Albert and Graves 1988). In summary, then, the European beet sugar industry is long established, as is the tradition of protection for that industry.

The contemporary European Community sugar market regime came into full effect in 1968. The regime has not been substantially altered since that time, apart from the introduction of more complete producer financing in 1981. The principal mechanism by which producers have been supported is a common support price. This price was meant to be an average of the support prices in the original six member countries. In the political bargaining that ensued, however, it was actually set closer to the high support prices that applied in Italy and Germany prior to the introduction of the EC sugar regime. As a consequence, support for the EC sugar industry was never open ended, but was always limited by production quotas in order to limit the EC's financial liability for supporting its sugar industry. The quotas were introduced on a temporary basis, to be removed after seven years. They have been maintained ever since, however, subject to periodic review, as the cut in the support price to get an equivalent control over production has proved politically unacceptable.

The total EC quotas for sugar and isoglucose are given in table 1 over the history of the regime. Only marketing years in which the quotas were changed are shown.[2] As we explain more fully in the next section, the quota system is two-tiered, with sugar under the *A* quota receiving a higher net support price than sugar under the *B* quota, although the gross support price is the same for all quota sugar. The *A* and *B* quotas taken together constitute the "maximum quota" for a given country. The quotas are allocated to governments—which in turn allocate them to individual enterprises (companies or cooperatives)—on the basis of their historical production. The quotas were originally set to meet existing consumption, plus the expected growth in consumption, and thus allowed for production surpluses from the start. Table 1 also shows the preferential quota allocation to the ACP states under the Lomé Convention, as well as the quotas applied to isoglucose production.

Because the EC production quotas are based on historic national production levels, their relationship to consumption varies widely between EC member countries. Table 2 shows that maximum country quotas vary from well below 100 percent self-sufficiency (for Portugal and the United Kingdom) to nearly 200 percent or more (for Belgium, Denmark, France). It also shows the level of *B* quota relative to *A* quota for each country. Countries with higher sugar production costs (Spain, Italy, Portugal, and Greece)—tend to have smaller *B* quota percentages because of the much higher incidence of levies on *B* quota production and, hence, the lower net returns. The UK case is an anomaly, as its total quota was held down to ensure a place for ACP cane sugar in the EC market.

When the allocation of quotas is reviewed periodically, the EC looks at whether producers have filled their quotas in previous years. As a result, the system builds in an incentive for production over quota, as producers aim to offset year-to-year variability in sugar yields by producing C sugar as a safe-

TABLE 1.   EC Production Quotas for Sugar and Isoglucose (million metric tons, wse[a])

Marketing Year	Quota Type	EC Total[b]	ACP Protocol	Isoglucose[c]
1968/69– 1972/73	A Quota Maximum Quota	6.480 8.530		
1973/74	A Quota Maximum Quota[d]	7.820 8.685		
1974/75	A Quota Maximum Quota[e]	7.820 10.751		
1975/76	A Quota Maximum Quota[e]	9.136 13.250	1.305	
1976/77– 1977/78	A Quota Maximum Quota[d]	9.136 12.335	1.305	
1978/79– 1979/80	A Quota Maximum Quota[f]	9.136 11.648	1.305	0.1471 0.1876
1980/81	A Quota Maximum Quota[f]	9.136 11.648	1.305	0.1471 0.1876
1981/82– 1985/86	A Quota B Quota Maximum Quota	9.516 2.242 11.758	1.305	0.1576 0.0404 0.1980
1986/87– 1990/91	A Quota B Quota Maximum Quota	10.540 2.289 12.829	1.305	0.2407 0.0503 0.2910
1991/92– 1992/93	A Quota B Quota Maximum Quota	11.187 2.488 13.675	1.305	0.2407 0.0503 0.2910

Source: Commission of the European Communities, *EEC Sugar Market Organisation*, Revision 1992, Brussels, table 1.

[a] White sugar equivalent.

[b] The data are for the EC-6 for marketing years 1968/69 to 1972/73, the EC-9 for 1973/74 to 1980/81, the EC-10 for 1981/82 to 1985/86, the EC-12 for 1986/87 to 1990/91, and the EC-12 with a unified Germany from 1991/92.

[c] Isoglucose is the EC term for high fructose corn syrup. Figures are given on a dry basis.

[d] The B quota was a maximum of 35 percent of the A quota.

[e] The B quota was a maximum of 45 percent of the A quota.

[f] The B quota was a maximum of 27.5 percent of the A quota.

TABLE 2. EC Beet Sugar Production Quotas Relative to Consumption, by Member State, 1986/87 to 1990/91 (wse)

	A Quota	Maximum[a] Quota	Average Consumption[b] 1986/87-1988/89	A Quota Relative to Consumption	Maximum Quota Relative to Consumption	B Quota Relative to A Quota
		thousand metric tons			percent	
Denmark	328	425	193	169.9	220.2	29.5
Germany	1,990	2,602	2,158	92.2	120.6	30.8
Greece	290	319	298	97.3	107.0	10.0
Spain	960	1,000	984	97.6	101.6	4.2
France	2,996	3,802	2,011	149.0	189.1	26.9
Ireland	182	200	126	144.4	158.7	10.0
Italy	1,320	1,568	1,533	86.1	102.3	18.8
Netherlands	690	872	555	124.3	157.1	26.4
Portugal	64	70	318	20.1	22.0	10.0
Belgium-Luxembourg	680	826	376	180.9	219.7	21.5
United Kingdom	1,040	1,144	2,327	44.7	49.2	10.0
EC-12	10,540	12,828	10,879	96.9	117.9	21.7

Source: Authors' calculations, based on EC Regulation 1785/81, as amended.
[a] A Quota + B Quota.
[b] Inclusion of more recent years in the consumption averages would have distorted the consumption data, given the effects of German unification in 1990 and the liberalization of the formerly communist countries of Eastern Europe.

guard against shortfalls in quota production. Such shortfalls are limited in practice. Residual C sugar not needed to ensure that quotas are filled is sold on world markets without any direct EC subsidy. When world prices are rising, C sugar production also tends to increase as world prices become more attractive.

2.2 Mechanics of the EC Regime

The EC sugar regime is typical of the Common Agricultural Policy of the EC in that it includes a variety of foreign trade interventions to maintain the administered support prices.[3] In particular, as with other CAP commodity regimes, it includes both variable import levies prohibitive to imports when world prices are below EC levels (the normal situation), as well as variable export subsidies to ensure that the EC can export its surplus quota sugar to the world market.[4] The sugar regime is unlike most other CAP regimes in that it has mechanisms—variable export taxes and a strategic stock that can be run down if necessary—to prevent EC domestic market prices from rising above the institutional support band when world sugar market prices exceed EC levels.

Two institutional support prices—the "intervention price" (a floor price) and the "threshold price" (a minimum import price)—form a band within which the domestic EC market price moves. The threshold price is meant to ensure that domestic market prices can rise toward a "target price" without being undercut by third-country imports. Support is given to processed sugar, because sugarbeet cannot be stored: national agricultural intervention agencies that found it necessary to purchase beet in order to support their price would not be able to store the product. As a result, processors are covered by the regime, though the regime is directed to farmers. Processors earn revenues on both sugar and molasses derived from the beet, and are obliged to pay beet growers a minimum price for the amount of beet necessary to fill the sugar quotas. Since the intervention price is a minimum price of sugar in the EC, the institutional processing margin included when setting support prices constitutes the minimum revenue for covering industrial processing costs and generating profits. The institutional relationships between the white sugar intervention price, the minimum producer price for beet, and the processing margin are illustrated in table 3 for marketing year 1989/90.

Figure 1 tracks the movement in average monthly world sugar prices and EC intervention prices from 1968/69 to 1989/90. The intervention price rose at an average annual rate of 6.7 percent over the period, the world price at 7.3 percent. The rate of increase of the intervention price accelerated, though with a lag, in response to the world price spikes of 1974 and 1980.

Intervention buying is rarely used in practice. Instead, export refunds are used to support internal EC market prices by enabling exports of the surplus of "free circulation" sugar to world markets: the export refunds are set so as to make selling to intervention less attractive than exporting.[5] The export refunds are bid for at weekly tenders by international commodity traders and some of the larger EC sugar processors, so ensuring a level of competition as export licenses are awarded to those who will accept the smallest rates of unit export refund. The competitive bidding holds down the financial costs of the export refund system, and provides periodic information on market conditions.[6] The EC awards refunds on the basis of a relatively constant target export volume (to avoid destabilizing world markets) and a maximum unit rate of refund it is prepared to grant, set to ensure that the unit rate of refund does not exceed the difference between the intervention price and the futures quotations on the world white sugar market. Although bidders at the tenders do not have to pay for the licenses, they are heavily penalized if the licenses, once granted, are not fulfilled.

From the start of the sugar regime, sugar producers were responsible for contributing to the cost of exporting *B* quota sugar. In the 1970s, however, the production levies contributed by producers were not set to cover the full cost of the export refunds. GATT panels in 1979 and 1980 criticized the

TABLE 3. Derivation of Processing Margin for Community Sugar, 1989/90

	ecu per 100kg of white sugar	U.S. cents per lb[c] of white sugar
Basic Beet Price	4.007	2.0035
White Sugar Intervention Price	53.10	26.55
Target Price	55.89	27.95
Processing Margin		
(A) Revenue: Intervention Price	53.10	26.15
molasses[a]	1.89	0.95
	54.99	27.50
(B) Expenditure: beet value[b]	30.82	15.41
transport, reception	3.70	1.85
	34.52	17.26
(C) Processing margin, (A) - (B)	20.47	10.24

Source: International Sugar Organization (1990, Annex I).

[a] One metric ton of beet yields 0.130 metric tons of sugar and 0.385 metric tons of molasses. A notional price of 6.40 ecu per 100kg molasses then generates revenues of 1.89 ecu per 100kg sugar.

[b] With 0.130 metric tons sugar per metric ton of beet, the beet value per 100kg of sugar is 4.007/0.130 or roughly 30.82.

[c] Conversion rate week 8 November 1989 to 14 November 1989: 1 ecu = 1.10150 $U.S., so that 1 ecu per 100kg equals roughly 0.5 cents per pound.

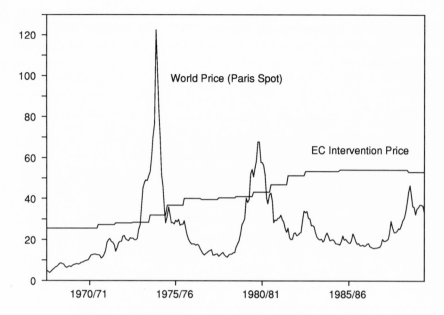

**FIGURE 1.   Monthly World Market Price and EC Intervention Price
for White Sugar, 1968/69–88/89 (ecu/100kg)**

EC's sugar policy for not having any effective limitation on the amounts of export refunds, among other issues (Osteras 1981). As a part of its response, the EC increased the rates of producer levies in 1981/82 so that the regime would be "self-financing." Under this principle, producers are responsible for funding the cost to the Community budget of exporting surplus sugar through a variety of levies they are charged.[7]

Though *B* quota producer levies were raised from a maximum rate of 30 percent to 39.5 percent in 1981/82, and levies were introduced at two percent on *A* quota, the levies still did not cover fully the cost of quota sugar exports. Since 1986/87, however, the producer levies have been varied annually to cover fully the deficit arising in the year of production, plus the accumulated deficit from the previous five-year period.

The distinction between *A* and *B* quotas is related to the proportion of producer levies they bear. For *A* quota—approximately equal to EC domestic consumption—only a small levy is payable, and the minimum producer price (the intervention price less *A* quota levies) is virtually stable. *B* quota—currently equal to 22.2 percent of *A* quota for the EC as a whole—receives a lower and more variable price as it carries the majority of the cost of the producer levies. *C* sugar is sugar produced in excess of the quotas. It does not receive EC support, and has to be exported to world markets without receiving any export refund. The majority of *C* sugar production in the EC comes from France, Germany, the Netherlands, and the United Kingdom.

Table 4 shows Community production levels of *A*-quota, *B*-quota, and *C* sugar for marketing years 1979/80 to 1989/90. It also shows the white sugar

TABLE 4. Producer Prices and Quantities for *A*, *B*, and *C* Sugar, 1979/80 to 1989/90 (ecu/100kg wse, unless otherwise noted)

	White Sugar Prices		Producer Levies Charged		Minimum Produce Prices[c]	
Marketing Year	Intervention[a]	World[b]	*A* Quota	*B* Quota	*A* Quota	*B* Quota
1979/80	41.09	32.32	-	12.0300	41.0900	29.0600
1980/81	43.27	53.58	-	3.4700	43.2700	39.8000
1981/82	46.95	30.82	0.9390	15.0240	46.0110	31.9260
1982/83	51.41	24.07	1.0282	20.3070	50.3818	31.1030
1983/84	53.47	26.14	1.0694	21.1207	52.4006	32.3493
1984/85	53.47	19.92	1.0694	21.1207	52.4006	32.3493
1985/86	54.18	19.88	1.0836	21.4011	53.0964	32.7789
1986/87	54.18	17.31	2.2161	30.4316	51.9639	23.7484
1987/88	54.18	18.43	1.9852	25.8715	52.1948	28.3085
1988/89	54.18	28.04	2.0870	27.8806	52.0930	26.2994
1989/90	53.10	37.66	1.7733	13.9405	51.3267	39.1595

	Sugar Production (1,000 metric tons wse)			Weighted Average Minimum Receipts	
Marketing Year	*A* Quota	*B* Quota	*C* Sugar	Quota Sugar	All Sugar
1979/80	9,005	1,792	1,446	39.09	38.29
1980/81	8,910	2,111	1,191	42.61	43.68
1981/82	9,382	2,125	2,531	43.41	41.14
1982/83	9,366	2,053	2,425	46.92	42.91
1983/84	9,268	1,660	951	49.36	47.50
1984/85	9,270	1,916	779	48.97	47.08
1985/86	9,300	1,926	1,222	49.43	46.69
1986/87	10,343	2,182	1,312	47.05	44.23
1987/88	10,236	2,163	819	48.03	46.19
1988/89	10,296	2,205	1,593	47.54	45.34
1989/90	10,239	2,235	2,273	49.15	47.38

Source: Authors' calculations based on European Commission worksheets.
[a] Common level.   [b] Paris spot market.
[c] Common white sugar intervention price net of producer levies.

intervention price payable for *A* and *B* quota sugar, and the world white sugar price earned by *C* sugar. Note the dramatic difference between producer levies on *A* quota and *B* quota sugar: as shown in the table, these levies imply very different minimum producer prices for the two categories of sugar. Also shown are the weighted average minimum producer prices—for quota sugar and for all sugar. It should be noted, however, that in most EC Member States processors pay weighted-average prices for beet covering all within-quota sugar. Thus, the impact of changes in minimum producer prices is masked for farmers, though it is fully felt by processors.

Figure 2 gives a graphical representation of the revenues earned on the three categories of sugar in 1987/88, with the volume in each category on the horizontal axis and the minimum producer price on the vertical axis. *A* quota sugar clearly generates the vast majority of revenues—some 87 percent in 1987/88.

The effect of the producer levy mechanism is that, at least for *B* quota, producer returns in the EC are variable and related to world prices: the lower are world prices, the higher is the cost of export refunds and hence the size of the producer levies to pay for these. (In two years of the period covered by table 4, net prices for *B* quota sugar were actually lower than world prices because of the incidence of the levies.)

C sugar production receives, in the first instance, the world price, although in several EC countries some form of averaging is applied by beet sugar processors between within-quota production and *C* production. Averaging, where it happens, implies that producers receive returns above world market prices on their *C* sugar exports. Even without such averaging, *C* sugar can be profitable for producers because fixed costs are covered by within-quota production. On this basis, it can be argued that *C* sugar is implicitly subsidized,[8] although this situation is little different from that in other major exporting countries (e.g., Australia, South Africa, and Thailand) where prices paid to producers are averages of domestic and world market prices.

In principle, common agricultural support prices apply throughout the Community: this is particularly not the case for sugar, for several reasons. First, there are small extra elements (termed "regionalization elements") included in the intervention prices of the United Kingdom, Ireland, and Italy, which are meant to increase the flow of sugar to these deficit areas. More importantly, National Aids to agriculture are still permitted in Italy, which result in beet growers receiving up to 35 percent more than the EC's common minimum beet price. Finally, Spain negotiated, as part of its accession arrangements, being able to maintain a support price much higher than the common level until 1995/96. We will argue that these kinds of exceptional arrangements can lead to the perpetuation of high-cost production in some countries.

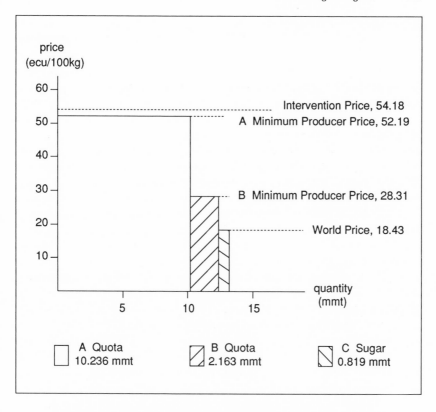

**FIGURE 2.   EC Sugar Production and Minimum Producer Prices,
1987/88 (white sugar equivalents)**

2.3 The ACP Arrangements

The historical origin of the preferential treatment of the ACP (African, Caribbean and Pacific) countries is the 1951 Commonwealth Sugar Agreement, which allowed Commonwealth countries preferential import access to the United Kingdom and Canada. The agreement marked a formalization of the traditional preferences for the sugar of the British colonies.[9] As one of its central objectives in the negotiations for its entry into the EC in 1973, the United Kingdom insisted that equivalent arrangements should be made.

The current EC-ACP arrangements (in a Sugar Protocol) are explicitly of "indefinite duration" and are carried over from one Lomé Convention to the next.[10] The Sugar Protocol provides that for 1.305 million metric tons of white sugar equivalent, the Community (not the United Kingdom) shall give the ACP countries free access to the EC market and a guarantee that they will receive the same price as EC producers. Although at one stage the EC tried to reduce the total of the ACP preferential quotas by not reallocating short-falls in the amount shipped, the total 1.305 million metric tons has applied in full since 1983/84, as shown in table 5.

Several comments on the ACP arrangements are in order. First, there is a very significant rent to the ACP quotas, given the wide gap between their guaranteed EC price and the much lower world market price. This rent, which accrues to the exporting ACP countries, is essentially an aid flow. It is of major importance to the ACP sugar exporters with quotas. The resource transfer to the ACP states is especially obvious for those ACP producers unable to fulfill their EC quotas from domestic production and who have to import sugar from the world market to release domestic sugar for export to the EC. Second, the effect of the arrangement is not only to transfer resources to the sugar industries of the ACP States, but also to differentiate between the ACP States and other developing countries that do not have access to the EC market. The ACP regime induces sugar production in the exporting countries that might not otherwise have occurred. This additional production, most visible in the reexportation from the EC of a quantity of sugar equal to its ACP imports, depresses world prices. Koester and Schmitz (1982) estimated that in 1979 the ACP States had a net welfare gain of 194 million ecu (there were U.S. $1.3706 per ecu in 1979), while other develop-ing country sugar exporters lost 154 million ecu due to the price depressing effects for world markets (partially offset by a 63 million ecu gain by developing country sugar importers). Lastly, we should note that the commercial implementation of the arrangements so far has been through the EC's port refiners (in the United Kingdom, France, and Portugal), which ensures that virtually all the preferential quotas are shipped in the form of raw sugar for refining, thus discouraging the development of value-added pro-cessing to white sugar in the ACP as well as the marketing of high-quality ACP sugars for direct retail sale in the EC.

2.4 Origins of the Current Market Situation

EC sugar production grew rapidly during the 1970s, in part due to rising yields, but principally due to the over-reaction of EC policy-makers to the worldwide sugar shortage of 1974, which led to a 53 percent increase in the maximum quota (A quota plus B quota) for the EC-9 between 1973/74 and 1975/76, as shown in table 1. Table 6 shows that apparent EC-9 sugar consumption peaked in 1973/74 at 10.414 million metric tons. This peak level of consumption included a significant level of sugar hoarding by consu-mers due to the impact of the 1974 worldwide sugar shortage. In reaction to

TABLE 5. EC Sugar Quotas for Preferential Imports from ACP Countries (metric tons, white sugar equivalent)

Quota Years (July/June)	1975/76 & 1976/77	1977/78	1978/79	1979/80	1980/81	1981/82	1982/83	1983/84	1984/85 & 1985/86	1986/87 to date
Barbados	49,300	49,300	49,300	49,300	49,300	49,300	49,300	49,300	50,049	50,312.4
Belize	39,400	39,400	39,400	39,400	39,400	39,400	39,400	39,400	40,104	40,348.8
Congo	10,000	10,000	4,957	4,957	4,957	4,957	4,957	8,000	10,000	10,168.1
Fiji	163,600	163,600	163,600	163,600	163,600	163,600	163,600	163,600	164,862	165,348.3
Guyana	157,700	157,700	157,700	157,700	157,700	157,700	157,700	157,700	158,935	159,410.1
India	25,000	25,000	25,000	25,000	25,000	0	0	10,000	10,000	10,000.0
Ivory Coast	-	-	-	-	-	-	-	2,000	10,000	10,186.1
Jamaica	118,300	118,300	118,300	118,300	118,300	118,300	118,300	118,300	118,300	118,696.0
Kenya	5,000	5,000	93	93	93	93	4,000	4,000	5,000	0.0
Madagascar	10,000	10,000	10,000	10,000	10,000	10,000	10,000	10,000	10,573	10,760.0
Malawi	20,000	20,000	20,000	20,000	20,000	20,000	20,000	20,000	20,618	20,824.4
Mauritius	487,200	487,200	487,200	487,200	487,200	487,200	487,200	487,200	489,914	491,030.5
St. Christopher and Nevis	14,800	14,800	14,800	14,800	14,800	14,800	14,800	14,800	15,394	15,590.9
Suriname	4,000	3,199	2,667	2,667	1,634	0	0	0	0	0.0
Swaziland	116,400	116,400	116,400	116,400	116,400	116,400	116,400	116,400	117,450	117,844.5
Tanzania	10,000	10,000	10,000	10,000	10,000	10,000	10,000	10,000	10,000	10,186.1
Trinidad and Tobago	69,000	69,000	69,000	69,000	69,000	69,000	69,000	69,000	43,500	43,751.0
Uganda	5,000	5,000	409	0	0	0	0	0	0	0.0
Zimbabwe	-	-	-	-	-	6,000	25,000	25,000	30,000	30,224.8
Total[a]	1,304,700	1,303,899	1,288,826	1,288,417	1,287,304	1,266,750	1,289,660	1,304,700	1,304,700	1,304,682.0

Sources: Regulation 3225/80 (Protocol No.7) giving the text of the Second Lomé Convention. Regulation 1255/82 on Zimbabwe's accession to the Lomé Convention. Regulation 1243/84 partially restoring India's quota. Regulation 1764/84 giving the Ivory Coast an ACP quota. Regulation 1763/84 giving full ACP membership to St. Christopher and Nevis and Regulation 1256/82 doing the same for Belize. Council Decision 75/456/EEC of July 15, 1975, on India's sugar quota. Notices of the Commission in Official Journal C112 (May 13, 1978), C97 (April 18, 1979), C108 (April 29, 1982), C124 (May 15, 1982), C328 (December 14, 1982) and C278 (October 16, 1987). Reallocation of Trinidad's shortfall by Commission Decision.

[a] Owing to rounding, individual figures may not add precisely to the totals shown.

the jump in consumption, EC production was allowed to expand dramatically, as shown in the table. This expansion in production led to a reversal of the shift to the EC's status as a net importer that followed the accession of the United Kingdom, Denmark, and Ireland in 1973: the EC reemerged as a net exporter in 1976/77. The original six member countries of the EC, however, have always been net exporters.

A coincidence of political events with the worldwide sugar shortage made

TABLE 6. Basic EC Sugar Statistics, 1968/69 to 1988/89 (million metric tons, wse)

Marketing Year[a]	Total Production	Total Consumption	Total Imports[b]	Total Exports[b,c]	Net Exports[d]	Self-Sufficiency Ratio[e]
EC-6						
1968/69	6.817	6.306	0.067	0.615	0.548	108.1
1969/70	7.435	6.410	0.065	0.562	0.497	116.0
1970/71	7.055	6.750	0.063	0.776	0.713	104.5
1971/72	8.081	6.325	0.046	1.348	1.302	127.7
1972/73	7.650	6.541	0.046	1.147	1.101	116.9
EC-9						
1973/74	9.516	10.414	1.418	0.979	-0.439	91.4
1974/75	8.570	9.561	1.718	0.097	-1.621	89.6
1975/76	9.703	9.535	1.429	1.405	-0.024	101.8
1976/77	10.003	9.036	1.444	1.666	0.222	110.7
1977/78	11.536	9.481	1.338	3.434	2.096	121.7
1978/79	11.774	9.544	1.266	3.231	1.965	123.4
1979/80	12.289	9.414	1.330	3.767	2.437	130.5
1980/81	12.088	9.246	1.162	4.592	3.430	130.7
EC-10						
1981/82	15.028	9.597	1.372	5.183	3.811	156.6
1982/83	13.942	9.474	1.333	5.207	3.874	147.1
1983/84	11.003	9.314	1.389	4.062	2.673	118.1
1984/85	12.500	9.555	1.368	3.832	2.464	130.8
1985/86	12.720	9.391	1.316	4.204	2.888	135.5
EC-12						
1986/87	14.096	10.907	1.562	4.506	2.944	129.2
1987/88	13.212	10.847	1.613	4.281	2.668	121.8
1988/89	13.915	10.885	1.561	4.749	3.188	127.8
1989/90	14.272	11.271	1.615	4.838	3.223	126.6

Source: Commission of the European Communities worksheets.
[a] 1968/69 through 1972/73 are July/June years; since 1973/74 the years are October/September.
[b] Sugar as such (excludes sugar in processed food products).
[c] "Free Circulation" sugar with export refunds plus C sugar "not blocked."
[d] Total exports less total imports.
[e] Total production divided by total consumption, multiplied by 100.

the expansion of production greater than it would have been otherwise. Smith (1981) points out that in negotiations with Commonwealth sugar exporters for access to the European market under the Lomé Convention, a deal was made in which European beet producers agreed to drop their opposition to preferential imports of ACP cane sugar, in return for the ACP agreeing not to object to increased EC sugar production and exports to world markets. (A cynic might suggest that the ACP states did not care what happened to the world market, as they were insulated because of their preferential access to the EC market.)

Moreover, the EC's emergence as a net exporter was aided by its nonmembership in the 1977 International Sugar Agreement (ISA). When the size of the world market available to ISA members was calculated, explicit allowance was made first for the exports from nonmembers (thus giving them a free-ride). Harris (1981) points out that between 1977 and 1980 the net exports of the EC rose by almost two million metric tons, while exports of potential ISA members were reduced by some two million metric tons from the level they otherwise would have been.

Table 7 shows that the EC share of net world exports rose rapidly in the second half of the 1970s to peak at 16 percent in 1981/2.[11] Its net exports rose to just over four million metric tons, though it had been a net importer following the first EC enlargement and a net exporter of less than a million metric tons prior to that. Since its 1981/82 peak, EC-9 production has been cut by almost a fifth (or about 2.5 million metric tons), however, with a consequent decline in exports.[12] The EC share of the world market has declined more slowly, however, because of a decline in the size of the total world market. (Table 7 shows world net exports peaking at 27.29 million metric tons in 1982, but dropping to 22.79 million metric tons by 1989). The decline in EC production since 1981/82 is principally due to the direct effect of lower world market prices for *C* sugar and the indirect effect through the impact on net producer returns for *B* quota sugar of the necessary increase in producer levies to fund the cost of export refunds, as documented in Section 2.2.

3. Economic Explorations of the Static Effects of EC Sugar Policy

3.1 Effects on World Markets

Results of economic explorations of the effects of EC sugar policy differ considerably among models and authors. One common scenario studied in recent years is the complete multilateral liberalization of all agricultural policies in the industrial market economies (IMEs). Table 8 shows various estimates of the effects of such liberalization on the world sugar price.[13]

Roningen and Dixit (1989) used the SWOPSIM model of the U.S. Department of Agriculture to estimate that the world sugar price would have increased by 52.7 percent over the 1986–87 base in this scenario. Anderson and Tyers (1989) estimated a 30 percent increase in the world sugar price for 1995 from a 1980–82 base. Similarly, Huff and Moreddu (1990) used the updated MTM model of the Organization for Economic Cooperation and Development (OECD) to estimate a 25 percent increase in the world market price relative to a 1982–85 base, as well as a 2.5 percent increase for a 10 percent reduction of producer subsidy equivalent (PSE) rates in the IMEs. A major reason for the differences in these findings is their differing base years, given the well-known price volatility of the world sugar market.

TABLE 7. EC and U.S. Sugar Balances with the World Market
(million metric tons, raw value)

Calendar Year	European Community[a,b]			United States[c]		
	EC Net Exports	World Net Exports	EC % of World Exports	U.S. Net Imports	World Net Imports	U.S. % of World Imports
1968	0.637	18.866	3.38	4.653	16.079	28.94
1969	0.260	16.670	1.56	4.431	15.720	28.19
1970	0.806	20.022	4.03	4.803	18.396	26.11
1971	0.894	19.225	4.65	5.068	17.800	28.47
1972	1.496	21.322	7.02	4.960	19.786	25.07
1973	-0.313	19.498	-1.61	4.831	19.498	24.78
1974	-1.036	19.336	-5.36	5.188	19.336	26.83
1975	-1.452	18.406	-7.89	3.312	18.406	17.99
1976	-0.209	19.249	-1.09	4.159	19.249	21.61
1977	0.966	25.445	3.80	5.271	24.056	21.91
1978	1.910	22.355	8.54	4.237	22.194	19.09
1979	2.102	23.397	8.98	4.422	22.472	19.68
1980	2.894	23.194	12.48	3.215	23.021	13.97
1981	4.049	25.179	16.08	3.697	24.257	15.24
1982	4.145	27.291	15.19	2.343	26.473	8.85
1983	3.394	25.298	13.40	2.466	24.059	10.25
1984	2.821	24.328	12.20	2.723	23.888	11.40
1985	2.953	24.202	12.33	1.910	23.017	8.30
1986	2.546	22.558	11.29	1.384	22.517	6.15
1987	3.737	23.440	15.93	0.632	22.758	2.78
1988	3.241	22.978	14.10	1.010	22.600	4.45
1989	3.434	22.785	15.07	1.221	22.630	5.40

Source: International Sugar Organization, *Sugar Year Book*, London, various issues.
[a] 1968–72 EC-6; 1973–80 EC-9; 1981–85 EC-10: 1986–88 EC-12.
[b] Net exporter, apart from 1973–76, when the EC was a net importer after the first enlargement.
[c] Net importer during the entire period.

In addition, Roningen and Dixit examined the effects of unilateral reform of EC and U.S. agricultural policies on the world market price of sugar, and estimated an 18.6 percent increase in the EC case and a 22.8 percent increase in the U.S. case. Anderson and Tyers also examined unilateral liberalization, and estimated for 1995 a 22 percent increase in the EC case and a 4 percent increase in the U.S. case. It clearly is difficult to argue that one of these policies does more harm than the other to the world economy.

Because of the residual nature of world sugar markets, recorded prices bear little relationship to production costs. For long periods of time, the world sugar price cycle is characterized by depressed prices at which not even the world's most efficient producers could survive. This makes econometric calculations based on record world prices highly sensitive to the assumptions made. It also means, for example, that producer subsidy calculations using world prices—as in the standard OECD format for calculating producer subsidy equivalents (PSEs)—are likely to overstate levels of support in the sugar sector, while revealing little about the distorted nature of world markets. Consumer cost calculations, as reported in Section 3.3, are subject to the same general caveat.

TABLE 8. Some Recent Estimates of the Effect on World Sugar Prices of Multilateral Liberalization of Major Agricultural Commodities

Study	Base Period	% Change in World Sugar Price	Model[a]
Martin, et al. (1990)	1980–83	60	RUNS
OECD (1987)	1979–81	10	MTM
Huff and Moreddu (1990)	1982–85	25	Updated MTM
Anderson and Tyers (1989)	1980–82	30	GLS
Roningen and Dixit (1989)	1986–87	53	SWOPSIM
Wong, Sturgiss and Borrell (1989)	1985	14	SUGABARE[b]

[a] The SUGABARE model is a detailed partial equilibrium model of the world sugar sector. The others are general equilibrium models of agriculture.

[b] Assumes partial liberalization of OECD sugar markets only. In a separate computation of the effects of partial liberalization of OECD sugar and wheat markets, there was no change estimated in the world sugar price.

3.2 Effects on the ACP Countries

As a simplifying assumption, we suppose that all ACP sugar exporters to the EC would, under free trade and with the higher world market price then expected to prevail, export at least as much as they now ship to the EC. The loss in their rents would then be the difference between their current EC price (U.S. $442 per ton) and the new world price (U.S. $291.7 per ton), times the volume of the ACP quota, 1.305 million tons, or U.S. $196.2 million.[14] The loss would in reality be larger, however, because some ACP countries import from the free market in order to fill their EC quotas. For those countries, the loss would equal the difference between the current EC price (U.S. $442 per ton) and the *current* world market price (U.S. $191 per ton), times the quantity reexported.

These estimates indicate the loss in *potential* rent for the ACP countries. Not all of them may actually gain all of that potential rent, however, mainly because of inappropriate domestic pricing policies. In particular, some ACP countries pay their producers a high price, thus inducing them to produce more than would be economically justified. The rational policy for an ACP state would be to produce no more than it can at a marginal cost equal to the world market price. If domestic production at that cost is less than needed to fill the EC quota, it is economically more rational to import the balance from the world market rather than to produce it at a higher marginal cost domestically.

3.3 Domestic Effects in the EC

In this section, we calculate changes in the surpluses or rents to EC domestic producers, consumers, and taxpayers, based on the price and quantity changes estimated by Roningen and Dixit for a complete liberalization of all IME agricultural support policies. Our calculations apply to the same 1986–87 base year as in their study. We have not explicitly taken into account cross effects (such as changes in land values) from other agricultural commodities. They are taken into account implicitly, however, as the new equilibrium prices and quantities come from a complete multicommodity model.

The average producer price (the farm-level equivalent of the white sugar price) would decrease from U.S. $364.0 to U.S. $291.7 per metric ton, or by 20 percent. The quantity produced would decrease from 13.423 to 13.020 million metric tons, or by 3 percent. From these changes, we calculate a loss of producer rent of U.S. $957 million.

The consumer price would decrease from U.S. $884.0 to U.S. $732.7 per metric ton (assuming that the retail margin is constant in absolute terms), or by 17 percent, while the quantity consumed would increase from 10.438 to 11.290 million tons, or by 8.2 percent. This increase in consumption results from the demand elasticity of -0.48 assumed by Roningen and Dixit. It appears relatively high compared with other estimates. To be achieved, it would appear to involve a replacement of glucose by sugar in food uses, which would be dependent on the relative movement of cereal prices. We calculate on the basis of the findings by Roningen and Dixit, an increase in consumer rent of U.S. $1663 million.

Finally, there would be only a small effect on the EC budget, because of the financial neutrality of the regime since 1986/87. There would only be budgetary savings due to the reduction in the cost of reexporting a quantity of sugar equal to ACP imports. This can be approximated by the loss in ACP rents of U.S. $196 million. Therefore, the overall economic welfare gain for the European Community would be the gain to consumers and the EC budget, net of the loss to producers, of some U.S. $902 million per year.

4. Dynamic Effects on the European Beet Sugar Industry

The existence of quotas and self-financing allows support prices for sugar to be maintained (while cereal prices have come down), as the sugar regime does not create significant budgetary costs and runs smoothly without creating sugar "mountains" domestically. The policy of price differentiation among *A*, *B*, and *C* sugar, at the level of beet growers, differs by EC country because of the different forms of price averaging employed. The effect is that the impact of the different producer prices for *A* and *B* quotas, and in some cases even *C* sugar, is masked for beet growers. The differences, however, are fully felt at the processor level.

One would assume a priori that the existence of quotas per se, and the difficulty of negotiating changes in their levels, as well as the continuation of National Aids for Italy, would have resulted in an inefficient industry. We can only speculate about the outcome in terms of efficiency improvements or specialization in production within the Community, had quotas not been applied. However, one of the effects of the 1992 program in the Community will be that the payment of those National Aids will come under more and more pressure. Moreover, the historical record suggests an industry in which there have been sufficient economic pressures to generate significant changes: in particular, nominal support prices for sugar were last increased in 1983/84, so that in real terms prices have been significantly squeezed.

For example, over the 20 years of the sugar regime's existence, productivity per hectare has grown steadily. White sugar yields, for the twelve countries now in the Community, averaged 5.51 metric tons of white sugar per hectare over 1968/69–1970/71, compared with 7.32 metric tons of white sugar per hectare in 1987/88–1989/90, an increase of one-third. EC cereal production, however, has done as well, so the sugar industry cannot claim to be unique in this regard.

Table 9 shows that the number of beet processing factories in the Community has been cut by more than 40 percent during the same 20 years, while average factory size—measured by metric tons of beet handled—has more than doubled.[15] As table 9 shows, productivity per employee has doubled as well.

International cost comparisons, despite their methodological and data difficulties, confirm the impression that the European beet industry taken as a whole is relatively competitive. Table 10 shows, for example, that French beet sugar rates among the lowest-cost sugar in the world, with even lower costs than cane from Thailand. Beet from Belgium, West Germany, Denmark, and the United Kingdom is rated as lower-cost than U.S. beet and cane. There are significant cost variations within the EC, however, and unit costs in Italy are double those in France. The apparent competitiveness of the Community beet industry in global terms appears to confirm the finding of Roningen and Dixit that multilateral trade liberalization would have a small effect on the volume of EC sugar production—that the industry would more-or-less maintain its present size.[16] At the same time, the EC sugar market regime clearly results in large rents flowing to the EC beet sugar industry. Successful reform would, of course, mean a reduction in these rents. EC policy makers have been unwilling to contemplate this prospect—except in the context of global CAP reform—because of the importance of sugarbeet to the arable sector as a whole.

5. Similarities and Differences with U.S. Sugar Policies

There are many similarities between the sugar policies of the EC and the United States. First, both operate with administered institutional price

TABLE 9.   Productivity Changes of EC Beet Processors

Marketing Year	Number of Factories	Total Employees	Average Factory Size[a]	Average Employed per Factory	Average Beet Sliced per Employee[a]
1968/69	276	91,979	3,028	333	9.1
1973/74	247	75,894	3,566	307	11.6
1978/79	220	74,213	4,826	337	14.3
1983/84	191	65,286	6,196	342	18.1
1988/89	160	58,000	7,000	345	20.3

Source: Salomon Brothers (1990).
[a] Metric tons of beet sliced per day.

arrangements that ensure high domestic market prices. Second, both operate so as to avoid budgetary costs: the economic transfer to domestic producers comes from consumers. Third, import access is restricted—through quotas in the United States and through prohibitive (under normal circumstances) variable import levies in the Community. On the other hand, both entities have preferential import arrangements with developing countries with which they have traditionally had economic ties. Fourth, there is a long history of support for sugar production in both the United States and the EC. Fifth, by insulating domestic producers and consumers from world market prices, both the United States and the EC thrust all the adjustment burden caused by domestic crop variations onto the residual world market. Sixth, in both entities the effect of support has been to encourage domestic beet production at the expense of imported cane. Finally, the two have affected world markets to a similar extent in recent decades: the expansion of Community net exports in the 1970s is of roughly equal magnitude to the contraction of U.S. net

TABLE 10.   Comparisons of Raw Sugar Production Costs[a]

	1979/80 to 1982/83 (index values; weighted world average = 100)	Second Half of 1980s (U.S. cents per pound of raw sugar)
Japan (beet)	170	30
Trinidad (cane)	158	27
Italy (beet)	155	26
Spain (beet)	-	22
United States (cane)	107	20
Guyana (cane)	118	20
Ireland (beet)	-	19
United States (beet)	111	18
United Kingdom (beet)	102	17
Denmark (beet)	-	16
West Germany (beet)	92	16
Jamaica (cane)	97	16
Belgium (beet)	-	15
Thailand (cane)	90	15
France (beet)	73	13
Cuba (cane)	71	-
Australia (cane)	62	9
Fiji (cane)	60	-

Sources: The first column is from Harris (1987), the second from Salomon Brothers (1990).

[a] Salomon Brothers (1990) suggests that the advantage for EC members and other beet producers may be understated, in that they produce not raw sugar, but the final consumer product, white sugar.

imports in the 1980s, as shown in table 7. These two developments were probably the key factors for the world market in their respective decades.

On the other hand, there are some critical differences between the two sugar regimes. The EC has operated an unchanged policy for the last 20 years, while the United States has gone through a series of policies during the same period—from domestic production quotas coupled with import quotas (prior to 1974), to essentially unrestricted trade (for roughly three years, to November 1977), to deficiency payments (for eleven days in November 1977), to import protection through fees and duties (to 1982), and with import quotas since then. The continuity of policy has been an important factor for the EC sugar industry, as it has provided a supportive environment for investments that have led to increased sugar yields.

Another critical difference is that the EC imposed production quotas on isoglucose (HFCS) when it was first commercially produced in the Community in the second half of the 1970s. The United States let HFCS production expand and lost three million metric tons of sugar consumption, while in the EC sugar consumption has been maintained. Specifically, in the EC in 1971 sugar had 89.8 percent of the market for sugar and corn sweeteners, while glucose and dextrose had the remainder. By 1986, sugar had 83.2 percent and HFCS had only 1.7 percent. In political-economy terms, the imposition of these quotas has prevented the emergence of a new special interest that would have benefited from EC sugar policy, while it has maintained the benefits to the old special interests.

The EC has been able to maintain its preferential import quotas for part of the developing world unchanged since their introduction in 1975, while the United States has reduced its import quotas to a very major extent since their introduction in 1982. Moreover, the Community has a well developed stocking policy, the costs of which are paid by consumers through the storage-cost levies. These stocks have been used for commercial reasons in a counter-cyclical manner—being built up when world prices were low and run down when world prices are reasonably high. The United States does not have such a stocking policy, reflecting its traditional position as a net importer of sugar.

Finally, although both entities have insulated their domestic producers and consumers from world markets, this insulation is less complete for EC production, since all production in excess of quota (*C* sugar) is at the world price and about one-fifth of within-quota production (*B* quota) is influenced by world prices. Thus, the net exports of the EC tend to be more responsive to the world price than are the net imports of the United States. In this respect, the EC regime *at the margin* contributes less to price volatility in the world sugar market. The returns to *B* quota sugar may be close to, or as in 1988/89, even below world prices. Moreover, as figure 1 suggests, at the cost of a high average domestic price level the EC sugar regime protects consumers from upward movements in the world price, given that EC market prices have remained relatively close to the intervention price throughout the period. In contrast, the U.S. import quotas have not shielded U.S. consumers from upward price spikes in the world market, as the 1974 and 1980 episodes made clear.[17]

6. Conclusions

In this paper we have tried to explain the complex mechanisms of support for sugar production under the EC sugar regime, as well as some of its major effects. Recent empirical studies of agricultural policy reform in the industrial market economies suggest that the world sugar price is substantially depressed by these policies, though there is a wide range of estimated price effects. Studies that have examined unilateral agricultural liberalization by both the EC and the United States yield inconsistent results, though it is clear that the sugar policies of both entities are harmful to domestic and world economic efficiency overall. However, the EC has provided a continuous income transfer to the developing countries of Africa, the Caribbean, and the Pacific under the Sugar Protocol of the Lomé Convention since 1975/76.

Moreover, we have argued that the self-financing feature of the EC regime means that EC producer prices are fairly responsive to world price movements—certainly more responsive than in the United States. Finally, based on international cost comparisons at different points in time, it is clear that EC sugar producers for the most part have been successful in keeping their costs down during the period the regime has been in effect.

NOTES

We are grateful to Stephen Marks for his extensive editorial assistance. The views expressed in this paper do not represent those of British Sugar.

1. See Chalmin (1984) for detailed discussion on the bounties and the sugar diplomacy of the period.
2. The EC sugar marketing year is July to June throughout the Community. The production year varies between member states, however. The norm is October to September, but Greece and Italy use August to July, and Spain uses July to June.
3. See Harris, Swinbank, and Wilkinson (1983), the Australian Bureau of Agricultural Economics (1985), or Abbott (1990) for a more complete description of the regime.
4. The preferential quota allocations to the ACP states are exempt from the variable import levy, so that the ACP states earn the policy rents. These rents are guaranteed to them as the EC pays them the same price it pays its own producers.
5. The surplus of free circulation sugar includes both the surplus of within-quota sugar production and the reexport of a quantity of sugar equal to the preferential imports from the ACP countries.

6. For further details on EC allocation of export refunds, see Harris, Swinbank, and Wilkinson (1983).

7. Producers are not charged the cost of reexporting a quantity of sugar equal to preferential sugar imports from the ACP states, however, as this is regarded as part of the EC's development effort.

8. See, for example, Wong, Sturgiss, and Borrell (1990). However, this implicit subsidy is not universal. For example, Salomon Brothers (1990) reports that at least one facility in France produces only *C* sugar.

9. Britain's preferential treatment of sugar from its colonies had been of long standing. Even so, the Caribbean industry had become very run down before the Second World War. It was revived by war-time arrangements to ensure that sugar was available for Britain, despite its own lack of self-sufficiency from beet sugar.

10. The Lomé Convention constitutes the association agreements between the EC and the ACP states.

11. The export figures shown in table 6 differ from those in table 7 for two reasons. First, the former shows data for marketing years, while the latter is for calendar years. Second, the former shows quantities in white sugar equivalents (refined terms), while the latter is in raw terms. Conventionally, production of one unit of white sugar requires 1.07 units of raw sugar.

12. Table 6 reveals a corresponding drop in EC-10 production and net exports after 1981/82. Changes in levels of EC sugar stocks reduced the change in net exports relative to production.

13. For a review of the general results of several agricultural trade models, see Blandford (1990).

14. This loss would be offset to a small extent by a reduction in their transport costs, as they would no longer have to ship to the EC.

15. In the last three years a spate of mergers has been set off as companies, having achieved economies of scale at the factory level and confronted with a static domestic market and a depressed world market, have looked to financial scale economies and the need to bolster their market positions. This process has undoubtedly been encouraged by the EC-92 Single Market program, though not triggered by it.

16. This is not to say that the process of rationalization in the EC sugar industry would not go on, however, with increased specialization in areas of production and concentration in ownership.

17. See the graph comparing U.S. and world sugar prices in the paper by Schmitz and Christian in this volume.

REFERENCES

Abbott, George C. 1990. *Sugar*. London: Routledge.

Albert, Bill, and Adrian Graves. 1988. "Introduction." In *The World Sugar Economy in War and Depression 1914–40*, ed. Bill Albert and Adrian Graves. London: Routledge.

Anderson, Kym, and Rodney Tyers. 1989. *Global Effects of Liberalizing Trade in Farm Products*. Thames Essay No. 55. London: Trade Policy Research Centre.

Australian Bureau of Agricultural Economics. 1985. *Agricultural Policies in the European Community*. Canberra: Australian Government Publishing Service.

Blandford, David. 1990. "The Costs of Agricultural Protection and the Difference Free Trade Would Make." In *Agricultural Protectionism in the Industrialized World*, ed. Fred H. Sanderson. Washington, DC: Resources for the Future.

Chalmin, Philip G. 1984. "The Important Trends in Sugar Diplomacy Before 1914." In *Crisis and Change in the International Sugar Economy 1860–1914*, ed. Bill Albert and Adrian Graves. Norwich and Edinburgh: ISC Press.

Harris, Simon. 1981. "The Effect of Governmental Actions on the World Sugar Market, with Particular Reference to the EEC and ISA." In *Proceedings of Conference on International Policy and Legislation on Sweeteners and Alcohol*. London: World Sugar Journal.

———. 1987. "Current Issues in the World Sugar Economy." *Food Policy* 12 (no. 2): 127–145.

———, Alan Swinbank, and Guy Wilkinson. 1983. *The Food and Farm Policies of the European Community*. Chichester, England: John Wiley.

Heckscher, Eli F. 1922. *The Continental System: An Economic Interpretation*. Oxford: Clarendon Press.

Huff, H. Bruce, and Catherine Moreddu. 1990. "The Ministerial Trade Mandate Model." *OECD Economics Studies* 13 (Winter 1989–90): 45–68.

International Sugar Organization. 1990. *EEC Sugar Policy*. MECAS (90) 1, London. (Document prepared for the ISO by the Commission of the European Communities).

Koester, Ulrich, and Peter Schmitz. 1982. "The EC Sugar Market Policy and Developing Countries." *European Review of Agricultural Economics* 9: 183–204.

Organization for Economic Cooperation and Development. 1987. *National Policies and Agricultural Trade*. Paris: OECD.

Martin, John P., et al. 1990. "Economy-wide Effects of Agricultural Policies in OECD Countries: Simulation Results with WALRAS." *OECD Economic Studies* 13 (Winter 1989–90): 131–172.

Osteras, M. 1981. "GATT and Conciliation of Disputes Related to the Marketing of Sweeteners." In *Proceedings of Conference on International Policy and Legislation on Sweeteners and Alcohol*. London: World Sugar Journal.

Roningen, Vernon O., and Praveen M. Dixit. 1989. *Economic Implications of Agricultural Policy Reforms in Industrial Market Economies*. U.S. Department of Agriculture, Economic Research Service. Staff Report No AGES 89–36.

Salomon Brothers. 1990. *The European Sugar Industry*. European Equity Research Series. London.

Smith, Ian. 1981. "EEC Sugar Policy in an International Context." *Journal of World Trade Law* 15 (March/April): 95–110.

Wong, Gordon, Robert Sturgiss, and Brent Borrell. 1989. *The Economic Consequences of International Sugar Trade Reform*. Discussion Paper 89.7. Australian Bureau of Agricultural and Resource Economics. Canberra: Australian Government Publishing Service.

CHAPTER 6

World Sugar Policies and Developing Countries

Cathy Jabara and Alberto Valdés

1. Introduction

Sugar is produced widely in both developed and developing countries; thus
world sugar trade patterns are significantly affected by the agricultural trade
policies of the two groups of countries. Developed countries have traditionally subsidized sugar production and taxed sugar consumption, while
developing countries often tax agricultural exports, either directly or through
anti-export, import-substitution industrializing policies. These trade biases
have resulted in a decline of sugar export market share for the developing
countries as a group, countries that generally have lower sugar production
costs than beet sugar producers in developed countries, and that at one time
supplied more than 80 percent of world sugar exports. Low world sugar
prices in the 1980s, combined with income growth and policies that tend to
subsidize rather than tax sugar consumers, have made the developing countries a growth market for sugar consumption and imports. This paper is
concerned with the role of developing countries in world sugar trade and with
the effect of government intervention in world sugar markets on that trade.
  Government intervention in world sugar markets and its effect on developing countries is of concern to development economists for three reasons.
First, many debt-laden developing countries are seeking ways to reorient their
economies toward greater market- and export-orientation under structural
adjustment initiatives supported by the World Bank and the International
Monetary Fund. Yet, in the case of sugar, many of these countries have been
forced by developed country policies, which lower world sugar prices, to
reduce production of export sugar and to switch to alternative crops. Second,
some developing countries have sought alternative domestic uses for sugar,
such as in ethanol production or in food and beverage industries. Diversification helps to mitigate the short-run adjustment costs to low world sugar
prices; however, diversification may also result in lower incomes for developing countries as compared to a situation where developing countries were
able to export sugar at free-market prices under trade liberalization. Third,
developed countries' trade restrictions on sugar have historically led to world
price instability, largely in the residual international market for export sugar.

To the extent that this price instability reduces the ability of government officials in developing countries to plan and to forecast foreign exchange earnings from sugar, then policy reforms could result in an important benefit to developing countries' sugar exports above any direct effect on export earnings.

It has also been argued that the higher-than-world-market prices offered to developing countries under developed countries' preferential sugar import schemes have offset the effects of developed countries' protectionism in sugar. Countries that participate in the European Community's (EC) program, which places a floor on the level of EC sugar imports, have benefited through higher export earnings, but countries that participate in the U.S. sugar quota have seen their export earnings fall because of declining U.S. imports. To the extent that both schemes limit expansion of developing countries' sugar exports and lower world prices, however, these schemes also contribute to the inefficiencies that plague the sugar market. The schemes also reduce longer-run employment and earnings opportunities in developing countries.

In the following pages, we will examine the role of developing countries in world sugar production, consumption, and trade, along with the effect of both developed and developing countries' sugar policies on that trade. We will also provide a simulation of the effects of trade liberalization on developing countries' sugar trade according to a partial equilibrium model of the world sugar market.

2. Trends in Developing Countries' Sugar Production, Consumption, and Trade

2.1 Developing Countries in World Sugar Production

Sugar is one of the most widely produced agricultural crops in the world. In 1988 more than 100 countries were producing beet or cane sugar or both. Seventy-nine were developing countries. Developing countries have increased their share of world sugar production in recent years, and in 1988 accounted for 57 percent of the 105 million metric tons (mmt) produced (figure 1). Developing countries in Asia account for 44 percent of the developing countries' share; those in Central America (including Cuba),[1] 25 percent; those in South America, 22 percent; and those in Africa, 9 percent (figure 2). Sugar is also produced in most developed countries, New Zealand being the main exception

Both climate and market factors have tended to favor sugar production in developing countries. A study of sugar production costs in the 1960s found that cane sugar exporters (that is, the developing countries, Hawaii, and Australia) had a marked absolute advantage over the beet sugar producers on

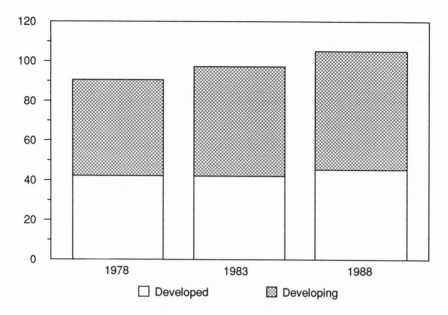

**FIGURE 1. Developed and Developing Countries'
Sugar Production, 1978–88 (mmt, raw value)**

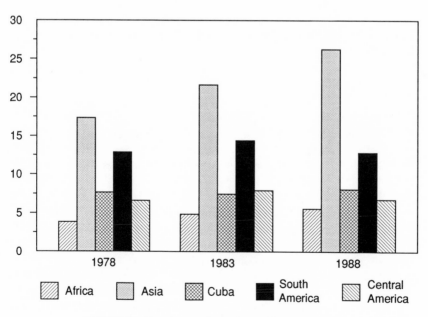

**FIGURE 2. Developing Countries' Sugar Production
by Region, 1978–88 (mmt, raw value)**

the whole (Grissa 1976). A more recent study of sugar production costs over 1979 to 1986 found that, on a refined value basis, the sugar production costs for 31 beet producers ranged from 25.5 to 29.5 cents per pound as compared with 17.5 to 20.6 cents per pound for 61 cane producers (U.S. Department of Agriculture 1989). Also found to contribute to the cost advantage over beet producers were cheap labor in cane-growing developing countries and the fact that tropical cane mills can operate for a much longer campaign than the temperate beet producers, which are limited to periods when cold weather prevents deterioration of the beets between harvest and processing.

Among the cane producers, production costs for raw cane sugar during 1979–86 were lowest for the African (11.7 to 14.5 cents per pound) and South American (11.3–15.1 cents per pound) producers on average, and highest in Asia and Oceania (13.3 to 16.8 cents per pound).[2] The five lowest-cost cane producers were Malawi, South Africa, Swaziland, Zambia, and Zimbabwe. Production costs in the seven largest cane exporters—Cuba, Australia, Brazil, Thailand, South Africa, Mauritius, and the Dominican Republic—averaged from 10.4 to 13.1 cents per pound over the period.

Between 1978 and 1988, several developing countries lost ground in their relative share of world production while others gained. The largest growth in sugar production (53 percent) occurred in the Asian developing countries (including the countries of the Middle East), with China having the largest increase (116.6 percent). Sugar production in the African countries as a group rose by 45 percent. Sugar production in South and Central America, excluding Mexico, stagnated or declined. With the exception of Thailand, where sugar production grew by 58 percent, production growth was generally largest in the developing countries where sugar is grown primarily for domestic consumption rather than for export.

One reason for these production shifts was the turbulence of prices in world markets. Specifically, the sharp increase in world prices from 1980 to 1981, followed by a prolonged period of depressed world prices, caused a disadvantage for many traditional sugar exporters from developing countries. These were the exporters who had to compete with subsidized exports from the EC. Developing countries also saw their export markets decline as developed countries closed their markets to sugar imports in order to protect domestic producers from low world sugar prices. Sugar producers in developing countries where sugar consumption is growing rapidly, and/or where sugar production is subsidized, were able to expand their production share.

2.2 Developing Countries in World Sugar Consumption

World sugar consumption grew at a fairly steady pace of about 2 percent per year during the 1980s to an estimated 106 million metric tons in 1988 (figure 3). Much of this growth occurred in the developing countries, whose sugar

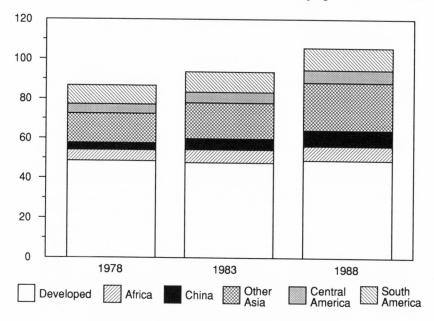

**FIGURE 3. Developed and Developing Countries'
Sugar Consumption, 1978–88 (mmt, raw value)**

consumption increased on average by about 5 percent annually during the same period.[3] In Western Europe, North America, and Japan, sugar consumption either stagnated or declined because of the high initial levels of per capita consumption, the sugar policies that tend to tax sugar consumption, the emergence of sugar substitutes, and the low rates of population growth. Five developing countries, China, India, Indonesia, Brazil, and Mexico, account for roughly 30 percent of world sugar consumption. Among the developing countries, the largest increases during 1978 to 1988 occurred in China (whose sugar consumption more than doubled), other Asian countries, Central America (primarily Mexico), and Africa.

Sugar consumption in developing countries has been encouraged by higher population growth rates, by policies that tend to promote rather than tax sugar consumption, by income growth, and by low initial per capita consumption levels in China, India, other Asian countries, and Africa (table 1). Some developing country exporters—Brazil, Mexico, and other countries in Central and South America—had higher per capita consumption levels that rival those in the developed countries. In these developing countries, sugar is an important source of food energy so that implementation of consumer taxation policies, such as those in the developed countries, would have particularly adverse effects on low-income consumers. For this reason, many developing countries that subsidize sugar producers—like Mexico and Brazil—also maintain sugar subsidies for consumers.[4]

2.3 Developing Countries in World Sugar Trade

Developing countries, as a whole, account for the bulk of world sugar exports, but their export share declined steadily from 1978 to 1988 (figure 4). In 1978, developing countries supplied roughly 70 percent of world exports, but by 1988 their export share had declined to 63 percent. The stagnant nature of the world sugar market resulted in absolute declines in the level of developing countries' sugar exports from 1983 to 1988.

Developing countries as a group account for the largest share of world sugar imports—54 percent in 1988, up from 40 percent in 1978. Thus trends in world sugar trade tend to show a reversal of the traditional trade patterns of 20 or 30 years ago, in which the developing countries supplied about 80 percent of exports, which went primarily to the developed countries. With rising consumption and stagnant exports, the developing countries' net export

TABLE 1. Per Capita Consumption of Sugar, Developed and Developing Countries, 1978 to 1988 (kg/person, raw value)

	1978	1983	1988
Developed Countries:	40.9	38.7	38.3
Developing Countries:	12.2	13.3	14.9
Egypt	24.3	33.8	34.2
Morocco	33.6	34.0	31.6
Other Africa	9.8	10.3	9.4
China	3.8	5.4	7.3
India	8.1	10.0	12.8
Indonesia	11.1	11.9	14.7
Iran	38.8	22.6	21.8
Philippines	23.7	23.2	20.9
Other Asia	10.8	11.9	14.0
Brazil	46.8	45.7	43.2
Other South America	36.2	34.4	33.8
Mexico	44.7	43.2	49.2
Other Central America	50.2	51.6	50.7
Other Developing	19.3	15.5	18.6

Sources: International Sugar Organization, *Yearbook*, London, various years; International Monetary Fund, *Financial Statistics Yearbook*, 1989.

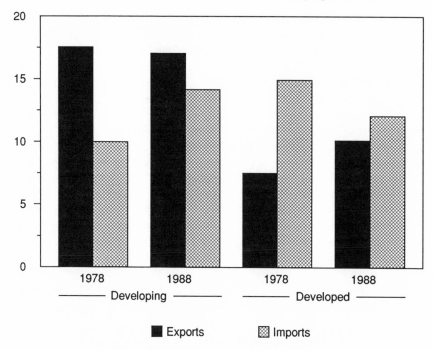

**FIGURE 4.   Developed and Developing Countries'
Sugar Exports and Imports, 1978–88 (mmt, raw value)**

position (exports less imports) has eroded, while the developed countries' trade deficit in sugar has almost disappeared. The developing countries' sugar exports exceeded their imports by about 3 million metric tons in 1988.

3. Developing Countries and Trade Protectionism in the World Sugar Market

It is generally recognized that developed countries give significantly greater protection to agriculture than to manufacturing, while many developing countries tax agriculture and protect manufacturing from import competition (Valdés 1987). These policy biases have generally constrained expansion of temperate and tropical agricultural exports from developing countries and have resulted in agricultural surpluses in developed countries. In this section, we will examine the extent to which developing and developed countries' sugar policies have an impact on world sugar trade.

Previous studies of the world sugar economy have discussed the trade protectionism that has resulted in rising self-sufficiency in sugar production on the part of both developed and developing countries (Grissa 1976; Harris 1987). Grissa found that producer-importers from both developed and developing countries raised their levels of self-sufficiency in sugar production (defined as the ratio of production to consumption) over 1951 to 1970, but the increase was largest for sugar importers in developing countries. However, because developed countries took the bulk of developing countries' sugar exports (more than 60 percent), the rise in developed countries' production-consumption ratios was largely responsible for slowing down exports from developing countries. For example, the EC, a major sugar importer in earlier years, became a net exporter in the middle 1970s. This change has not only limited sugar import growth, but also resulted in displacement of developing countries' sugar exports.

A more recent indicator of the degree of trade openness—the net import share of domestic consumption—is shown for the major sugar importers in table 2. Net import-consumption ratios declined among both the major developed and developing sugar importers from 1978 to 1988. However, the decline has been clearly the largest for the EC, the United States, and Japan. In those areas, import-consumption ratios declined by 101.5, 66.4, and 19.2

TABLE 2.   Net Import Shares of Consumption, Developed and Developing Country Importers, 1978 to 1988 (percent)

	1978	1983	1988
Developed Countries:			
Canada	86.1	90.2	84.0
EC[a]	-13.0	-24.9	-26.2
Other Europe	4.0	5.9	12.3
Japan	82.1	67.0	66.3
Soviet Union	31.3	45.0	30.0
United States	42.0	30.3	14.1
Developing Countries:			
Egypt	53.7	57.6	47.9
Morocco	41.1	31.0	36.5
Other Africa	75.2	62.6	57.3
China	36.1	30.0	46.2[b]
Republic of Korea[c]	99.9	91.0	123.6
Other Asia	59.0	50.8	41.6
South America	16.1	38.3	22.9

Source: International Sugar Organization, *Yearbook*, London, various years.

[a] Negative import-consumption ratio denotes net exporter.

[b] China's sugar imports in both 1988 and 1989 were double the levels of 1986 and 1987 because of a production shortfall. China's average import consumption ratio over 1986 to 1988 was 17 percent.

[c] Korea's self-sufficiency ratio in 1988 of more than 100 percent is due to stockholding. In general, Korea imports more raw sugar than it uses and re-exports the excess as refined sugar.

percent, respectively. These three areas accounted for 33 percent of gross sugar imports in 1978, but only 19 percent in 1988.[5] Among the developed countries, only the import-consumption ratio for Other Europe, which includes Eastern Europe and non-EC countries, increased during this period.

Import-consumption ratios among importers from developing countries, particularly China, Other Asia, and Africa, also declined but at much lower rates than in the developed countries. The 1983 to 1988 decline in import-consumption ratios in the African countries reflects the impact of the region's foreign exchange difficulties, of the macroeconomic adjustment programs that responded to these foreign exchange problems, and of the declining real per capita income during the 1980s (Mosley and Smith 1989). As a part of the adjustment programs, some African countries have raised tariffs on sugar, as well as other imports, to conserve foreign exchange earnings.

3.1 Trade Effects of Developed Countries' Sugar Policies on Developing Countries

Trade restrictions in major sugar-importing developed countries (the United States, Japan, and the EC) are based on variable import levies or restrictive import quotas, which allow domestic sugar prices to be maintained above world market levels. The EC, in addition, uses export subsidies to dispose of surplus sugar production on the world market. These policies lower world prices by artificially raising domestic production and reducing domestic consumption. Price and volume effects together translate into a loss to developing-country exporters of foreign exchange and welfare. On the other hand, the developing countries that are net importers of sugar have benefited from trade restrictions because protection has led to lower world prices of imports. By insulating their sugar producers from changing world market conditions, policies of developed countries also promote instability in world sugar markets.

Studies of developed countries' protection in the world sugar market have generally assessed the static effects of this protection on the world sugar market, on export earnings, on import costs, and on the resulting income gains and losses. In one of the earliest studies, Snape (1963) found that raw sugar prices in the major import markets of the developed countries were 60 to 105 percent higher than the free-market level. Snape found that if importing countries had protected their producers with deficiency payments,[6] rather than through high tariffs and excise taxes, the free-market sugar price would have risen in 1959 by about 16 percent, world sugar consumption would have increased by about 30 percent of net world trade, and developing countries' export earnings would have risen by half a billion dollars (1.4 billion in 1980 dollars). In a later study, Johnson (1966) found that if all support to sugar producers in developed countries were ended, free trade in sugar would increase the export earnings received by developing countries from the United States and the original six members of the European Community by three quarters of a billion dollars (2.1 billion in 1980 dollars).

More recent studies, summarized in Valdés (1987), indicate that world sugar prices would increase from 5 percent (Tyers and Anderson 1986) to 29 percent (Zietz and Valdés 1986) under trade liberalization (table 3). These results are not strictly comparable because (1) they estimate rates of protection and trade flows in different years, and (2) they apply different liberalization scenarios—total removal of protection versus partial liberalization, and unilateral (EC) versus multilateral (the United States, the EC, and Japan).

Zietz and Valdés (1986) found that foreign exchange earnings of exporters from developing countries were reduced between 2.2 and 5.1 billion in 1980 dollars per year as a result of the protection to sugar producers in industrial countries. This range of results reflects different assumptions about the domestic supply elasticities (see table 4). The increase in the developing countries' import bill was considerably smaller, ranging from about 310 to 480 million in 1980 dollars per year in additional imports.

TABLE 3.   Estimated Effects of Trade Liberalization on World Sugar Prices from Various Studies

Study and Year	Commodity	Effect on World Price (percentage change)
Valdés and Zietz (1980)	Sugar Confectionery	+ 6–8 + 9
Koester and Schmitz (1982)	Sugar	+ 12
Roberts (1982)	Sugar	+ 7–11
Matthews (1985)	Sugar	+ 11
Zietz and Valdés (1986)	Sugar	+ 13–29
Tyers and Anderson (1986)	Sugar Sugar	+ 5[a] + 3[b]
Wong, Sturgiss, and Borrell (1989)	Sugar	+ 8[c]

Source: Valdés (1987).

[a] Liberalization in industrial market economies only.

[b] Liberalization in all developing economies only.

[c] Relaxation of production controls to allow more sugar production to respond to world prices, combined with liberalization of consumer prices in OECD (Organization for Economic Cooperation and Development) countries.

TABLE 4. Changes Caused by Trade Liberalization in Sugar: Varying Domestic Supply Elasticities

Country Supply Elasticity	World Price	World Exports[a]	Developing Countries			
	percent		Foreign Exchange Earnings	Exporter Welfare	Import Bill	Net Welfare
			billions of 1980 dollars			
0.60 for all Countries	16.7	12.4	2.75	0.60	-0.33	0.08
0.06 for EC Members	13.6	10.4	2.19	0.46	-0.31	0.03
6.0 for all EC and 4.0 for all other Developed	29.4	31.3	5.11	1.25	-0.42	0.39
1.20 for all Developing	12.9	16.8	3.04	0.49	-0.48	0.09

Source: Valdés (1987).
a The sum of net exports of all net-exporting countries.

These estimates may be conservative, however, because trade liberalization modeling efforts do not capture all of the potential long-run gains that could result from a permanent reduction in trade barriers in industrial countries. Such a policy reform would probably encourage developing countries to direct more resources toward increasing agricultural production, to develop new export products and expand their processing operations, and, more generally, to help break the current climate in developing countries of "export pessimism" that inhibits the adoption of export-oriented policies in agriculture, as well as in other sectors.

3.2 Sugar Policies in Developing Countries

Government intervention in sugar sectors is widespread among developing countries. Many governments intervene in both agricultural and nonagricultural markets to support specific development objectives. Some specific sugar interventions are designed to counteract the price instability that characterizes the world's sugar market, although trade and domestic price interventions may not be the first-best way to achieve this.

In the preferential import schemes that developed countries have offered to certain developing countries, higher-than-free-market prices are granted for fixed amounts of sugar exports. However, these schemes invite government intervention and often promote inefficiency among sugar companies that divert resources to gain access to the preferred exports.[7] Many developing countries use the higher prices of the preferential markets to support their producer prices of sugar above free-market levels. It has been found that, at official exchange rates, protection for sugar in developing countries is often high, particularly in comparison to other agricultural commodities, though the intervention is much less than in developed countries (see Krueger, Schiff, and Valdés 1991).

Agricultural and trade policies of developing countries affect incentives for sugar production and consumption in two ways.[8] First, direct agricultural price interventions specifically affect the price of sugar and create a wedge between the producer or consumer price and the (world) border price (converted into local currency at the official exchange rate). As shown in table 5, developing countries that import sugar—illustrated by Egypt, Morocco, Pakistan, and Turkey—tend to implement sugar policies that support producer incentives above world market levels, except in a year like 1980 when world sugar prices were exceptionally high. Estimates of the direct nominal protection rates (NPRD) provided to producers at official exchange rates in these countries ranged from 14 percent to 1,296 percent in 1970 and 1984. These rates were comparable to nominal rates of protection for raw sugar of 222, 188, and 542 percent in the United States, the EC, and Japan, respectively, in 1986 (U.S. International Trade Commission 1990). The

TABLE 5. Sugar Price Intervention Measures for Selected Developing Countries, 1970, 1980, and 1984 (percent)

Country	NPRD 1970	NPRD 1980	NPRD 1984	NPRT 1970	NPRT 1980	NPRT 1984	NPRDc 1970	NPRDc 1980	NPRDc 1984	NPRTc 1970	NPRTc 1980	NPRTc 1984
Importers:												
Egypt[a]	25.0	-79.0	1296.0	-53.0	-81.0	52.0	18.0	-47.0	90.0	-17.0	-52.0	5.0
Morocco	66.0	-37.0	14.0	23.0	-58.0	-1.0	136.0	-25.0	19.0	117.0	-40.0	11.0
Pakistan	241.0	-58.0	18.0	95.0	-71.0	-12.0	n/a	n/a	n/a	n/a	n/a	n/a
Turkey[b]	n/a	192.0	172.0	n/a	10.0	16.5	n/a	-94.9	-87.5	n/a	n/a	n/a
Exporters:												
Dominican Republic[c] (1)	-44.0	-56.5	-30.7	-60.0	-70.9	-72.4	-18.5	-66.2	-64.7	-35.1	-76.4	-81.7
(2)	19.8	-55.3	77.4	23.3	-70.2	48.2	29.4	-65.2	-42.7	3.1	-75.8	-70.3
Philippines[d] (1)	-24.0	-23.0	-6.7	-37.0	-42.0	-24.0	-32.4	-31.6	10.6	-44.2	-48.2	-13.1
(2)	48.0	-54.0	37.3	22.0	-65.0	11.6	31.6	-59.0	62.7	8.6	-69.0	27.0
Thailand[e] (1)	23.8	-2.8	53.1	9.0	-13.0	34.0	68.6	55.6	161.3	48.5	38.6	128.4
(2)	n/a	n/a	n/a	1.0	-21.0	23.0	n/a	n/a	n/a	37.5	26.0	110.7

Source: Krueger, Schiff, and Valdés (1991).

Notes: NPRD = direct nominal protection rate at the producer level; it measures the difference between the domestic producer price and the border price evaluated at the official nominal exchange rate as a proportion of the border price; (+) = subsidy, (-) = tax. NPRT = total nominal protection rate at the producer level; it includes direct protection measures in NPRD and indirect measures such as exchange rate misalignment and other industrial protection policies; the NPRT measures this protection relative to the nonagricultural prices that would prevail in the absence of trade intervention; (+) = subsidy, (-) = tax. NPRDc, NPRDc = direct nominal protection rate and total nominal protection rate at the consumer level; (-) = subsidy, (+) = tax.

[a] The first year of the study is 1972.

[b] NPRDc is the nominal rate of protection on consumer prices relative to wheat prices; last year is 1983.

[c] (1) Border price equivalents are calculated using a weighted average FOB export price for Dominican raw sugar sold on the world and U.S. quota markets.
(2) Border price equivalents are calculated using the FOB export price sold on the world market.

[d] (1) Border price equivalents are calculated using the FOB export unit price.
(2) Border price equivalents are calculated using the spot price set by the International Sugar Organization Agreement.

[e] (1) The equilibrium exchange rate is computed ignoring the current account deficit.
(2) The equilibrium exchange rate is computed taking into account the current account deficit.

NPRDs were negative for the importing countries in 1980, which indicates that the price spike was not fully passed through to sugar producers in that year.

Second, economy-wide or indirect interventions, such as exchange rate misalignment and industrial protection for inputs and other goods along with services used by farmers, affect agricultural incentives, but more so in developing than in developed countries. Estimated total nominal protection rates (NPRT) shown in table 5, which include the direct price interventions plus the economy-wide or indirect interventions, indicate that economy-wide interventions have tended to tax sugar producers in the importing developing countries. While still positive in some years, the level of total support in most of the import-competing countries is substantially lower than when only the direct interventions are considered. For example, in Pakistan, the nominal rate of protection declined from 241 percent to 95 percent in 1970, and from 18 percent to -12 percent in 1984.

Estimates of the direct and total nominal protection rates for consumers (NPRDc and NPRTc) in the importing countries suggest that sugar consumers, in contrast to those in developed countries, have been spared much of the adverse effects of direct sugar price interventions. The estimates of NPRTc are negative or very low, indicating that sugar consumption is generally taxed at very low rates or is even subsidized in these countries.

Sugar-exporting countries, such as the Dominican Republic, the Philippines, and Thailand, also protected sugar producers relative to the residual world market price, except in 1980. For the Philippines and the Dominican Republic, estimated NPRDs and NPRTs are generally positive relative to the world free market (see footnotes c(2) and d(2) in table 5), but negative in relation to average FOB export prices (see footnotes c(1) and d(1) in table 5), which include sugar exports made under preferential arrangements. These countries were able to protect their farmers from low world sugar prices through the higher export prices offered in the preferential markets, but part of the quota's proceeds were taxed away by their governments.

The data in table 5 reveal, in general, that while sugar consumption may be subsidized in selected developing countries, taxation of sugar producers is relatively low. Thus, most of the distortion in world sugar trade patterns appears to be caused by the excessive protection in developed countries.

The data also reveal that among the developing countries considered, Thailand represents a unique case. In contrast to the other exporting countries, sugar consumers are heavily taxed rather than subsidized. In 1982 to protect its sugar sector from the precipitous drop in sugar prices that occurred in that year, Thailand implemented a two-price policy that effectively taxed sugar consumers to support a stable sugar price for producers. Moreover, as shown by its very low NPRD in 1980 (-2.8 percent), Thailand was the only

country that allowed the price spike of 1980 to pass through to sugar producers. In effect, Thailand's sugar policies resemble those of developed countries, rather than those of other developing country exporters, which may
explain much of its success as a sugar exporter during the 1980s.

3.3 Developing Countries and Preferential Sugar Markets

Preferential sugar import schemes have been maintained by the EC, the
United States, and the former Soviet Union (the latter for imports from
Cuba). Under these arrangements, beneficiary countries—primarily in
Africa, Central America, South America, and the Pacific—export fixed
amounts of sugar at prices well above free market prices. The preferential
schemes provide a product-tied income transfer to the beneficiary countries
whose size depends on the prices paid in the preferential market, the amount
allowed for delivery, and the world market price. In 1988, about 50 percent
of developing countries' exports were sold to preferential markets.

Studies of the effects of the EC and U.S. preferential schemes on developing countries have shown that, while some individual countries may benefit
from receiving high prices for a portion of their exports, developing countries
as a group would benefit far more from free trade in sugar. For instance,
Koester and Schmitz (1982) found that, with the exception of India, countries
that participate in the EC's preferential system have generally benefited from
this program in terms of increased sugar export earnings. The countries that
participate in this scheme are primarily small African and Caribbean producers, and some of these countries would not be able to compete in the world
sugar market under free-market conditions. Koester and Schmitz, however,
did not examine the long-term effects of the program on inhibiting export
expansion (particularly in some of the African countries), or its effect on sup-
pressing investment and employment opportunities in sugar refining
capacity.[9] In another study, Roberts (1982) calculated that the developing
countries as a whole could expect an increase in welfare of between $370
million and $570 million from the EC's trade liberalization in sugar,
compared with a loss of $170 million to the EC's beneficiary countries.

The U.S. program, on the other hand, has not only adversely affected the
developing countries as a group, but also most of the countries that benefit
from U.S. preferences. In contrast to the EC's sugar import policy of stable
imports, U.S. sugar imports declined steadily over 1983 to 1988. Thus,
despite receiving higher-than-world-market prices for their sugar exports
under the U.S. quota, sugar export earnings of U.S. trading partners fell
because U.S. sugar imports declined more than prices increased. Countries in
Central and South America, and the Philippines, have been affected primarily
by this decline. For instance, the Caribbean Basin countries alone have lost

more than $300 million per year in export earnings since 1986 because of sugar quotas, and their total losses from 1982 to 1989 have amounted to about $1.8 billion (Overseas Development Council 1989).[10] Net export losses of developing countries from U.S. sugar policies in 1989 are estimated at $700 million in 1989, despite the gain of about $135 million from higher preferential prices.

3.4 Government Intervention in the World Sugar Market and Export Trends in Developing Countries

The effects of both developed and developing countries' intervention in sugar markets during the 1980s can best be summarized through an analysis of changes in the export market shares of individual sugar exporters. As the price of sugar fell to around 5 to 8 cents per pound, raw basis, during this period and as few, if any, countries have production costs that low, the ability to survive in the sugar market during the 1980s basically depended on a country's sugar policies. The trend in export market shares from 1978 to 1988 is shown in table 6.

During the 1980s, sugar exports became more concentrated among sugar exporters in developed countries, particularly the EC and Australia, and among the top three developing-country exporters, Cuba, Brazil, and Thailand. The average export share in developed countries rose from 31.4 percent in 1978 to 1980, to 38 percent in 1986 to 1988, while the share of the top three developing countries rose from 38.5 to 40 percent. However, Brazil, Cuba and Thailand's combined share of total developing-country sugar exports rose from 56 percent in 1978 to 1980 to 64 percent in 1986 to 1988.

The success of these countries in maintaining a relatively large share of the sugar market is partly due to government intervention, which cushioned their sugar producers from the low world prices during this period. More than 80 percent of Cuba's sugar cane is produced on state farms that are managed to meet production targets. Cuba has also delivered more than 50 percent of its sugar exports to the former Soviet Union under preferential sugar arrangements.[11] However, while Brazil and Cuba maintained their export shares, Thailand's export share more than doubled. In addition to its export-oriented sugar policies, Thailand is also the only major exporter among developing countries that marginally participates in the preferential import schemes of developed countries.[12]

The export shares of other exporters among developing countries—except Swaziland, Mexico, Guatemala, and Mauritius—declined during 1978 to 1988. Mexico's increased exports followed from its sugar self-sufficiency program, which granted sugar producers large subsidies.[13] Guatemala implemented a major investment program for exports of plantation white sugar in the mid-1980s, with much of the increased exports being sold to the former Soviet Union; its maintenance of a favorable exchange rate against the U.S. dollar has also promoted sales to neighboring South American countries.[14]

Countries that experienced the largest declines in sugar export shares were generally those associated with the U.S. quota market. These countries' collective export share declined by 30 percent from 1978 to 1988, while developing countries that participated in the EC quota maintained their collective export share at about 8 percent of the sugar market. Swaziland and Mauritius, both low-cost African sugar producers, were able to expand or maintain their export shares as a result of the stable EC market. Mauritius

TABLE 6. Export Shares of Major Sugar Exporters,
1978 to 1980 and 1986 to 1988 (percent)

Exporting Country/Region	Annual Average 1978 to 1980	Annual Average 1986 to 1988	Percentage Change
Developing Countries:	68.6	62.0	-9.6
Argentina[a]	1.5	0.5	-66.7
Brazil[a]	8.4	8.0	-4.8
Cuba[b]	26.6	24.4	-8.3
Dominican Republic[a]	3.6	1.9	-47.2
Fiji[c]	1.7	1.4	-17.6
Guatemala[a]	0.7	1.3	85.7
Mauritius[c]	2.5	2.5	0.0
Mexico[a]	0.1	2.1	2,000.0
Philippines[a]	5.3	0.6	-88.7
Swaziland[c]	1.0	1.6	60.0
Thailand	3.5	7.4	111.4
Other Central America[c]	3.6	2.5	-30.5
Other Central America[a]	3.8	1.9	-50.0
Other Developing	6.3	5.9	-6.3
Developed Countries:[d]	31.4	38.0	21.0
Australia	8.2	10.3	25.6
European Community	14.8	17.7	19.6
South Africa	3.1	3.5	12.9
Other Europe	3.4	3.6	5.9
Other Developed	1.9	2.8	52.6

Source: International Sugar Council, *Yearbook*, various years.

[a] Indicates countries that sell more than 10 percent of their total sales under preferential access to U.S. sugar market.

[b] Sales to the former Soviet Union under preferential arrangements.

[c] Indicates countries that sell more than 10 percent of their total sales under preferential access to EC sugar market.

[d] Includes exports of centrally-planned countries.

exports 80 percent of its sugar to the EC and Swaziland exports 47 percent.[15] Swaziland also benefited from a 30 percent increase in its EC quota during this period.

The decline in exports by U.S. quota countries was accompanied by substantial social adjustment costs because sugar cane is often mono-cropped in developing countries and because sugar cane involves higher initial fixed investment costs when compared to beet production in developed countries. Some countries, particularly those in Central America, attempted to diversify out of exporting sugar and into converting sugar to ethanol, either for domestic use or for export. Domestic sugar use in food and beverage industries has also been encouraged.[16] Low export prices for sugar and high world petroleum prices in the early 1980s made the ethanol projects look economically sound, but this situation can easily be reversed when world petroleum prices decline. To the extent that these projects are profitable without subsidies, they mitigate the short-run costs of adjustment to reduced sugar exports and also raise income levels in the developing countries. However, to the extent that the resources used in diversification projects could yield greater output and earnings as sugar exports under free trade, then these projects (and reduced sugar exports) lower developing countries' incomes and standards of living as compared to a free-trade situation.

4. Sugar Trade Liberalization: Results from a Recent Model Simulation

In this section we will present simulation results of the effects of trade liberalization in the world sugar market on developing countries' trade. The analysis is based on a nonspatial price equilibrium model of the world grain, soybean, sugar, and meat markets that is described in detail in Zietz and Valdés (1990). However, only the sugar submodel is simulated. The model, which is comparative static in nature and partial equilibrium, is built around constant elasticity demand and supply functions that are modeled in terms of percentage changes from a base period. The model is an extension of the models cited in Valdés and Zietz (1980) and Zietz and Valdés (1986), but it goes beyond these and other studies of the world sugar market in that it incorporates the latest available information on the price incentives facing sugar producers and consumers in developing countries. An important omission of the analysis, but one that is consistent with other studies of developing countries' sugar trade, is that the model does not incorporate linkages with the corn sweetener market in the United States.

The model incorporates policy information through the use of producer subsidy equivalents (PSEs) and consumer subsidy equivalents (CSEs), the measures of policy intervention used in the Uruguay Round of Multilateral Trade Negotiations to compare policies across nations. PSEs for sugar are calculated by estimating the amount of income transferred to sugar producers by all policy measures that affect the incentives for the production of sugar in a given economy. These individual estimates are then added together to get an aggregate PSE, which is typically expressed as a percentage of the total value of production. CSEs are similarly calculated from the policy measures that affect sugar consumption.

Scenarios. The 1981–83 base represents actual average sugar production, consumption, trade, and prices from 1981 to 1983. Five liberalization scenarios are considered, each based on changes in PSEs and CSEs:

1. 20–year forecast with no policy change (base line run).
2. 10 percent reduction in U.S. PSEs and CSEs.
3. 50 percent reduction in U.S. PSEs and CSEs.
4. Reduction to zero of U.S. PSEs and CSEs.
5. Reduction to zero of PSEs and CSEs for the United States and all member countries of the Organization for Economic Cooperation and Development (OECD).
6. Reduction to zero of PSEs and CSEs for the United States, all OECD countries, and all developing countries.

Assumptions. The sugar trade model was simulated under the following assumptions:

1. No link exists through cross-price elasticities or income effects to other commodities (e.g., coarse grains in the case of the United States).
2. Income growth rates for agriculture-based developing countries enter into the model exogenously and do not exceed 4 percent per year.
3. Exogenous (price independent) production growth is limited to a maximum of 1 percent per year for industrialized countries. For the United States, the value is zero.
4. The income elasticities of sugar demand are set to 0.06 for all industrialized countries. They are limited to a maximum of 0.3 for all developing countries. (For further details, see Zietz and Valdés 1990.)

The Zietz-Valdés model ignores the complexities of the adjustment path to the new equilibrium. It assumes that all long-run changes occur simultaneously at the base prices. All exogenous changes are translated into excess demands at the base period, and the model projects the price adjustment needed to eliminate these excess demands. All quantities, prices, and protection rates apply to the period of 1981 to 1983. It may be noted in this context that the average protection rate for that period matches that for the end of 1989 or the beginning of 1990 fairly closely.

The model simulation results are shown in tables 7 to 10. Table 7 presents actual U.S. sugar production, consumption, and net imports in 1981 to 1983 and as predicted for 2002 under the six scenarios. For example, under simulation 4 (removal of U.S. PSEs and CSEs), U.S. net sugar imports increase from 2,843 (1981 to 1983 base) to 3,322 thousand metric tons in 2002, mainly as the result of an increase in consumption relative to the base line. The changes in the world sugar price and in U.S. quantities resulting from the various policy scenarios, as compared to the base line, are shown in table 8. With complete U.S. trade liberalization, the world price of sugar rises by about 2 percent from the base line scenario, but U.S. imports rise by about 40 percent. Under complete OECD trade liberalization, the increase in U.S. sugar imports is less than under complete U.S. liberalization because of the greater increase in the world sugar price that follows from the reduction in sugar producer subsidies in other developed countries.

Table 8 shows that global trade liberalization, including the developing

TABLE 7.   U.S. Sugar Production, Consumption, and Net Imports, 1981–1983, and Predicted for 2002 Under Various Scenarios (thousands of metric tons)

Simulation	Assumption	Consumption	Production	Net Imports
1981–83	Actual Values	8,164	5,321	2,843
1	20–year forecast	8,393	6,031	2,362
2	10 percent reduction, U.S. PSEs and CSEs	8,437	5,976	2,461
3	50 percent reduction, U.S. PSEs and CSEs	8,606	5,768	2,838
4	U.S. PSEs and CSEs reduced to zero	8,798	5,476	3,322
5	U.S. & OECD PSEs and CSEs reduced to zero	8,574	5,664	2,910
6	Global liberalization by all countries	8,867	5,421	3,446

TABLE 8.   Change in World Price and in U.S. Sugar Production, Consumption, and Net Imports Relative to Base Line (percent)

Simulation	World Price	Consumption	Production	Net Imports
2	0.2	0.5	-0.9	4.2
3	0.9	2.5	-4.4	20.2
4	1.8	4.8	-9.2	40.6
5	14.0	2.2	-6.1	23.2
6	-1.6	5.6	-10.1	45.9

countries, would depress world sugar prices as compared to the base line. This depression would result from developing countries producing more sugar and consuming (importing) less under trade liberalization.[17]

Tables 9 and 10 show the effects of the various trade liberalization scenarios on the developing countries. The base line shows that without any policy change, two regions (Asia and Sub-Saharan Africa) with developing countries that were net sugar exporters in 1981 to 1983 will be net importing regions in the year 2002 because of rapidly growing consumption. U.S. trade liberalization would result in greater net exports from Central and South America, as well as a reduction in net imports of the other regions (Asia, Sub-Saharan Africa, and North Africa/Middle East). With additional trade liberalization by other OECD members, however, the effect on the world sugar price and on developing countries' trade position is much greater: this simulation results in a 14 percent increase in the world sugar price from the

TABLE 9. Net Imports, by Developing Country Region, Actual for 1981 to 1983 and Predicted for 2002, Under Various Scenarios (thousands of metric tons)

Simulation	Asia	North Africa/ Middle East	Sub-Saharan Africa	Central/South America
1981–83	-1,413	4,454	-299	-11,017
1	4,301	8,555	1,759	-13,122
2	4,264	8,548	1,757	-13,144
3	4,126	8,522	1,747	-13,227
4	3,948	8,488	1,734	-13,334
5	1,718	8,076	1,573	-14,668
6	-361	7,753	1,374	-15,320

Note: Negative sign indicates net exports.

TABLE 10. Decrease (-) in Imports or Increase in Exports by Developing Country Region, Relative to Baseline (percent)

Simulation	Asia	North Africa/ Middle East	Sub-Saharan Africa	Central/South America
3	-4.1	-0.4	-0.7	0.8
4	-8.2	-0.8	-14.0	1.6
5	-60.1	-5.8	-10.4	11.8
6	-108.4	-9.4	-21.9	16.8

base line and in larger increases in developing countries' exports and/or reductions in net imports. Despite reduced U.S. imports under this scenario, as compared to the scenarios of U.S. trade liberalization only, net exports from Central and South American countries rise by 12 percent (compared to the base), and net imports in Asia decline by 60 percent from the base line.

With trade liberalization by the developing countries as well as by the OECD countries, the world price declines by 1.6 percent as compared to the base world price (scenario 6). The developing country regions experience a further increase in net exports or a decrease in net imports. The most notable change is in Asia, which becomes a net sugar exporting region in this scenario. The change in Asia's net sugar trade is due to a reduction in sugar consumption subsidies, as well as a relaxation of price policies that tax sugar producers in those countries. The decline in the world sugar price from the base line and the magnitudes of the changes in trade flows indicate that all developing countries would benefit from a situation of complete trade liberalization in sugar. Exporting countries would benefit through increased export volumes and earnings—despite the decline in the world price—and importing countries would benefit from the lower import price.

5. Conclusions

Traditionally, the world sugar market has been dominated by low-cost sugar exports from developing countries. In recent decades, however, trade protection by industrialized countries has resulted in a significant decline in developing countries' export share in sugar, while exports from developed countries have increased. High rates of import protection in industrialized sugar importers (the United States, the EC, and Japan, as well as others in Western Europe) and subsidized exports (primarily from the EC) depress world sugar prices and developing countries' export revenues. Although some developing countries are net sugar importers, and thus benefit through lower import costs, the developing countries as a group are net losers from these policies.

It has often been argued that developing countries' taxation of agriculture is an important factor inhibiting agricultural export growth; however, we did not find this necessarily to be the case for sugar. Many developing countries have supported sugar producers, particularly during periods of low world prices, but this protection is much lower than in developed countries. We do show that developing countries would gain in general from removal of the anti-export bias that taxes agricultural products, but they would have a greater incentive to do this if developed countries would eliminate their sugar protection and allow more export opportunities.

Contrary to supporters of U.S. sugar policies, some recent studies have found that developing countries have not benefited from the U.S. sugar quota.

Since 1981, U.S. sugar imports have declined sharply, along with sugar export earnings of U.S. quota countries. Moreover, the large difference in profits between world and U.S. quota sugar sales often promotes government intervention and inefficiency in quota countries because of the need to allocate the declining quota rents among different exporters. The EC, on the other hand, maintains a floor on its sugar imports, and export earnings of the EC beneficiary countries have increased under its preferential program. The EC's program, however, suppresses long-run export expansion and development of sugar processing activities, particularly in low-income countries in Africa.

From 1978 to 1988 sugar exports became more concentrated among the developed countries and the top three developing country exporters—Cuba, Brazil, and Thailand—countries that do not depend to a large extent on the U.S. sugar market and that also subsidize sugar production. Thailand, whose sugar export market share more than doubled, relies the least on preferential import schemes of developed countries. In 1982 it implemented a policy of taxing sugar consumers to subsidize sugar producers—a regime that follows the ones commonly adopted in developed countries. Developing countries that have traditionally depended on the U.S. market for a large part of their sugar sales (the Philippines and countries in Central America) experienced the largest decline in export market share (30 percent), while the export share of developing countries that traditionally sell to the EC remained constant.

Low world sugar prices and high petroleum prices in the early 1980s stimulated the interest of many developing countries in diversification from exporting sugar to converting sugar into ethanol. These kinds of diversification projects reduce the short run effects of lower sugar exports and foreign exchange earnings when world petroleum prices are high, but they are often not sustainable without subsidies in the long run. On the other hand, our results from a model simulation of trade liberalization in the world sugar market show that developing countries as a whole would gain if both developed and developing countries would agree to eliminate trade-distorting policies in the world sugar market. Such gains would come from higher export earnings as well as from lower prices for sugar imports. Both developed and developing countries would gain from improved resource allocation.

NOTES

The views expressed in this paper are not necessarily those of the World Bank or the U.S. International Trade Commission..

1. The Central America group includes the Caribbean countries and, when not explicitly excluded, Mexico.

2. In a study of agricultural pricing policy, Krueger, Schiff, and Valdés (1991) found that exchange rate misalignment, which has tended to raise the cost of inputs used in sugar production, is much higher in Sub-Saharan Africa than in other developing countries. If this misalignment were corrected, African sugar producers, on average, would probably be more competitive than sugar producers in South America.

3. The former Soviet Union and Eastern Europe were also growth markets for sugar.

4. A notable exception is Thailand, which implemented a policy of taxing consumers to support producer sugar prices following the decline in world sugar prices in 1982. However, Thailand's per capita sugar consumption of about 15 kg per capita per year is relatively low compared with other sugar exporters.

5. The decline in the EC's import-consumption ratio is due to stagnant imports and rapidly rising exports.

6. A proposal for a deficiency payment scheme to replace the current U.S. program for sugar producers was prepared by the Reagan Administration in 1987. However, the administration was unable to find the support it needed to introduce the proposal as a bill for consideration by the Congress.

7. While most multilateral and bilateral donors are promoting free markets and private enterprise in developing countries, developed countries' sugar policies tend to undermine these efforts.

8. Details on the methodology used to compute the various measures of intervention can be found in Krueger, Schiff, and Valdés (1988).

9. The adverse effect on the African countries is noted because more than 50 percent of these countries' sugar imports are supplied by the EC in refined form.

10. These estimates of earning losses from gross exports assume that in the absence of U.S. quotas, developing countries' exports to the United States would be the same from 1975 to 1981 (the pre-quota period) at a free-market price of 15 cents per pound. The estimates do not account for export earnings that have been generated by developing countries through diversion of sugar resources into other export-earning activities.

11. These trade benefits will likely be reduced in the future. In the past, Cuba sold its sugar to the Soviet Union in exchange for petroleum, other products, and rubles. The Soviets generally paid a premium over the prevailing world price. However, the governments of the former Soviet states and Eastern Europe planned to do business with Cuba in hard currency rather than in rubles starting in 1991. This change most likely will result in a reduction in the sugar premium, as well as in the volume of sugar purchased by the former Soviet states.

12. Less than 1 percent of Thailand's exports are sold to the United States.

13. Mexico was a net importer in 1989 and 1990 following crop shortfalls.

14. Guatemala has also benefited from quota-exempt sugar sales to the United States. Under this program, additional amounts of raw sugar can be imported into the United States, provided the sugar is reexported in another form. While the quota-exempt program does not add to net sugar trade, there is an equity effect to the extent that U.S. exports of processed sugar products promote developing countries' raw sugar exports and displace processed sugar-containing exports from the EC and other countries. For more on the trade in sugar-containing products, see Jabara (1989).

15. Mauritius implemented a successful sugar diversification program during the 1980s. Its dependence on sugar for foreign exchange earnings declined from 60 percent to 30 percent in the early 1980s.
16. In addition to Brazil, which has long had a program to produce ethanol from sugar, those that have examined the ethanol option include Costa Rica, the Dominican Republic, El Salvador, Guatemala, Jamaica, and the Philippines.
17. In his comments on an earlier version of this paper, Arnold Harberger pointed out that table 8 suggests a rough proportionality between the degree of U.S. liberalization (10, 50, and 100 percent in simulations 2, 3, and 4) and the effects on the world price, consumption, and production. He inferred from this proportionality that the model was highly "linear" in its construction, and noted the potential advantages of an alternative modeling approach: to identify by country or region the cut-off prices below which production would cease. Such an approach would be especially useful for analysis of major liberalizations—beyond 10 percent, for example—in which one would expect vastly expanded production in areas in which production is cheap and expandable, and abandonment of production in areas in which it has been maintained only at artificially high prices.

REFERENCES

Grissa, Abdessatar. 1976. *Structure of the International Sugar Market and Its Impact on Developing Countries*. Organization for Economic Cooperation and Development, Development Centre. Paris.

Harris, Simon. 1987. "Current Issues in the World Sugar Economy." *Food Policy* 12 (no. 11): 127–145.

Jabara, Cathy L. 1989. "Effects of Sugar Price Policy on U.S. Imports of Processed Sugar-Containing Foods." *Agricultural Economics* 3: 131–146.

Johnson, Harry G. 1966. "Sugar Protectionism and the Export Earnings of Less-Developed Countries: Variations on a Theme by R. H. Snape." *Economica* 33: 34–42.

Koester, Ulrich, and Peter Michael Schmitz. 1982. "The EC Sugar Market Policy and Developing Countries." *European Review of Agricultural Economics* 9: 183–204.

Krueger, Anne O., Maurice Schiff, and Alberto Valdés. 1988. "Agricultural Incentives in Developing Countries: Measuring the Effect of Sectoral and Economywide Policies." *World Bank Economic Review* 2: 255–71.

———. 1991. *The Political Economy of Agricultural Pricing Policy* (three volumes). Baltimore: Johns Hopkins University Press.

Matthews, Alan. 1985. *The Common Agricultural Policy and Developing Countries*. Dublin: Gill and Macmillan.

Mosley, Paul, and Lawrence Smith. 1989. "Structural Adjustment and Agricultural Performance in Sub-Saharan Africa 1980–87." *Journal of International Development* 1: 321–355.

Overseas Development Council. 1989. *U.S. Sugar Quotas and the Caribbean Basin*. Policy Focus Brief No. 6. Washington, DC.

Roberts, I. M. 1982. *EEC Sugar Support Policies and World Market Prices: A*

Comparative Static Analysis. Australian Bureau of Agricultural Economics. Working Paper No. 8213. Canberra: Australian Government Publishing Service.

Snape, Richard H. 1963. "Some Effects of Protection in the World Sugar Industry." *Economica* 30: 63–73.

Tyers, Rod, and Kym Anderson. 1986. "Distortions in World Food Markets: A Quantitative Assessment." Paper prepared for the *World Development Report, 1986.* World Bank. Washington, DC.

U.S. Department of Agriculture. 1989. *Sugar and Sweetener Situation and Outlook.* Economic Research Service. June.

U.S. International Trade Commission. 1990. *Estimated Tariff Equivalents of Nontariff Barriers on Certain Agricultural Imports in the European Community, Japan, and Canada.* Report No. 2280. Washington, DC.

Valdés, Alberto. 1987. "Agriculture in the Uruguay Round: Interests of Developing Countries." *World Bank Economic Review* 1: 571–593.

Valdés, Alberto, and Joachim Zietz. 1980. *Agricultural Protection in OECD Countries: Its Cost to Less-Developed Countries.* International Food Policy Research Institute, Washington, DC. Research Report No. 21.

Wong, Gordon, Robert Sturgiss, and Brent Borrell. 1989. *The Economic Consequences of International Sugar Trade Reform.* Australian Bureau of Agricultural and Resource Economics. Discussion Paper 89.7. Canberra: Australian Government Publishing Service.

Zietz, Joachim, and Alberto Valdés. 1986. *The Costs of Protectionism to Developing Countries: An Analysis for Selected Agricultural Products.* World Bank. Staff Working Paper No. 769.

———— (1990). "International Interactions in Food and Agricultural Policies: Effects of Alternative Policies." In *Agricultural Liberalization: Implications for Developing Countries,* ed. Ian Goldin and Odin Knudsen. Paris: World Bank/OECD.

Five Commentaries on Sugar Policy

Commentary

Bruce A. Gardner

I would like to talk about prospects for the sugar industry after the Uruguay Round. There are two general scenarios: (1) the Uruguay Round is successful, in the sense of coming up with an agreement that means something, or (2) it is unsuccessful, and we get no agreement.

First, suppose that an agreement is reached and that it is, at least in outline, consistent with the U.S. proposal, which would (1) convert import access restraints around the world to tariffs, which would then be phased down over a ten year period, (2) phase down export subsidies at a faster rate over the same period, and (3) phase down the internal supports that all countries have.

We do not need to have a complete phase-out over a very short period, but rather some significant rate of reduction in all of these three aspects of protection. What would then happen, in that scenario, to the sugar industry? Two kinds of analyses have been carried out: first, generic studies of liberalization, and second, studies of a specific proposal.

All of the academic studies familiar to me take the generic approach and fail to incorporate a dynamic context of gradually phasing out supports, with non-distorting assistance continuing. Instead they take a cold-turkey approach: what happens if we just remove all agricultural protection around the world? The results can appear quite shocking to any industry currently protected. But the kinds of answers these studies give depend very much on the assumptions made. Unfortunately, the assumptions made in generic studies make them academic in the worst sense of the word: complexly irrelevant. The findings depend on the base year from which protection is removed; they depend on the assumptions made about supply and demand elasticities; they depend on what policy instruments are disciplined and how they are disciplined; they depend on the assumptions made about the way markets are going to evolve in the absence of protection.

In the case of sugar, for example, we have results—and this is the main and perhaps only interesting finding from the generic studies—on what would happen to the world price of sugar if we had a multilateral agreement among countries to reduce protection of their sugar industries. These studies uniformly find that the world price of sugar would increase, because countries that now restrain access to imports would take more off the world

163

market, and that would be bullish for world prices. Countries that now subsidize exports would stop that practice, which too would take sugar off the world market, and be bullish for the world prices. But the amount of the price increase varies tremendously in the studies published to date.

One study from the Economic Research Service (ERS) by Roningen and Dixit has been quoted a lot:[1] I have heard it quoted more than I would have liked to have heard it quoted, because it is generic and does not provide an estimate of any actual proposal's results. Roningen and Dixit estimate that the world price of sugar would rise by over 50 percent if there were a complete removal of protection. This estimate is made on a 1986–87 base, however, when the world sugar price was quite low. An earlier study by Tyers and Anderson had more modest findings—about an 8 percent rise in the price of sugar.[2] More recent work within ERS by Bob Barry and Ron Lord finds a roughly 10 to 30 percent rise in the world price of sugar with multilateral liberalization.[3]

In comparing different countries, how the sugar industry fares depends on how the world price increase compares with the level of protection the industry had previously enjoyed, and of course that level varies across countries.

In the U.S. case, most of the calculations suggest that, for the industry as a whole, the current level of protection is greater than the price increase that could be expected when the protection is ended. Thus, the U.S. sugar industry loses revenue in the generic liberalization scenario. But that is a cold-turkey liberalization scenario, which permits no policies to remain in place.

In discussions with representatives of sugar producers, as with other industries, survival of the industry is often raised as an issue. The idea is that if a country's sugar industry can produce at a cost that is less than the world price which results from liberalization, then the industry can survive in a liberalized trade regime. This is a difficult concept to make operational or to forecast with confidence because of the slippery nature of the cost concept and the difficulty of measuring its components. The general assessment of costs in the U.S. sugar industry appears to be that the industry could survive with a "level playing field": the U.S. industry can produce at a cost less than the world price under a regime in which all countries protect their sugar industries at an equal rate. This implies that the U.S. industry would be able to survive with a completely liberalized world sugar economy, since all countries would then have zero protection. Even if this were true it does not address the question whether the sugar producers would be better or worse off in a free-trade regime for sugar, compared with the present situation.

Let me now consider the other possible outcome—that there is no agreement in the GATT. First of all, if we do not have a concerted policy change in the GATT countries as a result of a multilateral agreement, what do we assume about policies? One possible assumption is that the policies would go on just as they are. There are reasons why this might not be the case in many countries, however. The outcome depends on the kinds of policies that are in place—whether they have budgetary costs, whether they have consumers pay for the protection that producers get, and other features.

What factors might come into play in the United States? A few years ago, if we had played out a scenario in which the United States continued its sugar policy of the 1980s, we would have projected an end to sugar imports. The restraint we had to put on the world market to keep our domestic price at the level we wanted kept the quantity of imports shrinking. We went from 4 to 5 million tons of imports down to 1 to 2 million tons, and it looked like we would go to zero before long. After what has happened in the last couple of years, that outcome does not look as likely for the time being: our own projections do not show imports going to zero if we maintain our policies just as they are, but they do not show them increasing either. Perhaps this million tons or so of annual sugar imports is a more robust possibility than we earlier thought it would be.

However, it seems to me that this scenario could turn around again very quickly. Any kind of projection for long periods is fraught with large error possibilities, and it may well be that before long we will again be considering what are we going to do if or when we become self-sufficient in sugar. That scenario changes the policy options available considerably. Even if it does not come about, I do not think we should suppose that the present level of price supports and imports can be maintained indefinitely.

When all the likely political and economic factors are taken into account, it seems to me that it would not be so irrational for the sugar industry to come on board and accept the idea of multilateral liberalization. And I sense that the industry is not rejecting the idea of liberalization out of hand, as some of the reactions to the earlier studies might have led us to think it would.

NOTES

1. Vernon O. Roningen and Praveen M. Dixit, "Economic Implications of Agricultural Policy Reforms in Industrial Market Economies," U.S. Department of Agriculture, Economic Research Service, Agriculture and Trade Analysis Division, Staff Report Number AGES 8936, August 1989.
2. Rod Tyers and Kym Anderson, "Distortions in World Food Markets: A Quantitative Assessment," paper prepared for the World Bank, *World Development Report 1986.*
3. Ron Lord and Robert D. Barry, *The World Sugar Market: Government Intervention and Multilateral Policy Reform,* U.S. Department of Agriculture, Economic Research Service, Commodity Economics Division, Staff Report Number AGES 9062, September 1990.

Commentary

Thomas Hammer

The Uruguay Round was launched in September 1986, the eighth negotiating round since the GATT began in 1948. All to that point had dealt largely with industrial tariffs, and had achieved fairly progressive trade liberalization, so that the rates on industrial products and manufactured goods were no longer very high.

In the Tokyo Round of the 1970s, it was decided that nontariff barriers, and more or less transparent barriers, had become the rules of the game, and had to be dealt with. So there was an effort to move beyond the normal request/offer procedure, in which a principal supplier goes to a principal market and asks for a tariff reduction. That was normally the way the GATT had operated for 40 years.

The Tokyo Round negotiators tried to devise agreements and codes for nontariff measures, and came to the novel idea, resisted for decades by the United States, to try to include agriculture in those same codes. The Tokyo Round was considered a success, but many would argue that, with respect to agriculture, it probably was not a great success.

One of the turning points, however, was that the United States finally realized that it had a stake in creating rules of the game for agriculture. By that time nearly one in every three acres farmed in the United States was tied to the export market. So new rules became good business for us, even though we had been one of the original GATT signatories who argued sternly that agricultural rules should be different. As we entered the Uruguay Round, the United States was at the forefront of those pushing for agricultural reform, and I think there has been some injustice done in maligning the approach that the United States has taken. It provides at least a rational approach, and a worthwhile objective.

I do not believe we will be able to eliminate all of the export subsidies, internal subsidies, or import barriers in agriculture. We have not done so in the industrial area over the past 45 years, and there is no reason to expect that we can in agriculture. But in the Uruguay Round we are trying to make parallel rules for industry and agriculture. I applaud this effort, and believe it can work. And I believe that we will—over 10 to 15 years—reduce some of the tremendous economic distortions in agriculture. I think sugar has a lot to gain from such reforms. As to sugar market prospects after the Uruguay Round, I would instead consider prospects for the sugar market if the Uruguay Round is a disaster. We would be looking at more of the same. And that would not be a pretty sight.

Some have been greatly concerned that we not unilaterally disarm programs here in the United States—go over and sacrifice them all in the Uruguay Round. I would suggest that if we are not careful—given our own budget problems, and our own political pressures—we are going to do something akin to what we did back in the 1980s, when we took 80 million acres out of production in this country, to deal with our own internal fiscal problems, and immediately saw 80 million acres or so go into plantings other places on the globe.

To sum up, I would say that it is very important for all of agriculture that the Uruguay Round succeeds, that there be an agricultural agreement, and that there be one that works for all commodities, including sugar.

The current domestic sugar program is very divisive. Buyers and sellers have been pitted against each other for the last decade or more. If we do not settle this, we will have more of the same. And the program the producers offered Congress in the spring of 1990 showed that the patient was not doing very well: it went back to the supply management programs that we had in the 1950s and 1960s—and that we have tried to move away from. The USDA sent a letter to the chairman of the House subcommittee outlining in about three pages all the provisions in the proposal that were illegal in terms of the GATT.

So I think we all ought to put the shoulder to the wheel, and hope that the Uruguay Round succeeds. I think that will be better for the United States sweetener industry, as well as those efficient producers outside of the United States.

Commentary

Eiler C. Ravnholt

The U.S. sugar program has been an extraordinary success when measured by what has happened under the program. Since 1981, we have had very stable sugar prices, and we have maintained the U.S. domestic sugar industry. Prices for sugar on the retail level in the United States have increased by only six percent since 1981, significantly less than the increase for the "high sugar content products" whose producers are the principal opponents of the sugar program. Candy prices are up 30 percent; cookies and cakes are up 48 percent; cereals are up a whopping 70 percent; and carbonated soft drinks are up 25 percent, despite the fact that the soft-drink industry switched to lower-cost high fructose corn sweetener.

The dramatic plunge in the "world price" of sugar in the early 1980s was one that the U.S. domestic sugar industry obviously would not have been able to survive, and that was the reason for the current sugar program.

The emergence of the corn sweetener industry may have been accelerated somewhat as a result of the existence of our sugar program, but that expansion was already well under way in 1981. In fact, most of the capacity that came on line over 1982–84 had been planned prior to the 1981 passage of the program. The program not only has permitted the use of a lot of corn for corn sweetener, it has also saved the federal taxpayer some $500 to $700 million a year in reduced deficiency payments for corn, according to the USDA, because of that assured outlet for corn.

The cost to the U.S. consumer of the sugar program, by at least one measure, has been more than adequately dealt with by Schmitz and Christian.[1] There are a couple of other measures that we could examine. One is the price of sugar in the United States compared to the price in other countries. The average retail price of sugar, as of last November, was 40 cents per pound in the United States, versus 44 cents on average in the other countries surveyed.

Another is to compare consumer prices in the United States to those in Canada, a developed country that has free access to world market price sugar. In Canada, the average retail price for 1980 through 1988 was 33 cents per pound; in the United States, the average retail price for that period was 37 cents per pound. So it appears that our sugar program cost us four cents per pound, or $672 million annually.

Well, not quite. More than 40 percent of the market in the United States that previously used only sucrose today utilizes HFCS, and HFCS sells for 65 to 75 percent of the price of sugar. Therefore, during the 1980–88 period the price of HFCS to the soft drink industry and other buyers in the United States was actually some six cents per pound below the average Canadian price for sucrose. Therefore, if one measures the total true expenditures for sweetener in Canada versus the United States, one finds that Canada's may in fact be slightly higher. Moreover, U.S. prices were more stable. Annual average prices in Canada ranged from 23 cents to 62 cents during the 1980s; in the United States, from 34 cents to 43 cents.

Change in U.S. sugar policy is pushed as a consumer benefit. I would note that industrial sweetener users would hardly be so interested in modifying the U.S. sugar program if they intended to pass through all of their cost reductions to consumers. They may like more volatile sugar prices, as they have in the past shown a penchant for using higher sugar prices to justify product price increases—increases that were maintained when input prices fell.

Finally, while U.S. producers have benefited from the current program, so have most foreign exporters of sugar to the U.S. market. The findings described in the Borrell-Duncan paper only run through 1988, when the quota was at its low point.[2] If they had run through the present—with fiscal 1991 U.S. imports at 2.3 million tons—they would find that quota rents to most exporters to the U.S. market were indeed substantial. The potential impact on the world price from change in the U.S. program is very small, unless support reductions are of such magnitude as to drive U.S. farmers out of sugar production.

As U.S. sugar producers are average-cost producers, they believe they can survive in a world of free trade. Many will not survive the process of getting to that goal, however, if their support levels are reduced by the same percentage as are those for other producers who are currently supported well above their production costs, and if they must at the same time compete with efficient sugar industries in developing countries that may be granted special and differential treatment for their subsidy programs under a Uruguay Round negotiated agreement.

NOTES

1. Andrew Schmitz and Douglas Christian, "U.S. Sugar: A Review of Empirical Relationships," paper presented at the U.S. Department of State, Conference on Sugar Markets in the 1990s, May 23, 1990.
2. Brent Borrell and Ronald Duncan, "An Overview of World Sugar Markets," paper presented at the U.S. Department of State, Conference on Sugar Markets in the 1990s, May 23, 1990.

Commentary

Daniel R. Pearson

I would like to make three points. The first is that Cargill has an interest in sugar policy for two reasons: it is a major international trader of sugar and molasses worldwide, and is also a major producer of corn sweeteners domestically in the United States. We would like to see consumption, production and trade of sweeteners grow in response to underlying market realities. Our business is likely to grow only if the overall market grows. This market growth is most likely to occur in a world with liberalized trade, and nondistorting domestic policies in all countries.

The second point is that all sweeteners require policies that allow them to be fully competitive if they are to maintain market share. The rapid growth of high fructose corn syrup consumption in the United States—now to the point that corn sweeteners provide more than half of caloric sweeteners in the country—shows all too clearly how policies that restricted the ability of sucrose to compete accelerated the decline in sucrose market share: in 1975, refined sugar accounted for almost 72 percent of total sweetener consumption in the United States. That had fallen to slightly over 40 percent by 1988. Corn sweeteners, on the other hand, rose from 22 percent in 1975 to 46 percent currently, and artificials increased from 4.9 percent to 13.1 percent. So we clearly have a very dynamic market, with a lot of shifting going on.

Consumption of noncaloric sweeteners—now at 20 pounds per capita on a sucrose equivalent basis—is higher than HFCS consumption was in 1980. How much additional market share can nutritive sweeteners lose to artificials? I think quite a bit, since there is potential for extraordinary technological improvement in the end-use characteristics of the artificials. Moreover, the patent comes off Aspartame in 1992, which could well price that sweetener below the cost of nutritive sweeteners. Caloric sweeteners have an advantage now, because NutraSweet has a market segment only for dietary products. But if it suddenly becomes cheaper than HFCS (it is already cheaper than sucrose), a substantial market could develop for things that are sweet, regardless of whether they are high or low in calories, and that would allow NutraSweet to expand dramatically. These sorts of potential shifts in market share would be exacerbated by inflexible policies toward nutritive sweeteners, like the ones the House Agriculture Committee was considering in 1990.

The third and final point is that economic rationality can only be brought to sweetener markets through liberalized sweetener policies. This can be best accomplished multilaterally and gradually. If all countries phase in improved policies simultaneously, the adjustment costs for everyone will be easier to absorb. This is especially true now that sweetener markets are in some rough semblance of balance—a condition that did not exist for much of the 1980s. Cargill continues to hope that this type of outcome can be achieved in the Uruguay Round.

Commentary

D. Gale Johnson

I would like to emphasize the role of our sugar policy in a broad framework. I will not discuss the costs of the program. I think it is obvious that there are costs, and that they are substantial.

Instead, I would first like to tie the program to the Uruguay Round of multilateral trade negotiations under the GATT, because I think success in the Uruguay Round depends on the United States abiding by a strengthened Article 11 of the GATT.

Article 11 of GATT deals with the use of trade restrictions other than tariffs or taxes. It says that, under very limited circumstances, countries can use quantitative restrictions. But this GATT rule—which, incidentally, we wrote ourselves—has not been met by the sugar program, at least since the 1970s. The requirement is that any reduction in imports as a result of a domestic price support program be matched by a reduction in domestic production.

Since 1978, when we went back into the sugar control business, we have not kept one ounce of sugar from being produced in the United States. We have laid a profitable price on the table, and told the farmers to go ahead and produce as much as they want—in violation of Article 11. This has gone on long enough. And I think it is clear that the other major participants in the negotiations are not going to stand for the United States continuing to violate Article 11.

Indeed, the United States initially proposed in the Uruguay Round that Article 11 be eliminated from the GATT: tariffs would have been the only appropriate restriction at the border. We would have had to give up our 1955 GATT waiver of Article 11. But our sugar program is in violation of the basic GATT principles, and it is about time it came to an end. I hope that it does come to an end as a result of the GATT negotiations.

Our sugar program has also violated Article 16, which governs export subsidies. In 1987, we found we were uncomfortably laden with some couple hundred thousand tons of sugar, for which we found willing buyers—I think primarily China. And so we used export subsidies, which we have accused the EC of using indiscriminately, for sugar and many other products.

A second point that I would like to emphasize is the impact of the sugar program on U.S. exports. It seems to me that this is an important issue: when

172

we have reduced our imports of sugar, we have also reduced the capacity of a group of countries to buy from us, and those countries have been major agricultural importers.

According to the USDA, in 1970–74 we imported 5.2 million tons of sugar—not those little teeny short tons—but metric tons. In 1978–81 we imported 4.7 million tons—very little change in the 1970s. But in 1986–89 we imported a mere 1.25 million tons per year. Imagine the state of American agriculture if trade restrictions around the world had been as restrictive as our sugar policy—had reduced the quantity of our exports by 60 percent: our exports would be valued at maybe $10 or $12 billion, instead of $40 billion.

This program has had an adverse impact on a number of countries important to the United States in many ways—in the Caribbean, Central America, and South America. Do we really want to live with this? I think not.

My third point is that sugar should be included in any negotiated program to reduce trade barriers, and on the same basis as all other agricultural commodities.

Sugar is not unique, except that it makes us fatter than some other things do. Sugar production is carried out on farms—actually, on a relatively small number of farms—only about 10,000 in the United States. Nothing about its processing, which is also fairly highly concentrated, or its consumption merits special and differential treatment. The characteristic matched by few others is that it is exceptionally well-organized politically. In terms of economic and social implications, sugar does not differ from corn or wheat or a number of other products. And just as these other commodity programs should be on the line in the GATT negotiations, so should the sugar program.

And sugar has received separate treatment in recent times. First, it has been protected by an import quota, and only peanuts and dairy products, of the other major farm products, are so protected. Second, it has not been subject to a cut in its nominal support prices. In fact, it has had a sympathetic administration that has held the actual domestic price well above the support price required by law, under the guise that it was a sin to risk costing the U.S. Treasury any money, but it was alright to fleece the consumer. So the sugar program has not been under the same policy constraints as any other major farm products.

Finally, I would like to comment on the argument that price instability justifies maintaining our domestic sugar program. This is about as ironic as can be, because our sugar program is one of the major sources of price instability in the world sugar market. A number of studies indicate that if there were free trade in sugar, price instability in the world sugar market would be cut by 50 percent. So we ought to at least use a little rationality in our rationalizations of this program.

Contributors

Brent Borrell is an economist with the Centre for International Economics in Canberra and was previously with the Australian Bureau of Agricultural and Resource Economics, for which he has authored several studies of world sugar policies.

Douglas Christian is a graduate student in the Department of Agricultural and Resource Economics at the University of California at Berkeley.

Ronald C. Duncan is Chief of the International Trade Division, International Economics Department, of the World Bank in Washington, DC.

Bruce A. Gardner is the Assistant Secretary of Agriculture for Economics and professor of agricultural economics on leave from the University of Maryland.

Thomas Hammer is the President of the Sweetener Users Association, and was formerly the Deputy Under Secretary for International Affairs and Commodity Programs in the U.S. Department of Agriculture.

Simon A. Harris is Director for Corporate Affairs at British Sugar, PLC, and is an authority on international sweetener markets and policies. He is coauthor of a 1983 volume on *The Food and Farm Policies of the European Community*.

Cathy Jabara is acting Chief of the Agriculture Division at the U.S. International Trade Commission and was previously a Senior Research Associate at the Cornell Food and Nutrition Policy Program in Washington, DC.

D. Gale Johnson is professor of economics at the University of Chicago. He is author of a 1974 study, *The Sugar Program: Large Costs and Small Benefits*, for the American Enterprise Institute. He and Bruce Gardner are past presidents of the American Agricultural Economics Association.

Stephen V. Marks is associate professor of economics at Pomona College and the Claremont Graduate School and has been a visiting economist at the U.S. Department of State in the Bureau of Economic and Business Affairs.

Keith E. Maskus is associate professor of economics at the University of Colorado at Boulder and has been a visiting economist at the U.S. Department of State in the Bureau of Economic and Business Affairs.

Daniel R. Pearson is a public policy analyst for Cargill, Inc., a producer of corn sweeteners and a major worldwide commodity trader. He formerly was the agricultural legislative assistant to Senator Rudy Boschwitz of Minnesota.

175

Eiler C. Ravnholt is Vice President for Legislative Affairs of the Hawaiian Sugar Planters Association. He previously was an aide to Senators Daniel Inouye of Hawaii and Hubert Humphrey of Minnesota.

Andrew Schmitz is a professor in the Department of Agricultural and Resource Economics at the University of California at Berkeley and is the author of several studies of the U.S. sugar program.

Stefan Tangermann is a professor at the Institute of Agricultural Economics at the University of Gottingen, Germany.

Alberto Valdés is an economist at the World Bank in Washington, DC, and was previously at the Institute for Food Policy Research. He has authored numerous studies of the effects of agricultural trade liberalization on developing countries.